Sustainable Urban De

Sustainable Urban Development Volume 1: The Framework and Protocols for Environmental Assessment discusses the objectives of sustainable urban development and sets out the framework and protocols for an environmental assessment of the planning, property development, design, construction, operation and use of buildings. Providing the knowledge stakeholders need to engage in the debate about the sustainability of urban development and professionals require to act upon government policy towards the built environment, this book offers:

- An introduction to the principles of sustainable urban development
- The framework, vision and methodology of sustainable urban development
- The protocols to follow in evaluating the sustainability of urban development
- The assessment methods available to undertake such evaluations
- State-of-the art case studies on the use of the assessment methods for evaluating the sustainability of urban development
- The latest thinking on how to integrate the framework, protocols and assessment methods when evaluating the sustainability of urban development.

This is the first of three volumes on the research and debate of the BEQUEST (**B**uilding, **E**nvironmental **QU**ality **E**valuation for **S**us**T**ainability) network funded by the European Commission. Together the books provide a toolkit of interest and value to policy makers, academics, professionals and advanced level students in Urban Planning, Urban Property Development, Urban Design, Architecture, Construction and related areas of the built environment.

Contributors:
Peter Brandon, Ian Cooper, Steven Curwell, Simin Davoudi, Mark Deakin, Andy Hamilton, John Hudson, Patrizia Lombardi, Martin Symes and Vincenzo Bentivegna.

Steven Curwell is Professor of Sustainable Urban Development at the University of Salford. **Mark Deakin** is Senior Lecturer and Teaching Fellow in the School of the Built Environment, Napier University. **Martin Symes** is Professor in the Cities Research Centre, University of the West of England.

Published by Routledge on research founded by BEQUEST
Editorial Board: Steven Curwell, Mark Deakin, Martin Symes

Sustainable Urban Development
Editors:
Steven Curwell, Salford University, UK
Mark Deakin, Napier University, UK
Martin Symes, University of the West of England, UK

Sustainable Urban Development Volume 1
The Framework and Protocols for Environmental Assessment
Steven Curwell, Mark Deakin and Martin Symes (eds)

Sustainable Urban Development Volume 2   Publishing 2006
The Environmental Assessment Methods
Mark Deakin, Peter Nijkamp, Gordon Mitchell and Ron Vreeker (eds)

Sustainable Urban Development Volume 3   Publishing 2006
A Toolkit for Assessment
Steven Curwell, Mark Deakin, Patrizia Lombardi, Gordon Mitchell and Ron Vreeker (eds)

These three volumes are based on the research and debate of the European BEQUEST network (**B**uilding **E**nvironmental **QU**ality **E**valuation for **S**us**T**ainability). Together the books provide a toolkit of interest and value to policy-makers, professionals and advanced level students in a variety of disciplines.

Sustainable Urban Development

Volume 1: The Framework and Protocols for Environmental Assessment

Edited by Steven Curwell, Mark Deakin and Martin Symes

Routledge
Taylor & Francis Group

LONDON AND NEW YORK

First published 2005
by Routledge
2 Park Square, Milton Park, Abingdon, Oxon OX14 4RN

Simultaneously published in the USA and Canada
by Routledge
270 Madison Ave, New York, NY 10016

Routledge is an imprint of the Taylor & Francis Group

Typeset in Akzidenz Grotesk by
Keystroke, Jacaranda Lodge, Wolverhampton
Printed and bound in Great Britain by
TJ International Ltd, Padstow, Cornwall

British Library Cataloguing in Publication Data
A catalogue record for this book is available from the British Library

Library of Congress Cataloging in Publication Data
A catalog record for this book has been requested

ISBN 0–415–32214–6 (hbk)
ISBN 0–415–32215–4 (pbk)

Contents

Contributors

Vincenzo Bentivegna: Professor at the Universiti degli Studii, Florence. He is an urban economist and teaches 'Real estate analysis' and 'Plan and project evaluation'. His key areas of expertise are the public decision process in urban planning and projects and in public–private co-operation in buildings. His scientific works are related to the efficiency of the decision process in public and private urban development and rehabilitation plans and projects, the integration between economic and environmental evaluation in urban planning, and the evaluation of urban plans and projects in the light of sustainability. He has professional experience in urban planning and urban development and renewal in Italy and other countries. He has participated in the following EU research projects: BEQUEST, JANUS, CRISP, KISS LUDA, INTELCITY and INTELCITIES.

Peter Brandon: Professor and former Pro-Vice Chancellor of the University of Salford. He has chaired a number of National Research Panels in the United Kingdom. His research interests range from construction economics and management to information technology and the evaluation of sustainable development, on which he had a new book published in December 2004. He lectures and publishes widely across the world.

Ian Cooper: Partner in Eclipse Research Consultants, Cambridge, England, founded in 1984. He is a specialist in research design, management and impact assessment, and in the sustainable procurement, management and operation of the built environment, and is a facilitator to the EU-funded BEQUEST concerted action. He has extensive experience of undertaking work to support 'futures' studies, and is convenor and editor for the RICS Research Foundation's (2001) futures study, *2020 Visions of the Future* and author of its introduction – *Preparing for the Future: A User's Guide*. He is also a facilitator for the EU-funded Roadmap, INTELCITY, which brought together two research and practitioner communities – sustainable urban development and ICTs – to envisage the intelligent sustainable city in 2030. He is currently a facilitator on INTELCITIES, engaging citizens in how to exploit ICTs for more sustainable urban development.

Steven Curwell: Professor of Sustainable Urban Development (SUD) and a leading European researcher in environmental and sustainability issues through his role in fourteen EU and UK national research projects to a total value of circa €15 million over the last fifteen years. He has extensive research collaboration experience with over 350 research groups, city authorities and IST companies via four EU projects: BEQUEST (FP4), CRISP, INTELCITY and LUDA (FP5). He has led exploration of innovative ways of inclusive, consensus-based research over the complex problems of SUD linking IT and new ways of e-working. He is the author or co-author of seventy-five publications; five books, fifty-plus research papers, two learning packages and two research websites. This includes the co-authorship of the prototype, Internet-based, urban decision-support aid known as the BEQUEST Toolkit, developed in 2000/1, the first to provide fully integrated approaches to SUD evaluation. In 2002/3 he successfully directed the INTELCITY (Intelligent Sustainable Cities) Roadmap project for the EC and is currently the Scientific Director of the INTELCITIES FP6 Integrated Project, which commenced in January 2004. This brings together nineteen cities, twenty ICT companies and thirty-five research groups to explore the application of ICTs for more Intelligent Cities.

Simin Davoudi: Professor of Planning and Environment and Director of the Centre for Urban Development and Environmental Management at Leeds Metropolitan University. She is the President of the Association of European Schools of Planning, Co-ordinator of the Planning Research Network that advises the UK Office of the Deputy Prime Minister on its planning research priority, a member of the RTPI Research and Knowledge Committee, and an expert adviser to the EU DG Environment. Her research focuses on UK and European spatial planning, the governance of strategic waste planning, and environmental sustainability. This research has been disseminated widely through numerous books and articles.

Mark Deakin: Senior Lecturer and Teaching Fellow in the School of the Built Environment, Napier University. Mark has carried out research for the Royal Institution of Chartered Surveyors (RICS), the British Know-How Fund, Overseas Development Agency and European Commission (EC). Since contributing to Brandon *et al.*'s (1997) *Evaluation of the Built Environment for Sustainability*, he has been a Partner in BEQUEST and Joint Leader, with Patrizia Lombardi, of the Environmental Assessment Methods Task Group set up to evaluate the sustainability of urban development. This has led him to publish a number of papers on BEQUEST. These papers provide an examination of the framework, protocols and assessment methods currently available to evaluate the sustainability of urban development. His most recent book publications include (with R. Dixon-Gough and H. Mansberger) *Models and Instruments for Rural* *and Urban Development* (2004), and *Property Management: Corporate Strategies, Financial Instruments and the Urban Environment* (2004). Mark's current research interests rest with the following: the INTELCITIES Integrating Project forming part of the EC's IST Programme; the LUDA Project funded by the EC's Environment and Climate Programme; the Modelling of Real Estate Transactions, funded under the EC's COST G9 Action; and the Research-led Teaching LINK initiative in architecture, planning and property, supported by the UK Higher Education Funding Council.

Andy Hamilton: Lecturer at the University of Salford since 1992 and researcher in the Research Institute for the Built and Human Environment since 1996. He is a specialist in information systems for collaboration generally, and for collaborative urban development control planning in particular, and a collaborator in writing the bids for, and played key roles in, the EU-funded projects: BEQUEST, INTELCITY and INTELCITIES. He was Communications Director and Toolkit designer for BEQUEST (1998–2001), and Communications Director for the INTELCITY Roadmap project (2002–2003).

John Hudson: Lecturer in the School of Construction and Property Management at the University of Salford. Within the University he is a member of the Research Institute for the Built and Human Environment and the Centre for Facilities Management. His current research interests are in issues of sustainable development and procurement in facilities management.

Patrizia Lombardi: Senior Lecturer and Teaching Fellow at the First Architecture Faculty of the Polytechnic of Turin. She has carried out research at both the national and international level. She was one of the promoters of BEQUEST and Joint Leader of the Environmental Assessment Methods Task Group, set up to evaluate the sustainability of urban development. She has co-ordinated the Mediterranean Regional Network of the INTELCITY Roadmap (EU-IST/2002) and she is currently leader of the visioning work-package of the INTELCITIES integrated project (EU-IST/2003). At national level, she has been project manager of the reorganisation of the central railway station 'Porta Nuova' area in Turin (2002/2004) and responsible for the 'Social reporting' on the strategic plans of Trieste (2000) and Modena (2002). She has co-organised several conferences in Italy, Europe and Asia, such as the *Environmental Impact Evaluation of Buildings and Cities for Sustainability* in Florence (September 1995) and the Millennium Conference on *Cities and Sustainability in Sri Lanka* (February 2000). She is editor of a number of national and international books on sustainability evaluation in planning and author of numerous specialised textbooks and scientific journals.

Martin Symes: Professor in the Cities Research Centre, University of the West of England. He has published widely in the area of urban renewal and co-edited *The Handbook on the Reuse of Redundant Industrial Buildings*, *Urban Waterside Regeneration* and *The Urban Experience: A People-Environment Perspective*. He is co-author of *Architects and their Practices: A Changing Profession*. He has won research awards from the Economic and Social Research Council, the Nuffield Foundation, Gatsby Foundation, British Council, Royal Institute of British Architects, Architectural Registration Council, Commission for Architecture and the Built Environment, the French Ministere de l'Aménagement. He is a partner on three other EU-funded projects: IANUS (indicators for urban services), HQE2R (sustainable buildings for sustainable neighbourhoods) INTELCITY; and an associate of CNRS UMR 7544 Laboratoire des Organisations Urbaines, Universite Paris X.

Foreword
Peter Brandon

One subject has begun to dominate the discussion on research in the built environment over the past decade. In the foresight exercises undertaken in several countries, sustainable development has come out as the top issue that researchers and industrialists think needs to be addressed for the longer-term future.

However, when people are asked about what they understand by 'sustainable development', often the answers they give are vague and imprecise. Partly this is because the definition has not been part of the public debate and partly because the debate itself has been widened to include the political and socio-economic issues related to sustainable communities arising from the concerns of Third World countries. Although the public debate is active there is a lack of structure and meaning regarding the components of sustainable development and if we are not careful it becomes a discussion on practically everything in which human beings engage. It then loses focus and can be dismissed by the sceptics on the grounds that it means what people want it to mean and there is no real substance.

The question is: How do we get out of this dilemma? It would appear that human beings recognise that over-consumption and inappropriate behaviour is possibly leaving future generations with a legacy which will close down their opportunities and quite probably their ability to enjoy the quality of life we have today. This concern for 'intergenerational justice' is at the heart of the issues regarding sustainable development. It is seen by many to provide the moral imperative by which to address such issues, so that succeeding generations will not be penalised by our own flagrant (mis)use of natural resources available to us. The question is: What sacrifices are we prepared to make now in order to ensure that future generations do not suffer in this way?

At the root of these questions is another more practical issue. How will we know if we have made progress towards a sustainable society? To answer this question it is necessary to have two issues addressed. One is the need for a structure, common language or common understanding of sustainable development, to which all stakeholders agree, in order to build the knowledge, discourse and understanding needed to tackle this extremely complex issue. The second is to find ways of assessing and measuring progress. If we can't measure or assess sustainable development then how do we know we have achieved or are achieving anything? It is one thing to identify the problem, it is another to provide benchmarks for its solution.

In 1995 a conference was held in Florence, Italy, to discuss these important issues, with many key people from Europe, the USA and Canada attending. A publication was forthcoming on the proceedings (Brandon *et al.* 1997) which provided a discussion of these important issues and contributed to the debate at the international level. It was recognised that one conference was not enough and that further discussion, and more importantly action, needed to be undertaken. In view of this, a group of experts in the built environment met in the English Lake District and decided that there was a need for concerted action on these matters at the international level. They applied for funding from the European Union and were successful in gaining enough for what was known as a 'Concerted Action Programme'. This enabled a series of meetings to take place in which papers were presented and key issues discussed. The group became known as BEQUEST (**B**uilt **E**nvironment **QU**ality **E**valuation for **S**us**T**ainability). As is suggested by this title, the main focus was evaluation of the present environment for the benefit of future generations and the bringing together of what was being developed to assess the sustainability of urban development. Part of the final result of these deliberations was a toolkit in which the discussions were distilled into a set of techniques helpful in persuading decision makers to consider the sustainability of urban development proposals. In addition the approach was further extended to provide a holistic and integrated approach which endeavoured to represent the needs of all stakeholders (present, potential and future ones) within a common framework, set of protocols and assessment methods. The framework, protocols and assessment methods form the substance of this book, its successor volumes in the series and the toolkit BEQUEST has developed.

The members of BEQUEST recognised the need for structure within which 'knowledge blocks' could be built for evaluation purposes but they also recognised that this was merely the start of a long process in which formal structures and theory would develop as in other disciplines. This one was more complex, however, and was multidisciplinary by its very nature. Much of the interesting research in the future will be at the interfaces between the traditional disciplines and it will require flexible and open minds to solve the problems posed. It provides a real challenge and there will be many false starts en route. It can be expected that it will be an evolutionary process whereby new ideas and thoughts emerge as we provide both positive and negative feedback from the ideas that are postulated.

This book provides a useful account of the discussions held and the thoughts that emerged from the BEQUEST initiative. It would be impossible to capture all the wealth of knowledge which emanated from the group comprising fourteen research groups from six EU member states together with other individuals who participated at various times in the three-year project. For all concerned it was a learning experience for which we are all richer. A particular thanks for this experience should go to Steven

Curwell who led the programme and did so much to hold the programme together. Without his wisdom and firm hand and the energy and foresight of his co-editors, Mark Deakin and Martin Symes, it is doubtful whether this book would have emerged.

REFERENCE

Brandon, P., Lombardi, P. and Bentivegna, V. (1997) *Evaluation of the Built Environment for Sustainability*, E&FN Spon, London.

Preface

This volume is the first in a new series: *Sustainable Urban Development*. The aims of this first volume are to: outline the concept of sustainable urban development (SUD) and examine the protocols to be followed in carrying out environmental assessments and evaluating the sustainability of urban development. Published together with this volume, *Sustainable Urban Development: The Framework and Protocols for Environmental Assessment*, will be a second volume in the series, examining how environmental assessment methods are currently being used to evaluate the sustainability of urban development. This second volume will appear as *Sustainable Urban Development: The Environmental Assessment Methods*. Accompanying these volumes will be a third, *Sustainable Urban Development: A Toolkit for Assessment*, providing integrated examples of best practice in evaluating the sustainability of urban development. These three volumes are based on research undertaken by a network of academics and practitioners, known as the BEQUEST (**B**uilding **E**nvironmental **QU**ality **E**valuation for **S**us**T**ainability) Network, and supported, in part, by a grant from the European Commission (ENV4-CT97-0607).

The first text published by members of the BEQUEST network appeared as Brandon *et al.*'s (1997) *Evaluation of the Built Environment for Sustainability*. A special issue of *Building Research and Information* was based on the work of BEQUEST, which arose from the collaboration generated by working on that first text, and appeared in March/April 2002. A number of the chapters in this new book draw on the articles included in that journal and bring their content up to date. This volume, and the two other volumes accompanying this new series, extend the findings of the network. They will be followed by others furthering debate on the qualities of urban environments and examining the economic and social challenges posed by sustainable development.

Acknowledgements

The editors wish to thank the chapter authors for their valuable contributions and the holders of copyright who have permitted the reuse of a number of illustrations and diagrams. We also thank Ian Cooper and Gordon Mitchell, who have read chapters in draft and made many useful suggestions, as well as other members of the BEQUEST team for their encouragement to take this publication forward. We are indebted to colleagues who attended the various meetings of the BEQUEST network and participated in discussions there, joining the extranet established at that time. We owe a special debt to Caroline Mallinder, Michelle Green and Helen Ibbotson at Taylor and Francis, our publishers, as well as to the production team at Keystroke, who have worked with enthusiasm to improve this volume and accepted delays and indecision on our part with unflagging good humour. Last but by no means least, we must record our gratitude to our families, who have tolerated our absences for long evenings at the keyboard and even longer meetings in far-flung corners of Europe – tolerance without which this publication, and the work on which it has been based, would never have been possible.

SOURCES

The Architectural Press: Figure 5.3
BEQUEST Consortium: Boxes 8.1, 9.1
Bradford Council: Figure 5.5 (courtesy of Bradford Council. © Bradford Council)
Eclipse Consultants: Figures 10.1, 10.2; Tables 10.1, 10.2
Steven Curwell: Tables 2.1, 6.1
Simin Davoudi: Figures 3.1, 3.2
Mark Deakin: Figures 1.1, 1.2, 9.1, 11.1; Tables 4.1, 4.2, 4.3, 7.1, 8.1, 9.1
English Partnerships: Figure 5.2
HQE2R Project: Figures 5.6, 5.7; Boxes 5.1, 5.2, 5.3, 5.4
IANUS Indicators Group: Figures 7.1, 7.2, 7.3, 7.4, 7.5
Anthony Oliver: Figure 5.1 (Barbican Centre, London © Anthony Oliver)
Urban Initiatives Ltd: Figure 5.4

Introduction

Martin Symes, Mark Deakin and Steven Curwell

This book is concerned with putting sustainable urban development into practice. It is based on the work of a European network, BEQUEST. Members of the network have begun to generate a context in which a focus on operational issues can be added to the continuing debate over the appropriate science, technology and institutions for sustainable development. They have taken the view that this practical context should have four principal components. The first, a framework, vision and methodology for analysing the sustainability of urban development. The second, a set of protocols that can guide the principal actors in urban development through their tasks, and suggest ways in which existing, often less sustainable, practices can continue to be improved, is the subject of this volume. The third, a directory of detailed assessment methods for evaluating the sustainability of specific urban development proposals, is outlined here but also covered in depth in a second volume. The fourth, a community of assessment specialists adept in evaluating the sustainability of urban development, is also discussed in general terms towards the end of this volume. But more detail is set out by the practitioners themselves in the extensive case studies of integrated urban development projects which they contribute to the third volume in this series.

SUSTAINABLE URBAN DEVELOPMENT

The foundations of concern for the impact of science and technology on the environment were laid by Rachel Carson (1965). Her work focused on problems of the natural environment but introduced many of the solutions which are promoted today in the broader context of concern for the man-made environment. These include: the need to conserve species variety, the need to approach changing natural processes with caution, the need to avoid taking unnecessary risks and the need to consider who has the right to make decisions which affect the future. The term *sustainable development*, which refocused the debate on the economic and social purposes of applying science to environmental problems, was coined by Barbara Ward in the mid-1970s (Holmberg and Sandbrook 1992). It has rapidly gained currency in governmental and non-governmental circles concerned with the changing quality of life. Dickens (2004) shows many more recent examples of the way in which man is now considered to be a part of nature, and how, as society transforms its environment, people's own natures are being transformed as well. But the terminology is highly contested. Pearce *et al.* (1989) list more than sixty detailed definitions of the term sustainable development, and Beckerman (1994) called for greater clarity in its analysis. Contributing to this latter process, Mitchell (Mitchell *et al.* 1995, Mitchell 2000) argued that in practice the various definitions can be summarised with reference to two well-known statements (see also Cooper 1997, Deakin *et al.* 2001). One is 'development that improves the quality of human life while living within the carrying capacity of supporting ecosystems' (IUCN 1991); the other is the much-quoted Brundtland definition: 'development that meets the needs of the present without compromising the ability of future generations to meet their needs and aspirations' (WCED 1987).

The United Nations 'Earth Summit', held in Rio de Janeiro in 1992, developed a programme of action, Local Agenda 21 (United Nations 1993). This was followed up with a Habitat Conference in 1996, in which special emphasis fell on the consequences of urban development, both because of its objectives for changing the quality of life and because of its environmental impact. In Europe, human settlement is already predominantly urban in form (two-thirds of EU citizens lived in towns or cities before the Union's enlargement to the east). As a result, many of the questions about sustainable development in Europe relate to matters concerning the future of the urban development process. The European Council held a major conference of cities and towns in Europe at which the Aalborg Charter (1994) was adopted. This referred *inter alia* to the need for establishing a strongly participatory process. The European Commission DG XI established an expert group on the urban environment and this reported in 1996 (CEC 1996). The report proposed an ultimate aim of reversing the present negative relationships between, on the one hand, economic growth and, on the other, environmental conditions and the quality of life. Its conclusions included the need to integrate economic, social and environmental policy objectives, and it stressed the importance of developing an approach to urban management which would emphasise integration and partnership mechanisms.

The emergence of much stronger levels of concern about environmental quality has already had some impact on local government in most European countries. After the Rio conference, local authorities have introduced Agenda 21 initiatives, and, depending on national administrative systems, revised their town planning and building control regulations. Young (1993) reported that officials who had previously been considered marginal, or of low status, have moved to more central positions in decision making, or found that their work has grown in prestige or authority. Hambleton and Thomas (1995) have shown that increasing concern for the broad implications of local action (sometimes associated with centralisation of control over budgets) has led to the increased use of environmental assessment methods to evaluate the sustainability of urban development. The use of environmental assessment in the evaluation of sustainable urban development (SUD) has become a key function of new forms of governance. Oestreicher (1995) suggested that this trend will continue, arguing that:

> From time immemorial, local communities have been concerned with shaping the . . . environment. . . . This will remain so. But in view of the threatened balance between the human and the non-human on our planet, we have to learn from the past and reconsider the foundations of local government.

Mitchell (Mitchell *et al.* 1995, Mitchell 2000) sought to address the problems currently experienced by today's local government, and others, in making the concepts of sustainable development more operational. He referred to the need to develop a common language and a framework for evaluating urban sustainability. He went on to show that various types of sustainability indicators have become available and set out a number of criteria by which the indicators themselves might be assessed. Many of these feature in the assessment methods to be introduced in Chapters 8 and 9 of this volume, and are considered in detail in the second volume of the series.

Mitchell also traced the widespread recognition of a need for objective indicators of sustainable development to the Earth Summit held in Rio de Janeiro in 1992. Programmes of indicator development have been set up at international and, later, national levels, with 'the most active development of sustainability at the sub-national level, where local governments have embraced Agenda 21 and led the drive for appropriate indicators'. Measurement issues are significant when debate moves on from scientific discussion to a debate about the possibility of corrective action. Indeed there has been a rapid expansion in the volume of data on the performance of 'human-environment systems' and in its availability.

In a recent review of the literature, Hatfield Dodds (2000) examined the scientific debate over the development of sustainability indicators, and how five different 'approaches' are used to build support for corrective action on matters concerning environmental quality and ecological integrity, to mention but a few of the issues. A similar classification of 'approaches' to achieving sustainability in architectural practice (six in this instance) can be found in Guy and Farmer (2001). Referring to the consensus of opinion that increasingly surrounds such action, Hatfield Dodds sets out the various 'approaches' which it is possible to adopt as part of the search for SUD as follows.

The first is referred to as the 'sustainable income approach'. This is the most common approach and starts from the position that past practice has taken insufficient account of environmental resources and the damage which can be imposed upon them. The response should be to include more environmental information and more complete economic indicators in decision-making models.

A second approach, 'maintaining ecological integrity', argues that it is not enough to take account of environmental costs, and that consideration should be given to the capital stock of resources consumed, special measures being taken to maintain 'natural capital'. Its loss may be irreversible and the impact of its reduction on ecosystem modification too uncertain for useful evaluations to be made.

The third of Hatfield Dodds's approaches is concerned with 'inequality, institutions and environmental impact'. This derives from the observation that the distribution of income and power shapes environmental impacts for a given level of resource use. Particular attention should be paid to the impact of sudden changes in affluence on developing areas: the 'carrying capacity' of local environments should be central to the assessment of change.

The fourth approach is focused on 'participation and sustainable well-being'. This is a demand-side approach, which draws attention to non-economic needs, biological requirements and social norms. It works to create non-declining well-being, emphasises the value of understanding the social construction of preferences and proposes the diffusion of more sustainable expectations.

The fifth and final approach in this classification is that which seeks 'alternative ethical approaches'. At their most extreme, the authors expressing this point of view trace the difficulty of achieving sustainability to 'mainstream ethics and religious traditions, which treat the environment as a commodity that exists only for human benefit'. They propose a variant termed 'deep ecology', because a total collapse of lifestyle can only be prevented if there is a 'return to the Earth and a relearning of Ancient Wisdom' (Hatfield Dodds 2000).

THE BEQUEST APPROACH

When the BEQUEST network members met they emphasised the significance of Hatfield Dodds's second, third and fourth approaches. Guy and Farmer include BEQUEST in their ecocentric logic, whose proponents are concerned with buildings and their place in nature. Indeed, this integration of ecological integrity, equality of resource consumption and participation in decision making was also seen by the network as providing an ethical basis for considering the future of urban development. This view was widely discussed in presentations made by the network to the 'extranet' of international experts who acted as a loose-knit steering group for BEQUEST.

The specific approach adopted by the BEQUEST network is founded on an application of goals outlined in the PICABUE model of sustainable development. PICABUE (Mitchell *et al.* 1995) condenses the complex and lengthy Agenda 21 document and the goals of the Aalborg Charter into a 'shorthand form'. It lays emphasis on the need for:

- ecological integrity
- equity
- public participation
- futurity.

After agreeing the model, network discussions turned towards the framework of analysis itself, towards the establishment of protocols and towards the creation of the directory of assessment methods needed to evaluate the sustainability of urban development. The central sections of this book develop the results of these discussions and the final chapter discusses again the community of practitioners which is emerging to undertake such actions.

THE BEQUEST FRAMEWORK

The first part of this volume is completed in Chapter 2 by a discussion of the vision and methodology of an integrated process of sustainable urban development set out in the BEQUEST framework. This draws on the broader debate which has just been outlined and gives a unified structure for the examinations of the protocols and assessment methods which appear in Chapters 3 to 7 and 8 and 9 of this volume, respectively. The BEQUEST framework is intended to establish a clear organisational basis for the urban development activities, issues, level and scales of analysis which should be taken into account when setting out the protocols to be followed in assessing the sustainability of urban development.

There are four other factors which constrain decisions and these provide the main structuring element for the framework. Each of these is subdivided by the BEQUEST framework into between three and nine categories, together giving an overall typology of SUD decisions. In the case of the first two factors, the categories are subdivided again to allow more detailed aspects to come into play.

The first of these factors is the life cycle of interrelated *activities* – planning, property development, design, construction and operation (use, demolition and recycling) – which make up the urban development process. The second factor is a set of *sustainability issues* that surface concerning the environmental, economic and social structures of urban development. The third factor is the *spatial level* of analysis. It identifies the territorial impact of urban development and shows that this can be at the city, district, neighbourhood, estate, building, component or material level. The fourth factor, the consideration of *time scales*, is intended to show that this impact can be short-, medium- or long-term in nature.

The fundamental factor which links the activities of development, each of which has its spatial levels and its time scales, with the overall aim of sustainability as set out in the PICABUE representation mentioned above, is the second factor of the BEQUEST framework. This defines the environmental, economic, social and institutional issues underlying the sustainability of urban development. These can be seen to embody the four aspects of the PICABUE model as follows. The environmental issues include consideration of how urban processes consume natural resources, whether they produce unwanted waste or emissions which pollute the atmosphere, as well as the effect this production may have upon the bio-diversity of habitats. This factor helps answer the question of whether an urban development process has the required *ecological integrity*. Economic considerations relate questions about the financing of the infrastructure, transportation systems and utilities to the more general employment of resources in the urban development process. The social issues relate to matters of *equity* and considerations of access, the safety and security of cities, and the health and well-being of their citizens. The institutional issues refer to the governance, justice and ethics of urban development. They raise concerns about *public participation* in decisions taken about the urban development process and hence their sustainability over time, or *futurity* of the city.

Underlying the use of this typology is a need to understand the system of *actors* involved in creating a more sustainable urban development process. The roles which these actors play and the expertise which they have at their disposal will provide the foundations of competence upon which any assessment process will have to rely. In the seminars held during the BEQUEST networking period, the ATEQUE model of roles in modification and management of the built environment was adopted as a reference. Its categories are the starting point for discussion of the variety of decision-making contexts addressed in the protocol chapters of the book.

Figure 1.1 illustrates the relationship between these dimensions of SUD: ecological integrity, equity, participation and futurity, their environmental, economic, social and institutional qualities. It also illustrates the key issues surrounding sustainable development: those of fairness for all and socially inclusive decision making. The nature of these relationships is elaborated in Chapter 2.

FIVE PROTOCOLS

The second part of this volume consists of five chapters which introduce the decision-making context, or protocols, for each of the key development activities (urban planning, property development, design, construction and operation). The BEQUEST network has published a glossary of terms used in the discussion of sustainable urban development and in this glossary the definition given for a protocol is that it represents 'the accepted or established code of procedure, rules, or formalities'.

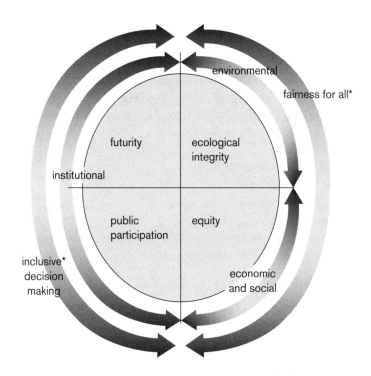

environmental

fairness for all*

futurity

ecological
integrity

institutional

public
participation

equity

inclusive*
decision
making

economic
and social

*fairness for all and inclusive decision making are discussed in Chapter 2's
examination of 'The BEQUEST framework: a vision and methodology'

1.1 The fourfold definition of sustainable urban development

These chapters, 3 to 7, outline protocols for the five development activities one by one. Each of them uses the framework already described to inform the protocol in question and prepare the ground for selecting the assessment methods appropriate for the evaluations which should be undertaken. Thus, for each of the five development activities, one of the chapters shows how assessment methods can be used to evaluate the sustainability of an aspect of urban development. It does this in three stages. First, each of these chapters uses the BEQUEST framework, and refers to the ATEQUE classification of actors concerned, identifying the issues (environmental, economic, social, institutional), or sub-issues, which can usefully be addressed when undertaking the tasks the relevant actors normally include in this stage of activity. Secondly, each chapter considers the range of spatial levels (which could be global, national, urban region, city, district, neighbourhood, estate, building, component or material, or some combination of these) at which the activity and relevant issues should be discussed. Thirdly, the chapters deal with the implications of various time scales (long-term, mid-term, short-term) for this discussion. On the basis of this classification, a set of assessment methods can be selected from the directory described in Chapters 8 and 9 and discussed in the second volume of the series.

The central sections of each chapter in this part of the volume seek to develop an understanding of the steps to be followed when establishing a process for using assessment methods to support decision making on the relevant issues in the activity concerned. In most instances these steps follow each other in a common sequence:[1]

- preliminary activities;
- planning of the assessment activity;
- what to do in assessing;
- carrying out the environmental assessment;
- carrying out consultations;
- taking into account the environmental report and the results of the consultations;
- providing information on the decisions;
- monitoring.

In order that this model of the assessment process should not remain an abstract model but become a valuable guide to practice, a *protocol*, each chapter attempts an explanation of the way assessments could (or should) be actually carried out in the area of activity with which it deals. Most of them contain an exemplary case study.

To generate and apply a protocol is not as simple as this description of decision making processes might make it sound. This is partly because what can be done to make urban development sustainable is heavily dependent on the uncertainties faced by each stakeholder and the risks they believe they are able or may be prepared to take. So the results in each of the five chapters do not all look exactly the same. These two particular characteristics – the degree of uncertainty that is experienced and the degree of risk which is thought possible to bear – have undoubtedly had an influence on the proposals presented here.

These points are well put by Brandon (1999) who, referring also to Cooper and Aouad (1998), presents them in the form of responses to questions a reader might ask, and suggests an interesting answer:

> First, 'how do I make a decision on sustainability where we are forecasting far into the future [and] we have no hard data?'

To which the answer given is:

> By creating a dialogue leading to a consensus between those with expert knowledge and those who benefit from the built environment.

And then:

> 'when should this dialogue take place?'

To which the suggestion made is:

> a consensus around a protocol would be beneficial . . . [one definition being] to define such protocols for [urban planning, property development, design and] construction with the identification of 'soft' and 'hard' gates you encounter when proceeding with a development . . . [so that] sustainability issues could be forced into the agenda at each 'hard' gate.

Brandon's answer, the definition of a 'hard' gate, being:

> the point at which the process cannot continue unless there is an agreed consensus or a permission, e.g. planning given for the next stage to proceed. In some cases compliance with . . . regulations will force the issue, in others it may be the demand of [a] client.

Each of the BEQUEST framework's five development activities has generated a different type of protocol for the use of assessment methods, each one appropriate for the depth of scientific knowledge which is available and the opportunities for good governance which have been envisaged. All five protocol chapters take the reader through the same sequence (preliminary, planning and so on, as described above), but for each the approach taken to the stages of this sequence varies, and in each the arguments about the need for (or existence of) 'soft' or 'hard' 'gates' at each of these stages will therefore be seen to differ.

Finally each of these five chapters provides a summary of the argument for the selection of a particular approach to sustainability assessment by the *actors* concerned with its particular activity and identified in the earlier chapter, thus illustrating the value of combining the ATEQUE structure of roles with the BEQUEST framework. Each chapter also gives pointers to the further examples of best practice which will be found in the second and third books of the series.

Indeed, both the protocols and the examples of practice have been written with the following objectives in mind:

• SUD requires assessments to be environmental, economic and social evaluations.
• It is necessary to go beyond rules and regulations and inspect the proposals as a whole.

- The actors must be at the centre of the process and work together on behalf of all stakeholders.
- Actors and stakeholders have expertise which must be exploited to the full.
- Building a consensus on the actions to be undertaken is fundamental to the process.
- Sustainability should become the rule and not the exception.

Arguably, to achieve these objectives equally well in all member states of the European Union will take many years of experimentation, and may require important innovations in governance, as well as local, national and European directives. These five chapters are seen as standing at the beginning of this process and a stimulus to further scientific investigation and to further debate.

Individually, the five chapters cover the major focus of attention for this volume. Chapter 3, on urban planning, emphasises the need to understand the scope of this activity and the issues surrounding development as well as the need to establish appropriate spatial levels and time scales of sustainable urban planning. Chapter 4 is a contribution on urban property development and examines the transformation property development is currently undergoing in making property market analysis, valuation and investment appraisal sustainable. This chapter goes on to outline the actions and guidelines decision makers should check when selecting the assessment methods needed to evaluate the sustainability of urban development. Chapter 5, on urban design, examines the need to distinguish between the processes and products of design and explores the complexities of integrating environmental, economic and social issues in an assessment methodology. Chapter 6 is on construction of the urban environment and deals with pre-project, pre-construction and construction phases. It covers a wide range of concerns which are vital to the physical development of cities, considering landscape and infrastructure construction as well as that of individual buildings. Chapter 7 is on the operation and use of the built environment: it defines urban development as social and economic, seeking to show how and when the use of the built environment interacts with this process. As a new profession, facilities management, has emerged to deal with some of these issues and its role is discussed in depth. In addition, more general questions are raised concerning the adequacy of present-day institutional arrangements. All five of the chapters in Part II include case study material illustrating best practice in a variety of European contexts.

THE ENVIRONMENTAL ASSESSMENT METHODS

The third part of the volume moves on to consider BEQUEST's post-Brundtland Directory of Environmental Assessment Methods. The trend has been for the methodology to turn towards investigating the *ecological integrity* of resource consumption. As argued above, this is a key aspect of the PICABUE description of sustainable urban development adopted by the BEQUEST network. It is possible to suggest that the advantage of this transformation lies in the opportunity it provides for applying the so-called 'hard' certainties of the bio-physical sciences to the more uncertain, and risky, sphere of economic and social relations. In so doing it has subsequently become necessary to take the growing interest in the ecological integrity of resource consumption a stage further: to emphasise the co-evolutionary nature of the bio-physical, economic and social factors in a framework of analysis which integrates them and, in so doing, allow the five protocols to guide decision makers towards those assessment methods capable of evaluating the sustainability of urban development most fully. It is argued that this integration can be achieved by the protocols being adopted as guides for action and as checks on the environmental appraisals and impact analyses to be described in the second volume of this series on SUD. For this, methodologies have been selected which cover the environmental, economic and social issues which underlie SUD. They raise questions about the capacity of conventional urban development processes to carry the ecological integrity, equity, public participation and futurity needed for sustainable development, and should stimulate innovation and integration in development activities.

There are two chapters on environmental assessment. Chapter 8 refers to the watershed created by the 1987 report of the World Commission on Environment and Development. It reports on the findings of a survey, carried out by BEQUEST members, which classified the types of environmental assessment method available 'post-Brundtland' to evaluate the sustainability of urban development. The survey on which it is based showed that there has been a process of transition from the basic assessment of the environment, to the development of advanced methods with broader, more complex, environmental, economic and social evaluations.

There follows a second contribution on assessment methods in Chapter 9. This explores how the various classes of environmental assessment method have been applied to evaluate the sustainability of urban development. This contribution maps out how the methods have been applied to plans, property development, designs, construction, and the uses of the built environment. It goes on to highlight the gaps that exist in the issues, spatial levels and time scales which most existing evaluations cover. Set within the classification of the urban development process provided by the BEQUEST framework and protocol, this mapping exercise highlights the way it should be possible to push environmental assessment methods beyond the 'state-of the-art' applications and cover the issues, spatial levels and time scales previously left out of sustainability evaluations.

THE ASSESSMENT COMMUNITY

The fourth part of the book examines the scientific and professional community undertaking such evaluations. It shows that this is increasingly becoming a 'networked' community or virtual organisation, using decision support systems underpinned by modern communications and information technology.

Chapter 10 argues that further development of 'post-Brundtland' approaches to integrated environmental assessment, as described in all of the first three volumes of this series, depends on the emergence of these communities and on their interaction with decision makers. The communication system which underpins this work has been, and will continue to be, both international and local, and supported by web-based information technology. It is unlikely that the decisions which need to be taken will be made without this technology or that the effort which is required for all appropriate sectors of an increasingly concerned, and well-informed, society to become involved in taking such decisions, shall be sustained without it.

LINKS AND CONNECTIONS

Figure 1.2 draws the relationships between the four dimensions of SUD, the framework, protocols and assessment methods together, giving them both form and content. As can be seen, it illustrates the relationship as a linear progression which can be read from the four dimensions to the framework, the protocols and assessment methods and which leads to the evaluation of SUD. The relationship is represented in this form because it is perhaps the most simple way to link them together and connect one with the content of the other. While useful for the links and connections it draws together for the reader, in the chapters that follow this assumption about the science and technology of sustainable development being read as a simple linear relationship is relaxed, so as to represent the truly complex nature of the material which is being dealt with: that of the urban development activities and sustainability issues which underlie SUD – activities and issues which are in reality far from linear and which are more logically speaking highly iterative in nature. Highly iterative in the sense that the relationships under examination need to be both 'back cast' and 'run forward' and to become the subject of reflection, critical evaluation and synthesis before a knowledge and understanding of SUD can be set out in all the true complexity which is needed for stakeholders to act upon.

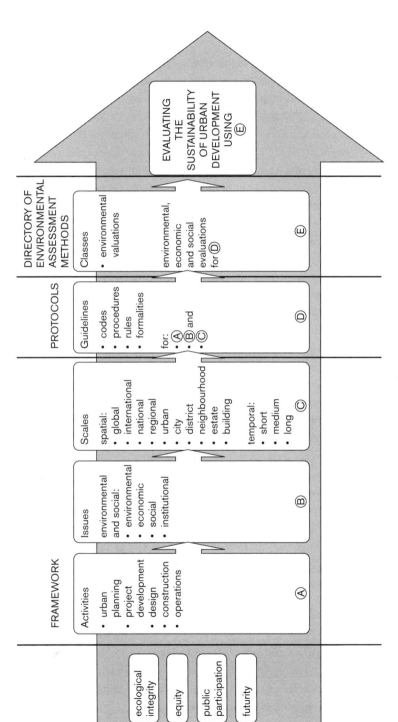

1.2 Framework, protocols and directory of environmental assessment methods

CONCLUSIONS

The eleventh and final chapter argues that this volume has reported on an international framework for the debate about the vision and methodologies needed for an integrated sustainable urban development, about the categories for an analysis, and about ways in which protocols for the planning, development, design, construction and use of the built environment can provide guidelines for decision makers to use when undertaking assessments. The work of BEQUEST, a European Community-funded network, suggests that the advances which are being made in SUD lead in a particular direction and that this is towards the development of protocols to follow in preparing for and carrying out environmental assessments. The chapter draws particular attention to the challenges the framework, protocols and environmental assessment methods pose for those in the scientific and professional communities who are responsible for evaluating the sustainability of urban development.

The final chapter also provides a link with the framework and the remaining two volumes in the series. This first volume has focused attention on five protocols, but the growing academic maturity of the field suggests that the strengths and weaknesses of technical advances in environmental assessment should be examined further. This will be the purpose of the second volume of the series. An opportunity also arises for speculation about new developments in assessment methodology appropriate for the evaluation of SUD. A recent review of the international agenda for improved environmental management (Dunn and Flavin, 2002) reports that the level of agreement on the scientific basis of the environmental crisis has changed dramatically since the Rio conference. It also suggests that the political will to implement such international agreements as the Kyoto protocol on climate change has become much stronger. These developments are working their way through to the national, regional and local levels and hence to urban development policy at the present time. For this reason, the increasing experience of practice in this field will be displayed in the third volume, which includes a range of case studies, giving examples of protocols and assessment methods in use. The concluding chapter closes by asking whether a new form of assessment methodology will in future be required for a more complete evaluation of the sustainability of urban development.

NOTE

1   This sequence of actions is based on the forthcoming European Directive (OJ 16.5.2000: Doc 52000AG0025). This is expected to provide a very particular official protocol framework for processes concerned with very large projects but its structure is generally applicable to assessment at most scales of development.

REFERENCES

Aalborg Charter (1994) available at: www.iclei.org/la21/echarter.htm

Beckerman, W. (1994) Sustainable development: is it a useful concept? *Environmental Values* 3: 191–209.

Brandon, P. S. (1999) Sustainability in management and organisation: the key issues? *Building Research and Information* 27(6): 391–397.

Carson, R. (1965) *Silent Spring*, Harmondsworth, Penguin Books.

CEC (Commission of the European Communities) (1996) *European Sustainable Cities: Report of the Expert Group on the Urban Environment*, Luxembourg, Office for Official Publications of the European Commission.

Cooper, I. (1997) Environmental assessment methods for use at the building and city scale: constructing bridges or identifying common ground. In Brandon, P., Lombardi, P. and Bentivenga, V. (eds) *Evaluation of the Built Environment for Sustainability*, London, E&FN Spon.

Cooper, R. and Aouad, G. (1998) Development of a general design and construction process, PDT Conference, Building Research Institute, Garston, March.

Deakin, M., Curwell, S. and Lombardi, P. (2001) BEQUEST: sustainability, assessment, the framework and directory of assessment methods, *International Journal of Life Cycle Assessment* 6(6).

Dickens, P. (2004) *Society and Nature: Changing our Environment, Changing Ourselves*, Cambridge, Polity Press.

Dunn, S. and Flavin, C. (2002) The climate change agenda: from Rio to Jo'burg and beyond, *International Journal of Technology Management and Sustainable Development* 1(2): 87–110.

Guy, S. and Farmer, G. (2001) Reinterpreting sustainable architecture, *Journal of Architectural Education* 54(3): 140–148.

Hambleton, R. and Thomas, H. (1995) Urban policy evaluation: the contours of the debate. In Hambleton, R. and Thomas, H. (eds) *Urban Policy Evaluation: Challenge and Change*, London, Paul Chapman.

Hatfield Dodds, S. (2000) Pathways and paradigms for sustaining human communities. In Lawrence, R.J. (ed.) *Sustaining Human Settlement: A Challenge for the New Millennium*, North Shields, Urban International Press.

Holmberg, J. and Sandbrook, R. (1992) Sustainable development: what is to be done? In Holmberg, J. (ed.) *Policies for a Small Planet*, London, IIED/Earthscan.

IUCN-UNEP-WWF (1991) *Caring for the Earth: Second Report on World Conservation and Development*, London, Earthscan.

Lawrence, R.J. (ed.) (2000) *Sustaining Human Settlement: A Challenge for the New Millennium*, North Shields, Urban International Press, editorial introduction.

Lombardi, P. and Brandon, P. (1997) Toward a multi-modal framework for evaluating built environment quality in sustainability planning. In Brandon, P. Lombardi, P. and Bentivegna, V. (eds) *Evaluation of the Built Environment for Sustainability*, London, E&FN Spon.

Mitchell, G. (2000) Indicators as tools to guide progress on the sustainable development pathway. In Lawrence, R.J. (ed.) *Sustaining Human Settlement: A Challenge for the New Millennium*, North Sheilds, Urban International Press.

Mitchell, G., May, A. and Macdonald, A. (1995) PICABUE: a methodological framework for the development of indicators of sustainable development, *International Journal of Sustainable Development World Ecology* **2**.

Oestreicher, J. (1995) Governing local communities: a view back and a look forward, *Trialog* 45: 33–35.

Pearce, D. W., Markandya, A. and Barbier, E.B. (1989) *Blueprint for a Green Economy*, London, Earthscan.

United Nations (1993) *Report of the United Nations Conference on Environment and Development, Rio de Janeiro, vol. 1: Resolutions*, New York, United Nations.

WCED (World Commission on Environment and Development) (1987) *Our Common Future*, Oxford, Oxford University Press.

Young, S. (1993) *The Politics of the Environment*, Manchester, Baseline Books.

Part I

The Framework

2

The BEQUEST Framework

A Vision and Methodology
Steven Curwell, Mark Deakin and Patrizia Lombardi

INTRODUCTION

The concepts of sustainable development that have emerged in the 'post-Brundtland' era are explored in terms of laying the foundations for a vision of sustainable urban development (SUD) and a methodology for its implementation. The integrated vision of SUD described here results from the activities of an international network called BEQUEST. Through a project funded by the European Commission (EC), the members of the network have built consensus across a wide range of stakeholders – planners, property developers, designers and contractors – involved in the creation, operation and use of the built environment. The result is a collaborative, urban re/development process, or methodology, in which the built environment is gradually adapted over space and time to suit more sustainable lifestyles. This consensus-building has in turn led to the development of a framework for analysing the stakeholder interests and activities underlying this collaboration and for evaluating the ecological integrity, equity, participation and futurity of urban development. This in turn provides the opportunity to integrate such values within the environmental, economic and social issues of SUD at various spatial levels and temporal scales of the urban development process and use them to assess the sustainability of cities.

After emphasising the environmental problems of cities, this chapter sets out the vision and methodology of consensus building and how this is shared across stakeholder interests collaborating over the planning, property, design, construction and operational stages of urban development. It then goes on to examine some impediments to the realisation of the vision and methodology set out in the BEQUEST framework. These include the lack of consideration given to the ecological integrity and equity of the urban development process and the drive towards their environmental, economic and social integration. In particular they relate to the absence of agreed sustainability targets and indicators. As will be seen, other impediments to which attention is drawn refer to the lack of appropriate protocols for SUD and methods by which to assessment it. Such protocols and assessment methods are essential for cities to deploy because they provide the means to properly evaluate the sustainability of urban development and provide a more rational basis for decisions affecting the future of towns and cities.

CITIES AND THE DECLINE OF ENVIRONMENTAL QUALITY

Cities, home to more than half the world's population and nearly 80 per cent of citizens of the EU (Buisquin 2000), are at the forefront of the battle to implement sustainable development. Cities can be seen simultaneously as a static receptacle of cultural heritage and as a dynamic mechanism, a machine with all the mobility, accommodation and other functions for supporting modern lifestyle needs. Clearly both views are relevant and BEQUEST has attempted to embrace them both. As the economic and cultural powerhouses of nations, cities provide an abundance of benefits that are essential to meeting our development aspirations. However, they are the most significant consumer of ecosystem resources and services. For example, it is estimated that in the developed countries around six to ten tonnes of building materials are used per person per year and 75 per cent of energy is consumed in the use of the built environment (BRE 1996). This exerts impacts from the local to the truly global scale, and yet most city dwellers feel little connection to the natural environment they rely so heavily upon. Unsurprisingly, despite some improvement in some areas in recent years, many of the environmental signals remain negative (EEA 2000).

Economies of scale have eroded, and continue to erode, the quality of the urban living environment and the social stability of cities, so that well-tuned efforts have to be made to reconcile environmental demands with economic and social goals (Orishimo 1982). In fact, the negative view of the 'unsustainable city' was summarised by Ekins and Cooper (1993) as:

- an environment which has degraded and become polluted, with an overloaded or degenerating and inefficient infrastructure, which is unacceptably detrimental to human well-being;
- an economy that has ceased to be able to support the population's expectations for either 'wealth creation' or 'quality of life';
- a society that has become dysfunctional, resulting in increased stress and fear of crime, alienation, high crime rates, and subsequent outward migration.

This represents a widespread consensus of what is 'wrong' with many existing inner-city areas, particularly in the post-industrial cities of affluent countries. This means that achieving urban development that is more sustainable is crucial, not just for improving the lives of urban populations, but for the well-being of the remainder of the planet, both people and ecosystems, impacted upon by all the activities of the inhabitants of cities. Thus the major challenge addressed by BEQUEST is the need to ensure economic, social and ecological sustainability of cities now and into the longer-term future.

UNDERSTANDING SUSTAINABLE URBAN DEVELOPMENT

What constitutes SUD is a complex and intractable problem. How to move towards SUD in existing cities, and how the sustainability of urban development proposals can be assessed and evaluated, has been explored through a series of ten interactive workshops and through the activities of an electronic network, known as the BEQUEST extranet. This involved discussion between the project team (twenty-four researchers from fourteen partner organisations in six EU countries) and around 120 representatives of all actors and a wide number of disciplines representing both the demand and supply sides of the property and construction sectors during the period 1998–2001. The network members, drawn mainly from European countries, also included a significant proportion from a wide range of other nations across all continents. Web pages were established and maintained as a means of supporting the networking activities, and the main outcomes and emerging policy issues raised in the workshops were reported in information papers available on the Web (BEQUEST 1998a, b, 1999a, b, 2000, 2001). Through this iterative networking process BEQUEST has engaged in a more structured discussion of sustainability issues and assessment methodologies, with a broader range of actors across a wider range of interests involved in the urban environment, than has been seen to date.

The iterative, interactive discussion process, described as a 'concerted action' – the EC's formal title for this type of research where knowledge and experience are pooled together – has provided the basis of the concepts and consensus that will be elaborated in this chapter. In this context the BEQUEST 'vision' of sustainable urban development is primarily that of a collaborative process represented by the BEQUEST framework described further below, rather than a utopian vision or blueprint for some idealised form of 'sustainable city'. Consideration of physical models was not a key objective of BEQUEST; however, a number of case study examples were examined in order to recognise aspects of 'good practice' in SUD (BEQUEST 1998a, b, 1999a, b, 2000). The outcomes of this collaboration, in terms of good practice protocols and assessment methods, were grouped together in a prototype electronic decision support system – the BEQUEST toolkit[1] – which provides a methodology for improving the sustainability of any particular urban re/development. This book considerably expands the original output from the BEQUEST project, by bringing together much of the good practice in SUD and its assessment which has previously been described (Deakin *et al.* 2001, 2002, Hamilton *et al.* 2002; see also BEQUEST 2001–2), with new material and insights and the more advanced understanding of SUD and its assessment which has emerged in the ensuing years.

The conceptual foundations of the BEQUEST framework stem from the continuing concerns about the negative aspects of cities, i.e. the 'unsustainable' city described earlier, and include the basis of sustainable development (SD), new ideas from 'green' economics and business, as well as emerging ideas for sustainable cities. A number of these 'building blocks' are briefly explored, before examining the framework in detail.

PRINCIPLES OF SUSTAINABLE DEVELOPMENT

The world-wide decay in environmental quality and the gradual depletion of natural resources has been a dominant theme for research and public policy in the latter part of the twentieth century and looks set to remain so for the first quarter of the next. The European Union and the majority of member states have placed sustainable development at the heart of policy making (Buisquin 2000). The global interest in, and current concepts of, SD can be traced back to the 1980 World Conservation Strategy published by the International Union for Conservation of Nature and Natural Resources (IUCN). In the section entitled 'Towards Sustainable Development' the main agents of habitat destruction are identified as poverty, population pressure, social inequity and the terms of trade which work against the interests of the poorer countries. This contributed to the concept of sustainable development (Hatcher 1996), although the real watershed in interest emerged from the Brundtland Commission on Environment and Development (WCED 1987). When the Commission tried to define sustainable development they were unable to agree on anything but this rather vague definition:

> Sustainable development is development that meets the needs of present generations
> without compromising the ability of future generations to meet their needs and aspirations.

This remains the 'benchmark' definition, but is often considered inadequate, and numerous other definitions exist, some good, others positively misleading. Nevertheless 'Brundtland' represented the emerging international consensus around the concept and the conflict between the demand for human development and protection of environmental systems into the future. The concept was further expanded at the Earth Summit, in Rio de Janeiro in 1992 (UNCED 1992), in the Agenda 21 'Policy plan for environment and sustainable development in the 21st Century'. In all, twenty-seven principles were agreed in the final declaration. All are important but ten of the more relevant in the context of urban re/development are shown in Table 2.1.

Table 2.1 'Agenda 21' principles of sustainable development – of particular relevance to urban re/development*

Principle 1: Human beings are the centre of concerns for sustainable development. They are entitled to a healthy and productive life in harmony with nature.

Principle 3: The right to development must be fulfilled so as to equitably meet developmental and environmental needs of present and future generations.

Principle 4: In order to achieve sustainable development, environmental protection shall constitute an integral part of the development process and cannot be considered in isolation from it.

Principle 5: All States and all people shall cooperate in the essential task of eradicating poverty as an indispensable requirement for sustainable development, in order to decrease the disparities in standards of living and better meet the needs of the majority of the people of the world.

Principle 7: States shall cooperate in a spirit of global partnership to conserve, protect and restore the health and integrity of the Earth's ecosystem. The developed countries acknowledge the responsibilities that they bear in the international pursuit of sustainable development in view of the pressures their societies place on the global environment and of the technologies and financial resources they command.

Principle 8: To achieve sustainable development and a higher quality of life for all people, States should reduce and eliminate unsustainable patterns of production and consumption and promote appropriate demographic policies.

Principle 10: Environmental issues are best handled with the participation of all concerned citizens, at the relevant level. At the national level, each individual shall have appropriate access to information concerning the environment that is held by public authorities, including information on hazardous materials and activities in their communities, and the opportunity to participate in decision-making processes. States shall facilitate and encourage public awareness and participation by making information widely available. Effective access to judicial and administrative proceedings, including redress and remedy shall be provided.

Principle 15: In order to protect the environment, the precautionary approach shall be widely applied by States according to their capabilities. Where there are threats of serious irreversible damage, lack of full scientific certainty shall not be used as a reason for postponing cost-effective measures to prevent environmental degradation.

Principle 16: National authorities should endeavour to promote the internalisation of environmental costs and the use of economic instruments, taking into account the approach that the polluter should, in principle, bear the cost of pollution, with due regard to the public interest and without distorting international trade and investment.

Principle 17: Environmental impact assessment, as a national instrument, shall be undertaken for proposed activities that are likely to have significant adverse impact on the environment and are subject to a decision of a competent national authority.

---

* It is accepted that as urban development is now all-pervading all twenty-seven Principles are relevant, but the ten above have the clearest implications for urban re/development.

The Agenda 21 principles have been criticised in terms of the human-centred nature of the recommendations; however, they should be judged together with the other agreements made in Rio, i.e. the Climate Change Framework Convention and the Biodiversity Convention. The twenty-seven principles interweave political, economic, legal, social and environmental dimensions. Thus a valid criticism is that the complex way in which they are framed undermines common understanding and appreciation. However, from the concepts underpinning the Brundtland definition, the Rio Agenda 21 principles, as well as a range of other views represented in the literature (Mitchell et al. 1995), there is widespread consensus on four underlying sustainable development principles, although not necessarily on their relative importance or interpretation. We can refer to these principles as those of ecological integrity, equity, participation and futurity.

Physical conditions for sustainable development

The principle of ecological integrity recognises the undeniable fact that humankind is entirely dependent upon the natural world, and that without the resources and ecosystem services it provides, life and development are impossible. Therefore, in order to maintain the viability of ecological systems in perpetuity, development must not degrade or deplete them to such an extent that they are unable to function effectively. The futurity principle recognises that the development aspirations of future generations must not be impaired by actions that we take today, and for this reason futurity forms one part of the concept known as inter-generational equity, or simply ensuring 'fair shares' for us and our descendants. Futurity demands that the value of all assets that are passed on to future generations, including natural resources, cultural heritage and human knowledge, should not decline, and is supported by the following guidelines:

- renewable resources must not be consumed faster than the rate at which they are renewed;
- non-renewable resources must not be consumed at a rate faster than they can be substituted for by a renewable resource;
- waste substances must not be discharged to the environment faster than it can assimilate them without impairment of ecosystem function.

Fairness for all

The equity principle, also known as social equity and, when considered with futurity, as intra-generational equity, requires that the most vulnerable people in society have a satisfactory quality of life, particularly with respect to access to resources and development opportunities, and freedom from threat. The equity principle arises through:

- enlightened self-interest, which argues that if social deprivation is reduced, less pressure is placed on critical natural systems upon which everyone depends;
- the view that social deprivation is morally undesirable.

SD requires transparent and inclusive decision making

From the above it is clear that there remains considerable scope for debate over the meaning of sustainable development, the objective goals associated with the concept and not least how best to achieve the desired goals in any given situation. There are heated arguments: for example, over the importance attached to species that have no obvious resource value, over what constitutes a fair allocation of resources amongst people, and over the nature of growth and development – the former associated with economic expansion, achieved through continued resource consumption, and the latter concerned with the quality of development, judged by its effectiveness at satisfying the higher 'quality of life' aspirations, whilst at the same time maintaining the ecological integrity of the environment. Such debates over the equity of resource allocation mean that another principle, i.e. 'participation of concerned stakeholders in decisions that affect them', is a critical consideration. The significance of participation is further elevated when it is considered that sustainable development is not about achieving a desired balance between competing demands placed on space, but about achieving this balance continuously over a long time frame, in a future where natural and human systems are dynamic and uncertain.

TOWARDS THE PRINCIPLES OF SUSTAINABLE URBAN DEVELOPMENT

Following the discussion of 'human development' appearing in the Brundtland Report and Agenda 21, and 'human settlement' in the UN Habitat Conference in 1996, BEQUEST sought to draw upon these definitions as a means of moving the EU towards a framework for common understanding of sustainable *urban* development. As identified above, in Europe human settlement is predominantly urban in form (80 per cent of EU citizens live in towns or cities). As a consequence, questions about sustainable development relate to matters concerning the future of the development process. In particular they relate to questions about the development of urban futures, cities of tomorrow and the protection of their cultural heritage, and how we build the capacity needed to not only conserve resources and protect the environment, but qualify whether such action is equitable. In turn this means such evaluation must foster public participation in decisions taken about the future of urban development because such inclusiveness becomes integral to SUD.

The PICABUE model of SD

BEQUEST began with the principles ecological integrity, equity, participation and futurity in a 'four-sided' model, known as PICABUE – see Figure 2.1 (ERC 1996). This combines the concern about the quality of the environment and the equity of resource consumption, and the participation of the public in decisions that affect their lives, particularly in understanding the future implications of decisions taken today on the environmental systems and on current and future generations. This four-dimensional description of sustainable development was used in the early stages of the project to explore common understanding and terminology for SD across the members of the network. This exposed significant gaps in the understanding and different prioritisation of the four principles between the various professional groups involved in urban re/development, which emphasised the potential barriers to concerted action across professional boundaries in order to deliver SUD in cities – see Cooper 2002 and Chapter 10. These activities provided BEQUEST with a common language, vocabulary and terminology to begin to address and communicate what is meant by SUD. The agreed vocabulary takes the form of a 'glossary', setting out the terminology thrown up by SUD.

Considering other models of SD

PICABUE was also used as the base model against which other models of SD could be tested and evaluated with a view to developing consensus over a conceptual model or framework for SUD. The review and testing embraced a wide range of SD concepts and models that had emerged from governments, non-governmental organisations (NGOs), industry and research, including the OECD Pressure State Response Indicator Model (OECD 1994), Pentagon Model (Nijkamp 1998) and Quantifiable

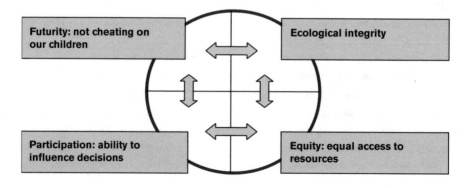

2.1 The PICABUE model of sustainable development

City (May *et al.* 1997). Some of these are represented in shorthand form in Figure 2.2 (see Mitchell *et al.* 1995, as developed by Cooper 1997). Another SD concept explored is the 'Natural Step', whose four 'System Conditions' (Figure 2.3) provide a good SD business philosophy, which is finding increasing application in a wide range of industrial sectors, including construction and development organisations. In the UK this includes notable companies such as the Sainsbury supermarket chain, the Cooperative Bank and the Carillion construction company. The vision underlying Natural Step and that of the 'Service Economy' concept (Figure 2.4) is of a more

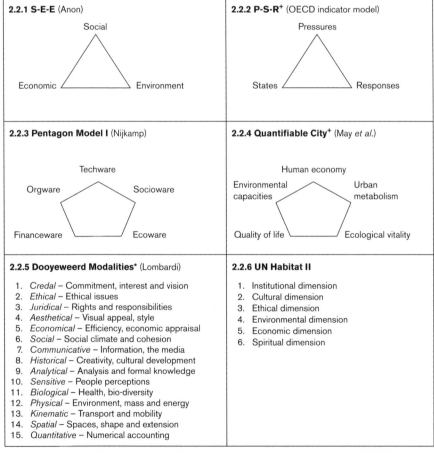

2.2.1 S-E-E (Anon)

Social

Economic — Environment

2.2.2 P-S-R[+] (OECD indicator model)

Pressures

States — Responses

2.2.3 Pentagon Model I (Nijkamp)

Techware

Orgware — Socioware

Financeware — Ecoware

2.2.4 Quantifiable City[+] (May *et al.*)

Human economy

Environmental capacities — Urban metabolism

Quality of life — Ecological vitality

2.2.5 Dooyeweerd Modalities* (Lombardi)

1. *Credal* – Commitment, interest and vision
2. *Ethical* – Ethical issues
3. *Juridical* – Rights and responsibilities
4. *Aesthetical* – Visual appeal, style
5. *Economical* – Efficiency, economic appraisal
6. *Social* – Social climate and cohesion
7. *Communicative* – Information, the media
8. *Historical* – Creativity, cultural development
9. *Analytical* – Analysis and formal knowledge
10. *Sensitive* – People perceptions
11. *Biological* – Health, bio-diversity
12. *Physical* – Environment, mass and energy
13. *Kinematic* – Transport and mobility
14. *Spatial* – Spaces, shape and extension
15. *Quantitative* – Numerical accounting

2.2.6 UN Habitat II

1. Institutional dimension
2. Cultural dimension
3. Ethical dimension
4. Environmental dimension
5. Economic dimension
6. Spiritual dimension

* Used here as a classification only, not a philosophy as originally conceived by Dooyeweerd (1958)
+ Each category subdivided one or more times to give increasingly more specific 'people-environment' factors

2.2 Some examples of people–environment factor classifications or models

The NATURAL STEP

The Four System Conditions

In the sustainable society, nature is not subject to systematically increasing . . .

    1. . . . concentrations of substances extracted from the Earth's crust
    2. . . . concentrations of substances produced by society
    3. . . . degradation by physical means

and, in that society . . .

    4. . . . human needs are met worldwide.

2.3 The 'Natural Step System Conditions'

cyclical industrial and economic process, rather than the current linear process of production, consumption and waste (Giarini and Stahel 1996). In the service economy citizens purchase services, e.g. photocopying, through a combined lease and maintenance package rather than owning the copier outright. The manufacturer retains ownership and will therefore seek to maximise value, e.g. through refurbishing the equipment or subcomponents or through recycling constituent materials at end-of-life. Thus design, manufacturing and maintenance strategies are aimed at considerably extending the service life of materials and components, and ultimately recovering a high percentage of the raw materials at the end of this extended life. Thus modern manufacturing could be 'dematerialised' in terms of reducing demand for raw materials to a very low level. Although, on the whole, buildings are long-lived artefacts, the Service Economy concept could be applied to extend the service life of those parts of buildings that are regularly replaced or changed due to wear and tear and through declining technical performance or appearance. Building services and fittings form good examples.

    Further emerging models of SUD such as the UN Habitat Programme (UNCHS 1996) or the Dooyeweerdian modalities (1958) as interpreted for urban development by Lombardi (1998) were also explored (see Figure 2.2). These identify, in addition to all the parameters already discussed, the importance of the cultural and spiritual background in terms of the built heritage and overall well-being of citizens. These point up important but difficult-to-quantify 'extra' dimensions of the quality of life of citizens. From an economic perspective, the built environment as cultural heritage is clearly an important 'good' that has measurable value, for instance, in terms of tourism.

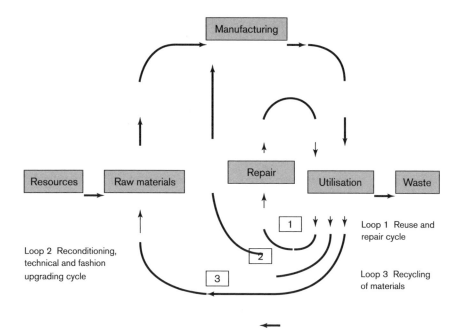

2.4 The service economy

Negative aspects of current policy and practice in urban re/development

The continuing decline in inner urban areas – the 'unsustainable city' (Ekins and Cooper 1993) mentioned earlier – means that improving the quality of the urban environment has become a key factor in the inter-competitiveness of urban areas within a city and between cities. This is focused on achieving income generation or other inward investment required to ensure the creative redevelopment of urban life in terms of the economic efficiency, competitiveness and required degree of social cohesion (Finco and Nijkamp 2001).

To address these issues, and in parallel with the review of various models of SD, BEQUEST also explored a number of case studies of urban development and regeneration. Each was selected because it offered some exemplary characteristics. However, the case studies collectively reveal an absence of any detailed and integrated investigation of SUD. Long-term consideration of environmental, economic and social effects is not common. Hence inter-generational equity, although recognised as an important principle, is not an effective part of active decision making at present (BEQUEST 1999a, b, 2000, 2001).

Instead the pressures to correct the problem areas of cities and the inter-competitiveness issues lead to what BEQUEST has described as the 'regeneration imperative'. Quick fixes are being adopted to the perceived problems such as industrial decline, environmental degradation or social malaise. This is compounded by the short time frames controlling allocation and use of various sources of financial aid available from EU, national, regional and local agencies to help with urban problems. Many commercial and political investment decisions are taken by the availability of such regeneration and re/development incentives. These factors link together to drive the normal pragmatic approach to setting objectives, spatial boundaries and time dimensions in planning of re/development projects. Thus the need for immediate action to improve an area suffering serious decay and/or decline typically overrides participation and futurity needed for consideration of the longer-term impacts of the development (BEQUEST 1999a, b, Curwell and Lombardi 1999).

This set of constraints favours a deterministic policy priority of (immediate?) physical change, which is expected to lead to economic and social improvements, ahead of measures promoting longer-term investment in people, through improvements in educational and skills capacity. In addition, the boundaries of political, administrative and economic jurisdictions form more important considerations than the potential 'footprint' of various environmental or social effects (e.g. over a river watershed, or in an adjoining community). In turn, this results in the assessment, and the majority of the tools that are used for the assessment, being restricted to short-term consideration of impacts within the specific 'site' or 'planning' boundaries set by the politico-economic drivers. The negative impact of these constraints on the longer-term sustainability of urban interventions and development appears to be a seriously un(der)addressed issue in current 'leading edge', 'good practice' in the EU, with important implications for policy at all levels.

Failure to develop an effectively balanced SUD policy, that is to say, without the required efficiency, competitiveness and cohesion, will tend to reinforce urban sprawl and run the risk of making cities more 'unsustainable'. The success of effective, well-balanced policies towards SUD depends on three determinants:

- Physical: the urban structure and morphology, i.e. population density, urban form, transportation and utility networks, urban heritage, etc.
- Behavioural: attitudes and behaviour of citizens, their lifestyle choices, mobility patterns, environmental awareness, etc.
- Governance: institutional factors in the management and organisation of the urban systems, public–private modes of co-operation, forms of participation, etc.

Targets and indicators

Whether a given urban development meets the dual aims of livability and sustainability is therefore co-determined by the targets set by policy makers. These have to reconcile conflicting demands and interests of various members of the community. The assessment systems and methodologies that are used to evaluate progress are critical. In the past twenty years many environmental assessment methods have been developed but these do not necessarily cover much of the wider set of criteria represented by SUD (Deakin et al. 2001, 2002).

Even in terms of minimising environmental impact, there is a lack of clarity and agreement about what overall sustainability targets should be set and which indicators of progress should be employed. A number of experimental building projects in the EU have achieved reductions in energy and/or resource consumption of in the region of Factor 10 to 20, when compared with normal practice (BEQUEST 1998a, b, 1999a, EGBF 2001), but the mainstream is a long way from such performance levels. This supports the view (expressed by Von Weizsaker et al. 1997 and Fudge 2000) that the technology exists to ameliorate the vast majority of current environmental problems in, or created by, urban centres, but only if all the best available technological practice could be generally instigated now. However, an immediate step change to Factor 20 reductions would bring with it a number of undesirable short-term consequences, and not just for the commercial viability of the construction industry, but for the whole economy. This is illustrated by developments in Holland, which began by setting a good international example in the late 1990s – to seek Factor 20 by 2050. However, a subsequent change in government means that this target seems to be quietly forgotten. The introduction of smaller year-on-year, aggregated improvements, such as those suggested by the Wuppertal Institute's *Modelling a Socially and Environmentally Sustainable Europe* (Wuppertal Institute 1998), appears a more viable route forward. The implications of attempting to achieve high levels of performance improvements for the EU construction sector have yet to become an area of serious (research strategy) debate, let alone practical action.

Very wide and varied sets of quantifiable criteria, or systems of indicators, have been developed internationally, and by local authorities through the local Agenda 21 process. However, it appears to be extremely difficult to operationalise such indicator systems and so there is no single unambiguous measure to help planners, urban designers and other urban policy makers with the 'change management' problem (Finco and Nijkamp 2001). In this confused situation BEQUEST has adopted and developed the classification used in the UN Working List of Indicators (UNCSD 1996), i.e. Environment, Economics, Social and Institutional, rather than others that might have been selected, such as that of the OECD. However, it should be noted that establishing a consensus view across all members of the BEQUEST research team in this area proved to be very difficult (Cooper 2002 and Chapter 10). Therefore selection of the four-sided environment, economics, social and institutional structure represents a compromise that provides a link with an established, recognised international system of indicators that is related to Agenda 21. It is important to appreciate that an EU concerted action, such as BEQUEST, is primarily about pooling of knowledge and development of a common approach and understanding. This is extremely difficult to achieve across the wide range of disciplines and cultural contexts that are embraced by the EU and SD. In this context the level of the consensus that the BEQUEST framework represents is a significant achievement. So too is the shared vision of the stakeholder interests and degree of collaboration experienced in dealing with the urban development process as a set of key environmental, economic and social issues underlying the sustainability of cities.

The principles of ecological integrity, equity, participation and futurity, described above, have a clear and distinct and strategic meaning for urban development and the built environment. They relate to land use, architecture, monument conservation, transport and infrastructure, housing, commercial buildings and public facilities. The spatial reality is that current urban centres consist of a complex amalgam of existing buildings, transport and infrastructure systems developed over a long time period. Ninety per cent of existing structures will be in use thirty years' time (CEC 2000). Thus SUD becomes a *process* for adapting the existing built environment over time in a way that supports more sustainable patterns of living and working. Priority needs to be given to addressing the political, economic and social barriers to implementing the emerging cleaner, resource-efficient technologies. At the same time, it ought to be recognised that the realisation of targets of urban sustainability may extend beyond the borders of the city (the 'ecological footprint'), implying that sustainable urban planning and development requires a more balanced portfolio of policy measures than is currently the case.

The principles of sustainable urban development

From this broad analysis of current understanding and practice it is clear that none of the models explored above, of themselves, provide an adequate 'picture' of 'sustainable *urban* development', but a number of important common factors emerge, which represent the key principles of SUD:

- SUD is a *relative* rather than an absolute concept.
- SUD is a *process* not a product or fixed destination.
- SUD relates considerations of *ecological integrity, equity, participation and futurity* of the urban development process.

- This in turn relates to the *planning, property development, design, construction and operational sectors* of the urban development process.
- Progress towards SUD *must integrate* Environmental, Economic and Social issues underlying the urban development process and sustainability of cities.
- Integration of the issues underlying the urban development process and sustainability of cities proceeds *within a given institutional setting.*

These points provide the terms of reference needed to 'frame' the relevant issues (structure them in space and time) and lead on to the formulation of the protocols needed to procure SUD and direct decision makers towards the assessment methods currently available to evaluate the sustainability of urban development, through which a more integrated view of the type that is set out below becomes possible.

THE BEQUEST FRAMEWORK

How do we know that the urban interventions we make today will lead to, or assist in supporting, more sustainable communities in the future? It is clear that the answer is very location-specific; it depends on the local environmental, economic and social constraints relevant in any particular urban area. Therefore BEQUEST does not attempt to impose an answer to this question directly. Rather it seeks to provide a frame of reference within which those who have to make such decisions can work and understand the context of the decisions taken.

The framework relates four main dimensions of SUD: the urban development activity, the sustainability issues (environmental, economic, social and institutional), spatial level and time scale (see Figure 2.5).

The urban development activities

As identified, SUD is a process. As such, good practice guidance on SUD and on the use and procurement of assessment methods needs to be integrated with the urban development process from strategic planning, on the one hand, to utilisation of the resulting built environment on the other. The main activities and their sub-activities are: Planning (strategic and local), Property development (public and private interests), Design (urban, building and components), Construction (new build, refurbishment and demolition) and Operation (use, facilities management and maintenance). Each of these involves a separate but interlinked process where specific methods of assessment are needed to evaluate the sustainability of urban development.

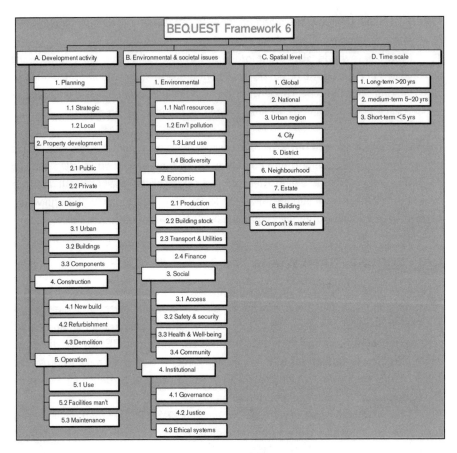

2.5 The BEQUEST framework

Environmental, economic and social issues

As outlined earlier, human activities create effects which are more or less sustainable. These activities are created by, or are consequences of, sources of environmental, economic and social stress. Environmental stresses include depletion of natural resources, pollution, and excessive land use with consequent loss of bio-diversity. Economic stress is often a cause and effect of loss of production, decaying building stock, and/or inadequate finance or incentives. Transport and utilities are important industrial sectors that affect and are affected by other economic sectors. Social stress may include lack of access to facilities, inadequate safety and security, poor health or general loss of well-being which is often associated with poor sense of community. Good governance is necessary to create equality of access to resources along with social participation, and judicial means of redress are all part of the institutional framework necessary to support SD. All these aspects, and the spiritual dimensions of life, are moral codes and ethical systems.

Spatial levels

Urban development can take place at various spatial levels from the whole city down to that of an individual building and its material components. Equally, the environmental effects or other socio-economic implications can be felt from local to global levels. A planning proposal can lead on to various new industrial and commercial consequences for the environment, economy and society from the level of the whole city down to that of the neighbourhood. The provision of new buildings can affect the extraction of raw materials and the manufacture of components, which, in turn, can create emissions that can have effects on the environment from the local to the global scale, and so on.

Time scale

The importance of long-term thinking to SUD has been emphasised above. The time scale used by BEQUEST, i.e. short-term 0–5 years, medium-term 5–20 years and long-term more than 20 years, represents the normal scale used in economic and strategic planning.

TOWARDS A PROCESS METHODOLOGY FOR 'MORE' SUD

It remains open to question whether urban re/development professionals will be able to fulfil the high expectations that SUD places on them as they find themselves confronted by one of the most important challenges of our time – the conflict or contradiction between:

- the immediate need to make improvements to towns and cities to reverse the negative trends of urbanisation (five years or less);
- the 'doomsday' predictions of some environmentalists – the short time period available to correct the numerous, serious environmental problems (e.g. twenty years or less);
- the long time frames necessary for both the social and political changes that will ensure adequate change towards much more sustainable lifestyles, as well as the necessary physical adaption of cities (e.g. fifty years or more).

A wide range of examples of good (and not so good) SUD policy and practice exist that can help address this challenge, and a number of these have been explored in the BEQUEST project. However, these are very location-specific and the lessons learned cannot be easily exported to other cultural or physical circumstances without broader understanding of SUD and so the protocols developed to date are fairly generic in order to be generally applicable. It is clear that there is a lack of awareness by many professional actors of the broad range of techniques (i.e. in terms of technological change, good practice and evaluation tools) that will allow them to achieve 'more' sustainable outcomes. This is contributing to the absence of detailed and integrated investigation of sustainable development effects beyond simple economic and environmental protection criteria. Clearly the BEQUEST approach can assist in the awareness-raising and capacity-building that is necessary to establish a broader and fuller SUD perspective.

The BEQUEST framework is predicated on the key finding identified earlier – that integrated SUD is a relative, adaptive process. This fact is important to establishing a methodology to be applied in urban re/development projects. In this context, the BEQUEST framework and toolkit (the electronic decision support system that operationalises the framework) are intended to help make 'better' decisions along the way – so that all stakeholders can be confident that the outcomes will be more sustainable. However, on its own, BEQUEST cannot overcome a number of wider social and political impediments that will tend to slow or constrain implementation of more integrated approaches to SUD, including:

- the overall lack of demand in some countries for more sustainable solutions;
- inadequate participation and empowerment in urban re/development decision making and loss of citizens' faith in governance in general;
- lack of clarity and agreement about what sustainability targets should be set and upon the indicators of progress towards a more sustainable built environment.

Final success (or failure) in any particular re/development situation will be dependent on two essentials. First, a closer **dialogue between all stakeholders**, addressing sustainability as an essential requirement for human settlements in future. BEQUEST offers a more defined and constructive language for SUD with which to frame these wider problems and build consensus on the issues in question. Second, greater **integration across various urban decision-making and professional disciplines**. In this context, urban policy makers, planners, property developers, designers (architects and engineers) and constructors need to see themselves as change-managers seeking innovative solutions to adapt and regenerate cities so as to support more sustainable lifestyles.

In order to achieve these objectives in any particular re/development programme or project, four steps are necessary:

1   Benchmark the current situation in environmental, socio-economic and institutional terms as the base on which proposals can be based.

2   Identification of a range of possible good practice policy and physical development options through collaborative work with, and the participation of, all stakeholders. This includes a long-term vision for the community through exploration of alternative scenarios for the future.

3   Analysis of and selection of the optimum outcome for the situation under consideration in terms of increasing the sustainability of the community.

4   Ongoing review to monitor progress and amend proposals, as becomes necessary, and to update the vision.

Over time this represents an iterative process in each of the activity areas – planning, property, design, construction (demolition and recycling) and operation (use). Although these steps are easily stated, the reality is that they are very difficult to achieve because of the complexity of the analysis and the lack of agreement over targets and indicators. They embrace a very wide range of issues and actors so that in all cases there is a clear need for a more defined methodology based on the application of SUD protocols, assessment methods and techniques that enable *objective*, fully evidence-based sustainability evaluations and provide sound information on the future implications of various options, both for decision makers and for the wide range of other stakeholders.

The full potential of the BEQUEST framework (as a methodological device linking SUD activities, issues, levels and scales to the protocols and the connection this has in turn to assessment methods) is still being investigated. The framework is already being used as a structuring device by other research groups, notably the European Green Building Forum (EGBF 2001), and in a project known as CRISP, exploring the range of Construction and City Related Sustainability Indicators (CRISP 2001), because of its recognised potential to identify various 'gaps' in understanding of SUD between a wide range of interests and stakeholders. These include the gaps between:

- the protocols for the planning, property, design and construction interests of SUD;
- fuller environmental, economic and social assessments;
- assessment methods used at the building scale and those at the urban planning scale;

and across three main groups of activities of SUD, i.e. those involved in:

- planning and property development;
- the provision and management of the infrastructure;
- the design, construction and management of buildings.

This 'gap analysis' has already influenced the approach of the individual research partners in their own portfolios of ongoing investigations in current research projects, the outcomes of which are to be included in later volumes of this series.

The BEQUEST framework, the vision of SUD that underlies it as well as the emerging methodology, offers an approach for integrating SUD across all scales of action, time frames, issues and stakeholders. It has provided a device for framing current thinking and to build consensus on the steps necessary to develop cities more sustainably. BEQUEST provides a common language and vocabulary for opening up a dialogue between relevant stakeholders and it provides comprehensive terms of reference for developing the protocols needed to manage such change in a suitably innovative way. Such protocols are needed in order to direct decision makers towards better practice options and the assessment methods which are currently available to evaluate the sustainability of urban development.

CONCLUSION

After setting out the physical conditions for sustainable development and the need for fairness and inclusive decision making, this chapter has examined various visions and models of SD that have emerged 'post-Brundtland' as a means of establishing a broader understanding and methodology for SUD.

BEQUEST has sought to identify the common issues underlying the growing interest in sustainable urban development and to structure them in such a way as to provide a framework for analysis. This has been done by first adopting the Mitchell et al. (1995) PICABUE definition of sustainable development, 'mapping out' the 'fuzzy buzzwords' associated with the concept as identified by Palmer et al. (1997) and then modifying it to include the issues underlying the urban re/development process. This has meant:

- foregrounding the question of urban development and representing it as a life cycle of interrelated activities;
- agreeing the sustainable development issues underlying the urban process;
- identifying the environmental, economic and social structure, spatial level and time frames involved in SUD.

Foregrounding urban development has emphasised its inherent processes, as well as the division of labour in the scientific and professional communities – planning, property, design, construction (demolition and recycling) and operation (use). Representing the process of urbanisation as a life cycle of inter-related activities allows a wide range of sustainable development issues to surface concerning the environmental, economic and social structure, spatial level and time scales of SUD. For example, the spatial level of analysis identifies the territorial impact of urban development. This illustrates that the impact can be at a host of spatial scales, from the city, district, neighbourhood, estate, building, component and material level. The consideration of time scales also shows that the said impact can be short-, medium- and long-term in nature.

The methodology proposed is that of an integrated, iterative process to catalyse change and improve the sustainability of cities by building consensus across stakeholder interests. In order to facilitate this, the BEQUEST framework of activities, issues, levels and scales of analysis:

- provides a 'model' of SUD that adequately represents, but simplifies, the breadth and complexities of the issues faced in consensus-building exercises of this type;
- forms the basis for common understanding and therefore for integration between a wide range of stakeholders;
- provides a framework for integrating analysis of SUD across activity, issue, level and scale;
- calls for a set of protocols that allow the planning, property development, design, construction and operational components of SUD to be integrated within, and as part of, the environmental, economic and social issues underlying matters concerning the sustainability of cities;
- allows decision makers in cities to select the assessment methods capable of evaluating the sustainability of urban development.

The chapters that follow in Part II will focus attention on the protocols, and those in Part III will focus on assessment methods available for all those involved in the change management of cities to use in evaluating the sustainability of urban development proposals.

NOTE

1   The development and functionality of the Toolkit is to be described in Volume 3 of this series.

REFERENCES

BEQUEST (1998a) *Information paper 1*: http://www.surveying.salford.ac.uk/bqextra

BEQUEST (1998b) *Information paper 2*: http://www.surveying.salford.ac.uk/bqextra

BEQUEST (1999a) *Information paper 3*: http://www.surveying.salford.ac.uk/bqextra

BEQUEST (1999b) *Information paper 4*: http://www.surveying.salford.ac.uk/bqextra

BEQUEST (2000) *Information paper 5*: http://www.surveying.salford.ac.uk/bqextra

BEQUEST (2001) *BEQUEST Toolkit*: http://www.surveying.salford.ac.uk/bqextra

BRE (Building Research Establishment) (1996) *Buildings and Sustainable Development*, Information Sheet A1, BRE, Garston, Watford, UK.

Buisquin, P. (2000) Foreword. In CEC *Design for Living – the European City of Tomorrow*, CEC EUR 19381, p. 3.

CEC (Commission for the European Communities) (1993) *Fifth Environmental Action Programme*, http://www.europa.eu.int/comm./environment/actionpr.htm

CEC (Commission for the European Communities) (2000) *Design for Living – the European City of Tomorrow*, CEC EUR 19381.

Cooper, I. (1997) Environmental assessment methods for use at the building and city scales: constructing bridges or identifying common ground? In Brandon, P., Bentivegna, V. and Lombardi, P. (eds) *Evaluation of the Built Environment for Sustainability*, E&FN Spon, London.

Cooper, I. (2002) Transgressing discipline boundaries: is BEQUEST an example of the 'new production of knowledge'? *Building Research and Information* 30(2): 116–129.

CRISP (2001) http://crisp.cstb.fr

Curwell, S. and Lombardi, P.L. (1999) Riqualificazione urbana sostenibile, *Urbanistica* 112: 96–103 (English summary 114–115).

Curwell, S., Hamilton, A. and Cooper I. (1998) The BEQUEST network: towards sustainable urban development, *Building Research and Information*, special issue, Sustainability: An International Perspective, 26(1): 56–65.

Deakin, M., Curwell, S. and Lombardi, P. (2001) BEQUEST: the framework and directory of methods, *International Journal of Life Cycle Assessment* 6 (6).

Deakin, M., Huovila, P., Rao, S., Sunnika, M. and Vreeker, R. (2002) Assessing the sustainability of urban development, *Building Research and Information* 30(2).

Dooyeweerd, H. (1958) *A New Critique of Theoretical Thought*, 4 vols, Presbyterian and Reformed Publisher Company, Philadelphia, PA.

Ekins, P. and Cooper, I. (1993) Cities and sustainability, a joint research agenda for the Economic and Social Research Council and Science and Engineering Research Council, SERC, Swindon, England.

ERC (Eclipse Research Consultants) (1996) Mapping commitment to sustainable development: a self-assessment technique for policy-makers and practitioners, ERC, Cambridge, England.

EEA (European Environment Agency) (2000) *Environmental Signals 2000*, European Environment Agency, Copenhagen.

EGBF (European Green Building Forum) (2001) http://www.egbf.org

Finco, A. and Nijkamp, P. (2001) Sustainable cities: an exploratory analysis, paper presented to an International Symposium – the Lisbon BEQUEST, 26–27 April, University of Lusofona, Lisbon, http://www.surveying.salford.ac.uk/bqextra

Fudge, C. (2000) Expert view. In CEC *Design for Living – the European City of Tomorrow*, CEC EUR 19381, p. 7.

Giarini, O. and Stahel, W. (1996) *The Limits to Certainty*, Kluwer, Higham, MA.

Hamilton, A., Mitchell, G. and Yli-Karjanmaa, S. (2002) Towards an integrated decision support system for urban sustainability assessment: the BEQUEST Toolkit, *Building Research and Information* 30(2).

Hatcher, L.R. (1996) The pre-Brundtland Commission era, in Nath *et al.* (eds) *Sustainable Development*, VUB Press, Brussels, pp. 57–80.

Lombardi, P.L. (1998) Sustainability indicators in urban planning evaluation. In Lichfield, N., Barbanente, A., Borri, D., Kakee, A. and Prat, A. (eds) *Evaluation in Planning*, Kluwer, Dordrecht, pp. 177–192.

May, A.D., Mitchell, G. and Kupiszewska, D. (1997) The development of the Leeds Quantifiable City Model. In Brandon *et al.* (eds) *Evaluation of Sustainability in the Built Environment*, E&FN Spon, London, pp. 39–52.

Mitchell, G., May, A. and McDonald, A. (1995) PICABUE: a methodological framework for the development of indicators of sustainable development, *International Journal of Sustainable Development World Ecology* 2: 104–123.

Nijkamp, P. (1998) Macro-economic perspective (on SUD), paper presented to the BEQUEST Workshop, Milton-Keynes, 4 December 1998 – see BEQUEST 1998–2, *Information paper 2*: http://www.surveying.salford.ac.uk/bqextra

OECD (1994) *Environmental Indicators*, Organisation for Economic Cooperation and Development, Paris.

Orishimo, I. (1982) *Urbanisation and Environmental Quality*, Kluwer, Dordrecht.

Palmer, J., Cooper, I. and van der Vorst, R. (1997) Mapping out fuzzy buzzwords – who sits where on sustainability and sustainable development, *Sustainable Development* 5(2): 87–93.

UNCSD (1996) *CSD Working List of Indicators*, United Nations Division for Sustainable Development, http://www.un.org/esa/sustdev/worklist.htm

UNCED (United Nations Conference on Environment and Development) (1992) *Earth Summit '92 (Agenda 21)*, Regency Press, London.

UNCHS (United Nations Conference for Human Settlement) (1996) *Habitat II*, United Nations, Istanbul.

Von Weizsaker, E., Lovins, A.B. and Lovins, L.H. (1997) *Factor Four: Doubling Wealth – Halving Resource Use*, Earthscan, London.

WCED (World Commission on Environment and Development (also known as Brundtland Commission) (1987) *Our Common Future*, United Nations, New York.

Wuppertal Institute (1998) Modeling a Socially and Environmentally Sustainable Europe, *Final Report to DG XII*, Wuppertal Institute for Climate, Environment and Energy, Wuppertal, Germany (www.wupperinst.org/projeckte/sue).

Part II

The Protocols

3

Urban Planning
Simin Davoudi

> Underlying virtually all urban environmental problems is the issue of land use, from lack of affordable housing, to recognition and pollution from motor vehicles, to inner cities marred by abandoned buildings. Indeed, urban form and land use patterns within a city are critical determinants of environmental quality.
>
> (World Resources Institute *et al.* 1996: 116)

All societies, bar the simplest ones, have some forms of planning by which a degree of forward looking in the management of space is pursued, often through mechanisms such as regulating the development and use of land, controlling property rights and providing urban services. This process of shaping and re-shaping places and spaces has a significant impact on cities' economic, social and environmental fortunes.

In Britain, town planning emerged from a series of radical, reformist ideas about tackling the public health, housing and sanitation problems associated with late nineteenth-century industrialisation and urbanisation. These social concerns, combined with architectural appreciation, underpinned the work of the 'founding fathers' of the planning movement. Ebenezer Howard and the garden city movement began to influence contemporary thinking and fuelled the demand for the extension of sanitary policy into town planning. The first Town and Country Planning Act (1947), which was prepared in the post-war climate of intense optimism and confidence and aimed at 'building a better Britain', provided the legal tools for the practice of planning and nationalised the right to develop land.

The 1947 Act put in place a system of public control over the use and development of land which was distinctly different from that in most countries in the rest of Europe. So, when elsewhere many countries adopted a system of zoning ordinance, Britain embarked on a discretionary planning system which combined certainty with flexibility through its twin elements of development plan and development control. While development plans provide the frameworks within which the criteria for making regulatory decisions are established, individual applications are determined on their merit, yet within the framework of relevant policies.

THE NATURE OF PLANNING

> The planning system regulates the development and use of land in the public interest. The system as whole, and the preparation of development plans in particular, is the most effective way of reconciling the demand for development and the protection of the environment. Thus it has a key role to play in contributing to the Government's strategy for sustainable development by helping to provide for necessary development in locations which do not compromise the ability of future generations to meet their needs.
>
> (DoE 1992a, para. 39)

An important characteristic of planning is that it is primarily a public sector activity. It is a process by which the state seeks to influence the activities of firms and households in 'the public interest'. The remit of planning is wide-ranging and covers a number of policy areas such as transport, inner cities, retail development, housing and pollution, each of which may be subject to other public sector policies. This implies that although planning is primarily concerned with the development and use of land, its activities may overlap with or complement other areas of public policy. The scope of planning as an overarching policy area is therefore dependent on, first, the accepted limits to public sector intervention in the market mechanisms and, second, the political salience given to the different aspects of planning at any given time (Rydin 2003b). So, for example, in the late 1980s, the rising significance of environmental issues in the public order of priorities and the subsequent political salience given to the sustainable development agenda have made environmental planning a significant part of the planning processes.

THE SYSTEM OF ACTORS IN THE PLANNING PROCESS

The BEQUEST network refers to the ATEQUE model of actors which influence the built environment. These are grouped into five 'poles':

- The pole of collective interest
- The pole of operational decision making
- The pole of design
- The pole of project carry-through
- The pole of use.

There are a number of weaknesses and inconsistencies in the ATEQUE model,[1] but it is beyond the scope of this chapter to provide a detailed critique of the model. Hence, using the approach adopted by the ATEQUE model, the following broad categories of key actors who are involved in the planning process can be identified:

- The state
- The professionals (planners, architects and contractors)
- The interest groups (environmentalists, economic development agencies, cultural heritage groups and community representatives)
- The development industry (the land, property and construction sectors)
- The wider stakeholders (citizens, business and cities).

The interactions between these actors, and between them and the contexts within which they operate, shape the highly political process of planning. A critical dimension of planning which has been brought to the fore by the rise of environmental concerns is its normative base, manifest in the contested notion of 'public interest'. There is an assumption that in regulating the land and property markets and protecting the environment, planners are acting in the public interest. The critics of normative planning theory have raised questions such as: how is this public interest to be defined? Should it be defined in terms of Pareto optimality or social justice? To what extent are planners capable of delivering this goal? And how?

These questions are central to the Collaborative Planning theory which, as Rydin (2003b) argues, is the contemporary manifestation of the hegemony of procedural planning theory during the post-war period. Collaborative Planning theory, as developed by Healey (1997), draws on Anthony Giddens's theory of structuration (Giddens 1984) and Jürgen Habermas's theory of communicative rationality (Habermas 1984).

The structuration theory is particularly relevant to the discussion of the actors and the ways in which their actions can influence the built environment. The emphasis is on the interrelationship between agency and structure (rules, resources and norms), between actors and contexts, between habitus and field, or in social philosophical terms between individual and society. The primacy of one or the other and the tensions between the two have been central to the debates in many academic disciplines. As Madanipour suggests, 'in city design, this distinction is often reflected in the private and the public spheres, where freedom to exclude others is distinctive from being in the presence of strangers' (2003: 122).

Drawing on the structuration theory, Healey (1997) argues that although there are powerful forces (i.e. structures) around us (i.e. actors) which are shaping our lives, our actions can still make a difference. Hence, although our actions are constrained by structuring forces, we are potentially capable of transforming these constrained situations, through conscious reflexivity. So, the Collaborative Planning theory sees the planning process as a site where actors operate in constrained situations but are potentially able to transform the situation and achieve their goals.

For this to happen, there is a need for reconstituting the public realm through open, public debate; through Habermasian 'communicative action'. As Healey elaborates, through

> communicative action, participants exchange ideas, sort out what is valid, work out what is important, and assess proposed courses of action. In this conception, planning becomes a process of interactive collective reasoning, carried out in the medium of language, in discourse.
>
> (Healey 1997: 52)

It is through such 'inclusionary argumentation' that a 'strategic consensus' may be built (Healey 1997). It should be noted, however, that 'argumentation is not a decision procedure resulting in collective decisions but a problem-solving procedure that generates convictions' (Habermas 1993: 158).

Planning, in all this, is considered as an important process

> which both reflect[s] and [has] the potential to shape the building of relations and discourses, the social and intellectual capital, through which links are made between networks to address matters of shared concerns at the level of neighbourhood, towns and urban regions.
>
> (Healey 1997: 61)

The role of planners is seen as mediating negotiations, enabling collaboration and empowering different voices. Collaborative Planning is an explicit normative planning theory which 'searches for a role for planners, a role which is addressed to solving pressing economic, social and environmental problems and yet is people-sensitive' (Rydin 2003b: 82).

This link-making potential of urban planning can be exploited to facilitate what has come to be called *governance*. The concept of governance, although freely used, is the subject of a growing body of literature focused on the underlying reasons for, and the outcomes of, the transformation from government to governance. In its *descriptive* sense, governance directs attention to the proliferation of agencies, interests, service delivery and regulatory systems which are involved in making policies and taking actions. In its *normative* sense, governance is defined as an alternative model for managing collective affairs. It is seen as 'horizontal self-organisation among mutually interdependent actors' (Jessop 2000: 15), of which government is only one and with only 'imperfect control' (Rhodes 1997: 8).

Within this context, the arenas of strategic planning have been considered as sites of emerging new forms of governance, with planners playing the role of co-ordinators. As Sellers (2002: 93) argues, within an urban region that faces common problems, the multiple local jurisdictions that typically divide up the urban space often must coordinate with one another or come together in collective action. Throughout the advanced industrial world urban and regional planning has emerged as one of the most important local means to this end.

PLANNING AND THE INTERPLAY OF ECONOMIC, SOCIAL AND ENVIRONMENTAL CONCERNS: A HISTORICAL PERSPECTIVE

The post-war history of the British planning system is an account of the interplay of economic priorities, social values and environmental concerns in relation to the regulation of land use and development. The conceptions of and the relations between these issues have been given different emphases in different times and places. The system has often witnessed a sidelining of the social distribution and environmental interests in favour of economic imperatives.

As regards the treatment of the sustainable development agenda in planning, there are two broad points of view. Some argue that environmental considerations have been a key concern for the planning system in Britain since the Second World War, and the sustainability agenda is no more than a new cloth to dress up what has always been practised (Raemakers 2000). Others argue that it has provided a new 'vision' for the planning system (Davoudi 2000) and has obligated planners to re-think their processes and methods. In practice, the answer lies somewhere between these extremes.

It is true that the regulatory power of the British land use planning system has played a significant role in the protection of the environment. However, the meaning given to, and the relative significance of, environmental issues as compared to other development priorities have changed over time. Newby (1990) argues that, until the turn of the last century the emphasis was on preservation of a pre-industrial past 'for the nation', but 'from the public', who were frequently regarded as unappreciative and a threat to 'national heritage'. After the Second World War, when the framework of the current planning controls emerged, this preservation from development was combined with regulation of development in order to safeguard communities' 'intangible amenities' such as natural beauty and pleasing landscapes. The 1950s development plans treated the environment as 'functional resources' to be conserved, and as amenities to be enhanced, yet still for human enjoyment and exploitation. Plans were dominated by an 'aesthetic utilitarian' approach which saw the environment as backcloth and setting (Healey and Shaw 1993). These conceptions of the environment were particularly echoed in the emphasis on protecting the countryside from urban encroachment.

In the 1960s and early 1970s, when the agenda of the wider environmental movement began to focus on tangible issues such as the scarcity of the earth's natural resources, the planning system remained largely preoccupied with accommodating and managing growth and its associated car-based expansion. Development plans, produced in a culture dominated by architects and engineers, continued to treat the environment as a recreational resource and backcloth. This is evident in many New Town plans of the early 1970s (see Davoudi *et al.* 1996). In fact, it was not until the late 1970s that planners embraced the growing initiatives for environmental care and management resulting from the 1960s expansion of urban development across the countryside. Within development plans, the countryside was treated not just as a setting to be conserved, but as a natural resource to be safeguarded, yet still for its amenity and economic value (Healey and Shaw 1993). Even then, the environmental care and management approach was short-lived. With the recession and less growth to manage, a rising agenda of economic and social problems faced planners, and environmental concerns became particularly vulnerable to the public reordering of priorities.

In the 1980s, in line with a neo-liberal agenda of the rolling back of the state frontier, the Thatcher administration launched a major attack on the scope and scale of planning and in particular the role of development plans in development control decisions. As a result, development plans became marginalised and sidelined as out-of-date (Thornley 1993). There had to be a 'presumption in favour of development' in all development control decision making (DoE 1995, Circular 14/85: 1). Within this pro-development climate, the quality of environment was treated as a commodity which, along with buildings and sites, could be packaged and traded. This 'marketised utilitarian' conception of the environment was combined with a narrow conception of conservation focused on heritage landscapes and wildlife sites (Whatmore and Boucher 1993).

By 1990 the language of sustainability and the request for sustainable development were well under way. Attention had begun to focus on global environmental change and on issues related to resource depletion and material constraints on rising living standards. Newby (1990) suggests that at this time, 'ecology' replaced 'amenity' as the focus of public debate. This re-emergence of environmental concerns, and particularly the EU requirement for formal Environmental Impact Assessment of main development projects, played an important part in the resurgence of the planning system and in particular development plans. New legislation enhanced the status of plans by putting them at the centre of decision making over land use. Planners were urged to 'reflect newer environmental concerns such as global warming and the consumption of new renewable resources in the analysis of policies that form part of plan preparation' (DoE 1992b, para. 6.3). The initial reaction to this governmental call was to 'turn plans green overnight', often through simplistic approaches such as putting the environment chapter at the beginning of the plan. However, gradually planners began to make genuine attempts to incorporate some of the principles of the 'new' environmental agenda, although not always with success (Davoudi *et al.* 1996). This is despite the fact that in the planning system 'the *concept* of sustainable development has been adopted more extensively, and more firmly on a statutory basis, than in any other field' (Owens, 1994: 87). What has not taken place yet is a systematic transformation of the planning agenda.

Despite the primacy of development plans, the planning system in Britain is still underpinned by presumption in favour of development, which to some is a sign of inherent contradiction with sustainable development. To others, it is the level of scrutiny to which the system subjects proposals that contributes to the sustainable development agenda (Raemaekers 2000). Nevertheless, it remains true that the government's policy on sustainable development and its implementation through planning mechanisms has failed to move beyond what is called 'weak' sustainability (Merrett 1994). At best, it can be seen as ecological modernisation (see Davoudi, 2000). Within this agenda, environmental objectives can always be balanced against economic and social issues and none should be regarded as imperatives (Davoudi and Layard 2001). By assuming that a balance between these objectives can be found, without clarifying limits, priorities and imperatives, the government and by extension the planning system has been able to avoid politically difficult choices. Planners are expected to 'grow the economy, distribute this growth fairly and in the process not degrade the ecosystem' (Campbell 1999: 252). In other words, planners are expected to strike a *balance* between these goals every time they make a decision on the use and development of land.

However, as Owens argues, planning is 'not simply a technical means by which sustainability is implemented but an important forum through which it is contested and defined' (Owens 1994: 87). It is where conflicts may emerge and solutions *have* to be negotiated. In practice, planners are often confronted with deep-rooted social, economic and environmental conflicts which cannot be wished away through a simple balancing exercise. Moreover, this balancing principle which underpins most planning decisions has poisoned the whole system and doomed the environment to incremental erosion (Levett 1999). A more recent study undertaken for the Royal Institute of Charted Surveyors Foundation concluded that the planning system needs considerable reform if it is to adopt a dynamic role in protecting the environment while forcing change in economic processes (Rydin 2003a).

SPATIAL LEVELS AND TIME SCALES OF PLANNING

Planning in Britain operates at various spatial scales ranging from national to neigh-bourhood level. The framework for planning policies is shaped by wider policy priorities that are set at international, national, regional and local levels. While the focus of the following sections is on the formal procedures of the planning system in England, which is embodied in a large number of statutes, rules, regulations and policy guid-ance, it is important to acknowledge that it is through the everyday informal practices and relationships that the system becomes operationalised. The processes of plan-ning, as mentioned above, involve a large number of stakeholders; and the planning arenas include a wide range of formal and informal fora.

Planning at the European level

The European level is exerting increasing influence on planning policies and practices in the UK. Its successive treaties, policies and initiatives have directly or indirectly influenced the development and implementation of national and regional spatial policies. The most obvious example is the EU Directive on Environmental Impact Assessment (EIA) which had to be incorporated into the UK planning processes. Although many of the EU sectoral policies have had spatial consequences for the regions of Europe and for national planning systems, there has been no explicit or homogeneous spatial strategy for the EU. However, a spatial development agenda has emerged over the last decade through the initiatives both of the Commission and of some proactive member states as well as an increasing level of trans-boundary planning activity. This is despite the fact that urban planning across Europe is understood in different ways. While in many countries (notably the UK) it is used as a generic term to describe a physical, land use regulatory system, in others it is used as a specific term to describe a method of co-ordinating and integrating the spatial dimension of sectoral policies. It is the latter which is predominantly used at the European level where spatial strategies are seen as a framework for formulation and implementation of sectoral policies (Cullingworth and Nadin 2002: 81).

The most significant development in this area has been the publication of the *European Spatial Development Perspective* (ESDP) in 1999 (CEC 1999). The ESDP has an indicative, not prescriptive, approach, and is not a legally binding document. It is a policy framework for better co-operation between Community sectoral policies and between member states, their regions and cities. The ESDP promotes a frame-work for integrated spatial policy and aims to achieve the following objectives:

- a balanced and polycentric city system and a new urban–rural relationship;
- parity of access to infrastructure and knowledge;
- prudent management and development of the natural and cultural heritage.

As regards the implementation of these objectives, the key priority is the promotion of voluntary co-operation at a horizontal level between sectoral policies, and in a vertical way between administrative areas. The key principles of the ESDP, such as the significance of polycentric development and the promotion of urban–rural relationships, are currently subject to major transnational studies under the EU-funded ESPON (*European Spatial Planning Observation Network*) Programme (see www. espon.lu). The outcome of these studies will provide a more robust basis for co-ordinating the spatial aspects of EU policy sectors and hence promoting coherence and complementarity between development strategies of the member states.

Planning at the national level

Although British planning practice is embedded in a system of law, a distinctive feature of the system is that central and local government bodies have been given a large measure of administrative discretion in interpreting and applying policies to particular local circumstances. There is little provision for external judiciary review of local planning decisions (Keene 1999). Instead, conflicts between planning authorities and developers are to be resolved through a system of appeal to central government. Decisions are based on the balance of public and private interests within the framework of planning policies. Hence, central government plays a quasi-judicial role of arbitration over what is fair and reasonable when the policies of a development plan or the decisions of a local planning authority over planning permission are challenged in inquiries or appeals.

Unlike many other European countries, the UK does not have a national land use or spatial plan. Hence, there are no policies or plans which are prepared for the whole country. Instead, national planning policy is conveyed through a growing body of national planning guidance. This is formulated by a central government department responsible for planning. This, in England, is the Office of the Deputy Prime Minister (ODPM). The Secretary of State has 'extensive formal powers . . . and has the final say on all policy matters' (Cullingworth and Nadin 2002: 47). These include the power to 'call in' a development plan for modification or a planning application for 'determination' on appeal.

The government's formal commitment to planning for sustainable development came from the White Paper on the environment: *This Common Inheritance* (HMSO 1990). This commitment to an environmental strategy was soon reflected in national planning policy guidance, which legitimised the role of land use planning in sustainable development and argued that,

> The planning system, and the preparation of development plans in particular, can contribute
> to the objectives of ensuring that development and growth are sustainable. The sum total

of decisions made in the planning field, as elsewhere, should not deny future generations the best of today's environment.

(DoE 1992a: para. 1.8)

While national planning guidance has had a considerable impact on planning practice, in some cases it has projected conflicting views. One example is the different explanations of the term 'sustainable development' in government guidance, which have created major concerns among planning practitioners (Land Use Consultants 1995). These concerns, combined with the changing government policy and a desire for further central control, have led to the production of an increasing number and a constant revision of guidance notes in the last decade. The new legislation (Planning and Compulsory Purchase (P&CP) Act 2004) seeks to provide more consistency in, and consolidation and simplification of, national planning guidance. However, the proposed new changes have not embraced the call for the development of a 'National Spatial Planning Perspective', which was particularly advocated by organisations such as the Royal Town Planning Institute (see *Town Planning Review*, 1999, vol. 70, no. 30).

Planning at the regional level

In England, there is no statutory planning at the regional level, partly because there is no democratically accountable statutory body to undertake it. However, this is not to say that there is no regional dimension to planning. Indeed, the last decade has witnessed a rising interest in regionalisation and strategic regional planning. The devolution to Scotland, Wales and Northern Ireland has further intensified the debate about the strengthening of regional powers, and regional planning as an integral part of it, in England, too. The government is now committed to the establishment of elected regional government in those regions which choose to vote in favour of it.

In the meantime, regional planning is carried out by the Regional Planning Bodies (RPBs) (often known as regional assemblies or regional chambers) in co-operation with Government Regional Offices. RPBs are mainly local authority led but include other regional stakeholders such as business and community representatives. They are responsible for preparing Regional Planning Guidance (RPG), which seeks to integrate a wide range of sectoral policies, such as transport and economic development, and their implications for land use policies. In 1997, following the new Labour Administration, the enthusiasm for regionalisation, which was partly a response to the developments at the European level, further highlighted the need for a stronger regional dimension to planning. Hence, the scope of RPG was extended beyond land use and its production became more inclusive and transparent. This 'new style' RPG intended to:

provide a broad development strategy for the region over a fifteen to twenty year period and identify the scale and distribution of provision for . . . [a wide range of development]. By virtue of being a spatial strategy it also informs other strategies and programmes, in particular . . . the regional context for the preparation of local transport plans; and it should also provide the longer term planning framework of the . . . regional economic strategies.

(DETR 2000: para. 1.03)

Despite this wide-ranging remit, the RPG's central purpose remains the provision of a regional planning framework for the preparation of local development plans. The new legislation (P&CP Act) aims to give the RPG (which is to be called Regional Spatial Strategies) a statutory status. As far as the sustainability agenda is concerned, the strategies are subject to two important procedures: first, they have to go through an Examination in Public before an independent panel appointed by the government, who will lead the discussion based on a list of selected topics. While participation in the discussion is by invitation, the hearing is open to the public. Second, the Strategies are required to go through an independent sustainability appraisal process and identification of clear targets and performance indicators (DETR, 1999). However, a study undertaken by ECOTEC showed 'the haphazard proliferation of targets and indicators' and the fact that 'there is little systematic consideration of indicators or targets in relation to the policy objectives; rather, they mostly represent general aspirations for the region, and the constraints of data availability' (Cullingworth and Nadin 2002: 90).

Planning at the local level

The day-to-day operation of the planning system takes place primarily in local planning authorities. They are responsible for preparing development plans and determining planning applications. Development plans and development control have remained the key mechanisms for delivering the sustainable development objectives within the planning system. While development plans provide the frameworks within which the criteria for making regulatory decisions are established, individual applications are determined on their merit, yet within the framework of relevant policies.

Development plan and sustainability appraisal

Although development plans have always provided the policy framework for individual planning decisions, their significance in the system has fluctuated over time from being land use-only master plans to becoming all-encompassing policy documents. Under the 1947 legislation, development plans were mainly concerned with broad strategies and major economic and social forces which shaped the process of urban and land use change (Davoudi et al. 1996).

The introduction of the plan-led system in the early 1990s was accompanied by a statutory requirement for taking into account the environmental considerations in the general polices and strategies of development plans. Another significant change, with regard to sustainable development objectives, was the requirement for plans to be subject to environmental appraisal (DoE 1992a). Many planning authorities began to undertake the appraisal. By 2002, 91 per cent of respondents to a major questionnaire survey conducted by Levett-Therivel consultancy firm had carried out an appraisal. More significantly, 53 per cent had done it as an integral part of plan preparation (*Planning* 2002).

While there are subtle differences between the approaches taken by various authorities, the most common is based on the DoE's guidance (DoE 1993) which begins with an assessment of the existing state of the physical environment and attempts to quantify the impact of the plan on this state. Policies are scored against the criteria according to whether they are judged to have a positive, negative or neutral impact on that aspect of the environment (see Figure 3.1). The adoption of a multi-disciplinary team approach helps reduce the arbitrary nature of appraisal and increase the quality of judgement.

Overall, it can be concluded that during the 1990s, the primacy and full coverage of the development plan, coupled with the environmental appraisal of plans'

Groupings of objectives* / Policies	Land use	Transport	Urban areas	Rural areas	Housing	Industry, commerce	Leisure and tourism	Health, education & social facilities	Wildlife, habitat	Built heritage	Agriculture, forestry & soil qualities	Minerals	Air quality and noise	Water quality, resources & supply	Waste	Energy

Suggested impact symbols

No relationship or significant impact	•	Uncertainty of prediction or knowledge	?
Significant adverse impact	x	Likely, but unpredictable adverse impact	x?
Significant beneficial impact	√	Likely, but unpredictable beneficial impact	√?

*Column headings should be expanded to reflect the local objectives identified under each topic heading where relevant to a particular area and type of plan

3.1 The policy impact matrix

Source: Adapted from DoE 1993

policies and proposals, 'turn[ed] the Development Plan into a potentially powerful instrument of environmentally sustainable development' (Raemaekers 2000: 34). However, making use of such an instrument has depended on the approach adopted by the planning authorities. While in some cases the use of appraisal has resulted in policy shifts during the course of planning and shaping the development (*Planning* 2002), in others, appraisals have been carried out too late and without consistent methodology and rigorous analysis (*Planning* 2003a).

As mentioned before, the planning system and in particular the development plan is in transition and is undergoing radical changes brought in by the P&CP Act. The proposed Local Development Framework (LDF), which will replace the current plans, is intended to deliver the long-term vision for the area (for a period of 10–15 years) and act as the spatial manifestation of the Community Strategy. It should cover policies for housing, business development, transport, waste and the historic environment. As regards environmental assessment, major changes are expected to take place. First, under the new legislation sustainability appraisal of plans will become mandatory and has to cover social, economic and environmental issues. Second, both regional and local plans will have to go thorough a Strategic Environmental Assessment (SEA) to satisfy the requirements of the 2001 EU Directive (2001/142/EC) which had to be implemented in the UK by July 2004.

Development control and the EIA

Development control is the cutting edge of the planning system. It provides the mechanism for controlling the development and use of land. It is through the development control system that many of the plans' policies are implemented. Following the 1986 EU Directive and its amendment in 1997, Environmental Impact Assessment (EIA) of all 'major' projects is an integral part of the development control process. In recent years, more than 70 per cent of all environmental statements produced have been for projects that fall to be considered under the planning system. The range of development types that require EIA has considerably expanded under the new regulations issued in 1999. Between 2002 and 2003, 90 per cent of planning authorities screened at least one proposal to determine whether EIA was needed (Wood and Becker 2003). However, while the use of size and scale as criteria has speeded up the screening process for environmental impacts of projects, socio-economic impacts exert less influence on screening decisions (ibid.). Local planning authorities' lack of resources and time constraints have been cited as major limitations.

In addition to the EIA, development control processes provide other opportunities to address sustainable development in planning, particularly through the Section 106 agreement which deals with issues of planning gains. For example, North Somerset Council has used this mechanism to create the largest EcoHome scheme in the UK to date. The agreement ensures that developers will deliver 1,470 homes (in Portishead) to the standards set by the Building Research Establishment for Eco-Home good rating. A further thirty homes will achieve excellent rating (Wilson 2003).

INTEGRATING SUSTAINABLE DEVELOPMENT INTO DEVELOPMENT PLANS: A GOOD PRACTICE GUIDE

In 1998, the Department of the Environment, Transport and Regions (currently ODPM) issued a good practice guide (*Planning for Sustainable Development: Towards Better Practice*) to assist planners by providing detailed advice on how the principles of sustainable development can be incorporated into development plans (DETR 1998). The guide focuses on those planning policy areas where sustainable development raises major new issues or requires a new approach. It is prepared not only to be used by planners but also by councillors who make planning decisions, the local community, developers and other built environment professionals involved in promoting and regulating new development.

A key thrust of the guide is to encourage development plans to develop an overall 'vision and action' which aims to create a more sustainable pattern of development by:

*   reducing the need to travel;
*   revitalising and regenerating urban centres;
*   reducing pressure for development of the countryside.

It advocates that plans should develop a *strategic vision* for what existing urban areas should be like in about twenty-five years' time when they are inherited by the next generation. They should indicate what development should be undertaken where, and how this can make towns and cities more sustainable. The emphasis is on developing a clear picture of what is sustainable, but also what is desirable and achievable (ibid.: 13). Such strategic thinking should take place at all regional, urban and local neighbourhood levels, and has to be linked into objectives.

The guide includes six chapters. Chapter 1 sets up the purpose and principles of the guide, with the following four chapters focusing on four areas which together should shape the content of plans and policies. The final chapter provides a methodology for integrating sustainable development into the process of preparing development plans.

The remaining part of this chapter will briefly outline the key points raised in chapters 1 to 5 of the guide and then focus on the final chapter to provide a more detailed summary of the proposed methodology.

Themes and principles of the guide

The guide identifies four key themes and principles with regard to sustainable development (ibid.: 10–13). These are as follows.

1 More sustainable patterns of development

At the *regional* level, a more sustainable pattern of development can be achieved by:

- exploiting access to existing infrastructure and services and using new public transport.

At the level of *urban areas*, the focus should be on managing growth in a way that leads to more sustainable forms by:

- concentrating major trip-generating developments in existing centres or near public transport nodes;
- raising densities of development around areas with high public transport accessibility and in public transport corridors;
- improving public transport accessibility.

At the *local neighbourhood* level, the vitality and viability of new centres should be improved by:

- building up local centres for the neighbourhood around existing focal points which have good public transport and local services;
- increasing density where necessary to support local services.

2 The sequential approach

Based on previous guidance for retail development, transport and housing, the guide advises local planning authorities to use the sequential approach in their development plan to identify appropriate sites for future developments at regional and urban levels. The aim is to manage the pattern of growth in the most sustainable way.

3 Changing the emphasis

Although it is acknowledged that planning policies continue to give weight to economic, social and environmental considerations, the guide aims to highlight where changes of emphasis are required. Such changes should emerge as a result of consideration being given to the need for:

- setting up clear objectives and well-integrated policies;
- taking into account the indirect and long-term secondary effects of development (such as energy use, emissions and cumulative impact);

- being sensitive to the needs of individuals and communities, such as access to services, affordable housing and employment;
- being transparent on the type of qualitative and quantitative information that is being used to draw up policies and plans;
- recognising that 'a high quality of urban design is not just a general objective of planning, but a specific requirement for sustainable development' (DETR 1998: 12).

4 Advising on process

Key to reconciling economic, social and environmental interests and integrating these through the planning system is to adopt a sustainable decision-making process. The guide provides advice on the process of assessing features of environmental importance to be taken into account in instances where the economic and social need for development outweighs an environmental interest. Another key point raised is the need for improving links between organisations and professions and forming partnerships to inform such decision-making processes.

The guide's advice on content of plans and policies

The main body of the guide is structured around four areas upon which the content of plans and policies should focus in order to achieve sustainable development through the planning process (ibid.: 15–124). These are as follows:

1 Realising the potential of existing areas by:

- encouraging mixed use development;
- re-using urban land;
- increasing urban densities.

2 Growing new urban areas by:

- extending at nodes and in corridors;
- considering new settlements.

3 Revitalising and enhancing the countryside by:

- reviving rural settlements;
- protecting landscape character and local distinctiveness;
- providing for recreation and leisure.

4 Incorporating other sustainability issues including:

- parking;
- nature conservation;
- renewable energy;
- energy efficiency.

Proposed methodology for integrating sustainable development into planning

The guide presents a methodology for integrating sustainable development into the process of preparing development plans. This is underpinned by three themes including:

- *strategic awareness*, which is reflected in the need to look further ahead in terms of both time scale and spatial context;
- planning for *people and places*, which requires ongoing community engagement and local distinctiveness;
- developing a *vision* of how an area might be structured or re-structured and what policies are needed to achieve this.

(ibid.: 130)

The main characteristics of the methodology are as follows:

- It is *iterative*, so the objectives defined as the starting points are then used to test emerging policy options.
- It involves *selectivity* and a recognition that some decisions are more central than others in determining a plan's policies.
- It requires developing *linkages* with a wide range of stakeholders and interests.
- Its success needs to be *monitored* frequently on the basis of how well the plan can be implemented and whether its implementation facilitates progress towards a more sustainable pattern of activities.

The methodology consists of a four-stage process (see Figure 3.2), which is similar to the procedure for preparing development plans in general but has the added dimension of trying to put 'sustainable development at the *heart* of plan preparation' (ibid.: 131).

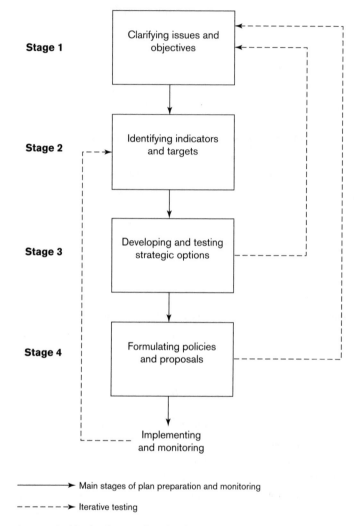

3.2 Integrating sustainable development into development plan preparation

Source: Adapted from DETR 1998: 132

The protocol for sustainable development planning

The above methodology, four-stage process and procedure may be seen as a protocol to follow in preparing the plans needed to deliver sustainable development. The four stages of this protocol for sustainable development planning are set out below.

Stage 1: Issues and objectives

The aim of this stage is to set the framework for an overview of the full range of topics involved in achieving sustainable development. Key actions for development plan preparation are as follows:

- Take part in identifying strategic issues and objectives for the region and sub-region.
- Use existing initiatives such as Local Agenda 21 to consult with as wide a range of stakeholders as possible about key concerns in local areas.
- Prepare Issues Reports as a focus for consultation and discussion in local forums.
- Try to be as spatially specific as possible in setting local economic, social and environmental objectives.

(ibid.: 133)

Stage 2: Indicators and targets

The aim of this stage is to identify indicators and targets for measuring progress towards achieving objectives. The guide emphasises that if indicators are to be helpful they must:

- be sensitive to environmental, economic and social change;
- be easily capable of being assessed;
- be readily understood so that people can identify with them and with the issues to which they relate;
- be cost-effective in terms of data needs and monitoring requirements;
- have specific identifiable thresholds (limits and targets) that indicate where significant changes are taking place.

(DETR 1998: 139)

For environmental indicators, it is important to differentiate between state, pressure and response indicators.

Key actions for development plan preparation are as follows:

- Select the key economic, social and environmental objectives where indicators are needed and select the type of indicators appropriate to the issue.
- Use existing data where possible to define indicators; share experience with other local authorities and national agencies.

- Involve the local community and councillors in deciding thresholds, particularly for qualitative issues.
- Use targets to signal the direction of change proposed in the plan and to monitor its success in moving towards sustainable development.

(ibid.: 139)

Stage 3: Strategic options

The aim of this stage is to develop and test options, particularly for the location of new growth, in order to determine the strategy for the plan. Key actions for development plan preparation are as follows:

- Select the key decision areas for strategy development (of which core topics for developing strategic options include: housing, employment, transport, environment and retail, with linkages to other areas, notably education, health, leisure and tourism).
- Develop options for the long-term future, based on different roles that the area could perform.
- Clarify the likely effects of the options in relation to the key objectives, using the 'Compatibility Matrix' suggested in *Environmental Appraisal of Development Plans* (DoE, 1993) to test the internal consistency of different elements of spatial strategy.
- Summarise the issues for further consultation or decision, using, for example, a Choices Report to summarise the results of option testing (the Vancouver City Plan of 1995 is used as an example: ibid.: 152).
- State the chosen strategy explicitly at the beginning of the plan to provide a vision for the area.

(ibid.: 146)

Stage 4: Policies and proposals

The aim of stage 4 is to add to the strategy the full range of policies and proposals that are needed to implement it. A development plan can have three types of policies: guidance, incentive and control. Each of these has a part to play in promoting sustainable development, by informing and raising awareness, by influencing the nature and location of development and by providing the basis for decisions on planning applications (ibid.: 153).

Key actions for development plan preparation are as follows:

- Develop policies that help to implement the overall strategy.
- Clarify the likely impact of the policies on the key local objectives.

- Make the contribution of each policy to achieving the plan's objective clear using the 'Policy Impact Matrix' suggested in *Environmental Appraisal of Development Plans* (DoE 1993), mentioned earlier.
- Test the practicality of policies and proposals by consulting via established channels.

(ibid.: 153)

The environmental assessments supporting such actions

From this representation of sustainable development planning, it is evident that EIA will be the main tool used to support such actions – be it in terms of SEA, or the newly emerging sustainability appraisals. The main reference points for this are:

- 1993 Environmental Appraisal of Development Plans
- 1997 EU Directives on EIA
- 1998 Good Practice Guide on Planning for Sustainable Development
- 1999 EU Directive on EIA
- 2001 EU Directive on SEA
- 2002 Statement on Sustainability Appraisals

These present significant milestones in the use of environmental assessment methods to evaluate the sustainability of development plans. However, it is noticeable that there are major concerns about the use of such assessments to support sustainable development planning. The most noticeable rest on the lack of resources, manpower, skills and expertise available to screen development proposals against sustainability measures set out in the plans. This in turn makes the sustainability of the said plans dependent, to a large degree, on the environmental statements provided by developers to support the socio-economic sustainability of their applications. This itself places a moral imperative on the development, design and construction sector to adopt the environmental standards and socio-economic obligations underlying such statements as measures of good practice in sustainable planning.

As a new form of governance, it is evident that such partnerships place an even greater imperative for planners, developers, architects and contractors to collaborate and build consensus over environmental standards and socio-economic obligations, not only as a policy discourse, but in terms of the methodology by which to guide development planning towards actions that are sustainable for citizens, businesses and cities. Viewed in light of this, it is possible to recognise the size of the task sustainable development planning faces.

CONCLUSION

Since its conception in 1947, concerns over environmental issues have been at the heart of the British planning system. However, the priorities given to environment when faced with economic imperatives have waxed and waned. Today, for the first time in the history of planning, the Planning and Compulsory Purchase Bill (2002) has defined a statutory purpose for planning which puts 'sustainable development' at its core. However, the way this is interpreted is at best ambivalent. Clause 38 of the Bill states that, 'it is a statutory duty for plans to contribute to sustainable development. This means high and stable level economic growth, social progress, effective protection of the environment and prudent use of resources' (P&CP Bill 2002: Clause 38).

While this reflects the breadth of issues covered within the sustainable development agenda and its holistic nature, there is a danger that the generality of this statement can detract from its core environmental concerns. These concerns have been voiced by a group of thirty-two voluntary organisations which called on the government to heed the advice of its own Sustainable Development Commission by adopting a more robust definition of sustainable development. They argued that the statutory purpose of planning as defined by the P&CP Bill is too weak and urged the ODPM to focus on six key issues including: quality of life, valuing nature, equity between urban and rural demands, the polluter pays principle, good governance and a precautionary principle (*Planning* 2003b).

Moreover, given the discretionary nature of the planning system and its balancing principle, it would be far too easy for the system to be pushed and pulled in different directions and hence, as has happened before, to experience the sidelining of environmental (and social) interests in favour of economic considerations. However, this is not inevitable. While the holistic concept of sustainable development remains a powerful long-range goal which links issues and provides a policy bridge, the sustainable society is not going to be reached in a single, holistic leap led by planners or indeed any other 'experts'. It has to be sought through day-to-day contested negotiations over a wide range of policies including those related to the built environment. It is the outcome of such negotiations which will constitute the evolutionary progression towards more sustainable practices. As O'Riordan suggests,

> The most important point to grasp about sustainable development is the paradoxical observation that it will only succeed by capturing and re-directing social and economic change, yet it also has to act as an accumulative role in the myriad of circumstances.
>
> (O'Riordan 2000: 31)

In this context, it is of paramount significance that the policies and proposals of development plans which set the strategic framework for future developments are subject to a rigorous sequence of appraisal processes. At the time of writing, the scope and the formal procedure of such processes are not finalised yet and are still subject to an ongoing debate amongst policy makers, academics and practitioners. Key to this debate is the concern over the implementation of the SEA. Current advice from the government is to integrate SEA, including the formal requirements of the Directive, with the sustainability appraisal approach to reduce duplication and save staff time and resources. However, this has raised some concerns about the extent to which environmental impacts can be traded off against economic and social interests, thus potentially diluting the aims of the directive. Furthermore, there are major differences between the two. While SEA tends to be baseline-led, starting from an analysis of the state of the environment, sustainability appraisal is objective-led, as outlined above. Also, while the latter aims for breadth of coverage across all aspects of sustainable development, the former focuses on depth of coverage around environmental issues. Environmental groups have made it clear that SEA should set the strategic scene by setting up thresholds and standards beyond which development would not be allowed to encroach no matter how pressing the social and economic requirements (*Planning* 2003c). However, this clearly is a contested proposition and one which will not fit in the current government agenda. Hence, the arenas of the planning system will once again be the key sites through which the social, economic and environmental interests, as voiced by the actors involved in the decision-making processes, will be played out. It is the outcome of such interplays that will help or hinder the planning system to realise its potential for making progress towards a more sustainable pattern of development.

NOTE

1   For example:

- It should be attributed to both built and natural environments because actions that influence the built environment will inevitably affect the natural environment, too.
- The model is merely a *list* (and not a *model*) of potential actors.
- No such lists can ever be comprehensive, and there is always the danger of missing key actors, as has happened here; landowners are not accounted for in any of the sub-categories.
- The list cannot be applied in different contexts. The role of different actors and the degree of their influence vary across time and space.
- The actors are somehow *boxed* into five categories with apparently no interactions between them.

- The poles implicitly depict a linear and sequential process which does not represent the complex reality of development processes.
- It is not clear why the public sector agencies (such as local authorities and politicians) are considered under the same pole as non-governmental organisations and why they are labelled 'collective interest'. Surely, a major distinction in terms of the degree of influence on the built environment can be made between, for example, the public sector regulatory agencies (such as central and local governments) and institutions such as universities and consumer organisations.

REFERENCES

Campbell, S. (1999) Planning, green cities, growing cities, just cities? Urban planning and the contradictions of sustainable development. In Satterthwaite, D. (ed.) *Sustainable Cities*, London: Earthscan Publications.

CEC: Committee on Spatial Development (1999) *ESDP: European Spatial Development Perspective: towards balanced and sustainable development of the territory of the European Union*, Luxembourg: Office for Official Publications of the European Communities.

Cullingworth, B. and Nadin, V. (2002) *Town and Country Planning in Britain*, 13th edn, London: Routledge.

Davoudi, S. (2000) Sustainability: a new vision for the British planning system, *Planning Perspectives* 15(2): 123–137.

Davoudi, S. and Layard, A. (2001) Sustainable development and planning: an overview. In Layard, A., Davoudi, S. and Batty, S., *Planning for a Sustainable Future*, London: Spon.

Davoudi, S., Hull, A. and Healey, P. (1996) Environmental concerns and economic imperatives in strategic plan-making, *Town Planning Review* 64(4): 421–436.

DETR (Department of the Environment, Transport and Regions) (1998) *Planning for Sustainable Development: Towards Better Practice*, London: HMSO.

DETR (Department of the Environment, Transport and Regions) (1999) *Planning Policy Guidance Note 12: Development Plans and Regional Guidance*, London: DETR.

DETR (Department of the Environment, Transport and Regions) (2000) *Planning Policy Guidance Note 11: Regional Planning*, London: DETR.

DoE (Department of the Environment) (1992a) *Planning Policy Guidance Note 12: Development Plans and Regional Guidance*, London: HMSO.

DoE (Department of the Environment) (1992b) *Development Plans: A Good Practice Guide*, London: HMSO.

DoE (Department of the Environment) (1993) *Environmental Appraisal of Development Plans: A Good Practice Guide*, London: HMSO.

DoE (Department of the Environment) (1995) *Circular 14/85*, London: HMSO.

Giddens, A. (1984) *The Constitution of Society: Outline of the Theory of Structuration*, Cambridge: Polity Press.

Habermas, J. (1984) *The Theory of Communicative Action*, London: Heinemann.

Habermas, J. (1993) *Justification and Application: Remarks on Discourse Ethics*, Cambridge: Polity Press.

Healey, P. (1997) *Collaborative Planning: Shaping Places in Fragmented Societies*, London: Macmillan.

Healey, P. and Shaw, T. (1993) Planners, plans and sustainable development, *Regional Studies* 27: 769–776.

HMSO (1990) *This Common Inheritance. Britain's Environmental Strategy*, Cm 1200, London: HMSO.

Jessop, B. (2000) Governance failure, in Stoker, G. (ed.) *The New Politics of British Local Governance*, London: Macmillan, pp. 11–32.

Keene, Hon. Justice (1999) Recent trends in judicial control, *Journal of Planning and Environment Law*, January, 30–37.

Land Use Consultants (1995) *The Effectiveness of Planning Policy Guidance Notes*, London: HMSO.

Levett, R. (1999) Planning for a change, *Town and Country Planning*, September.

Madanipour, A. (2003) *Public and Private Spaces of the City*, London: Routledge.

Merrett, S. (1994) New age of planning, *Town and Country Planning*, June, 164–165.

Newby, H. (1990) Ecology, amenity and society, *Town Planning Review* 61(1): 3–13.

O'Riordan, T. (2000) *Environmental Science for Environmental Management*, 2nd edition, Harlow: Pearson Education.

Owens, S. (1994) Land, limits and sustainability: a conceptual framework and some dilemmas for the planning system, *Transactions of the Institute of British Geographers* ns19: 430–456.

Planning (2002) Picking up the challenge: delivering sustainability through local plans, 4 October, 20.

Planning (2003a) Sustainability appraisals: should be an intrinsic part of plan-making, 10 October, 28.

Planning (2003b) Groups united in call for tougher statutory purpose, 29 August, 4.

Planning (2003c) Europe Sets a Green Agenda, 22 August, 18.

Raemaekers, J. (2000) Planning for sustainable development. In Allmendinger, P., Prior, A. and Raemaekers, J. (eds) *Introduction to Planning Practice*, London: Wiley.

Rhodes, R. (1997) *Understanding Governance – Policy Networks, Governance Reflexivity and Accountability*, Buckingham and Philadelphia: Open University Press.

Rydin, Y. (2003a) *In Pursuit of Sustainable Development – Rethinking the Planning System*, London: Royal Institute of Charted Surveyors Foundation.

Rydin, Y. (2003b) *Urban and Environmental Planning in the UK*, 2nd edition, London: Macmillan.

Sellers, J.M. (2002) *Governance from Below: Urban Regions and the Global Economy*, Cambridge: Cambridge University Press.

Thornley, A. (1993) *Urban Planning under Thatcherism: The Challenge of the Market*, 2nd edition, London: Routledge.

Town Planning Review (1999) 70(30).

Whatmore, S. and Boucher, S. (1993) Bargaining with nature: the discourse and practice of 'Environmental Planning Gain', *Transactions of the Institute of British Geographers* 18(2): 166–178.

Wilson, E. (2003) Planning's contribution to sustainability, *Planning*, 13 June, 21.

Wood, G. and Becker, J. (2003) An environmental evolution, *Planning*, 22 August, 16.

World Resources Institute, UN Environment Programme, UN Development Programme, and World Bank (1996) *World Resources: A Guide to the Global Environment – The Urban Environment*, Oxford: Oxford University Press.

Urban Property Development
Mark Deakin

Remarkable as it may seem, urban property development and sustainable development are matters that have not previously been linked together and, what is more, the connection which this in turn has to sustainable urban development remains unclear. One of the main reasons for this lies with the tendency to see urban property development as an exclusively technical exercise, linked to property market analysis, valuation and investment appraisal. As has recently been pointed out, this traditional representation of urban property has tended to limit our understanding of the development process to the analysis and pricing of market transactions without due knowledge of the environmental, economic or social structures forming the substance of urban property development. Wishing to break free from the limitations of purely market-based representations of urban property, a number of researchers have called for us to transform our understanding of the development process and base urban property development on a knowledge of its environmental, economic and social content. The challenge which this poses is considerable, for in responding to the call for us to break free from the conventions of urban property and transform our understanding of the development process, it is noticeable that the resulting representation of urban property development suggests little is still known about the environmental, economic, or social content of this process. As the majority of researchers point out, this is unfortunate because it limits not only our understanding of urban property, but also our knowledge of how the development process relates to the discourse on sustainable development – how in that sense urban property development breaks with conventions – be it of the traditionalist, or more radical, positions – and becomes sustainable.

This is, of course, the question this chapter will address and try to answer. In addressing this question it will examine the traditional models of the urban property development process and go on to study the criticisms of convention. This section of the chapter will study the structure of urban property, examine the shortcomings in the recent transformation of the development process and highlight the need to base urban property development on a stronger environmental, economic and social structure. The examination will then go on to expose the shortcomings of this transformation and uncover how BEQUEST has sought to overcome the prevailing hegemony of the urban property market and strengthen the environmental, economic and social structure of the development process. This will be done by relating the structure of urban property to the BEQUEST framework, drawing attention to the protocol this provides to guide actions aimed at assessing whether the transformation of urban property development is sustainable, and checking if the gateway this opens up beats a path towards the sustainable development of urban property.

In taking this form, the protocol for sustainable urban property development provides a tool linking the technical requirements of property market analysis, valuation and investment appraisal with the more substantial environmental, economic and social issues and connections such assessments in turn have to the evaluation of sustainable urban development. The instrument provides a tool to guide actions taken to link the technical analysis and substantive issues and check the connection such assessments have to the evaluation of sustainable urban development. In this respect the protocol is a valuable tool because the linkages and connections that it makes not only have the potential to guide actions aimed at overcoming the prevailing hegemony of the urban property market, but also check if the actions taken, guidelines adopted and checklists drawn up, to transform urban property development and make it sustainable, are sufficiently targeted. That is to say, sufficiently targeted not only to balance the formal requirements of property market analysis, valuation and investment appraisal with the environmental, economic and social content of sustainable urban development, but also to direct decision makers to the assessment methods needed to evaluate the sustainability of urban development.

The value of the protocol can be seen as lying in the potential the tool has not only to overcome the hegemony of the urban property market and strengthen the environmental, economic and social structure of the said development process, but also to provide a pathway – set of actions, guidelines and checklists – to follow in assessing urban property and evaluating the sustainability of its development process.

THE TRADITIONAL REPRESENTATION OF URBAN PROPERTY DEVELOPMENT

Discussing the question of urban property development, Cadman and Topping state:

> There are a variety of views on, and descriptions of, the development process. At its most simple, property development can be likened to any other industrial production process that involves the combination of various inputs in order to achieve an output or product. In the case of property development, the product is a change of land use and/or a new or altered building in a process which combines land, labour, materials and [capital]. However, in practice the process is complex.
>
> (1995: 2)

As the quote points out, at its most simple, property development can be likened to any other production process in the sense that:

- it is a process that takes a number of inputs to produce an output – the so-called 'pipeline analogy' of property developement;
- it has a number of 'upstream' activities associated with the production process and 'downstream' activities in connection with its distribution;
- it takes raw materials (land, labour and capital) and in combining them together succeeds in changing the use of land and increasing the productivity of sites through the application of labour and capital – the so-called 'transformation analogy' of property development.

However, as the quote also goes on to point out, 'in practice the process is complex' and as a consequence requires a further degree of characterisation. The reasons given for this are as follows:

- in addition to being seen as a technical process with a pipeline, upstream, downstream and transformative analogy, the property development process operates in a sector of the market that requires a great deal of entrepreneurial skill and management expertise;
- in practice the development process is what is called 'front-end loaded' with large amounts of expenditure on 'upstream' activities – often producing additions to the 'standing stock' on a 'speculative' basis – that is in anticipation, rather than direct response to, demand;
- the front-end loading of development – initiation, evaluation of a potential scheme and acquisition of materials – is fraught with technical, legal and financial difficulties and is often abortive;
- this is made even more difficult an exercise due to the fact that the use of land, any changes to the use thereof, or development, is regulated and tightly controlled under the statutory provisions of the Town and County Planning Acts;
- each development is unique in the sense of being site-specific, requiring architectural, engineering and construction skills in the production of additional stock;
- the high degree of professionalisation requires a clear management structure to make sure developments are of a given quality, to cost and on time;
- being speculative, a high proportion of expenditure goes into the marketing of the product under 'downstream' activities – marketing, lettings and sales;
- government policy also affects the cost, timing and magnitude of development through macro-economic policy and strategies towards the urban and regional regeneration of towns and cities.

While providing further characterisation, it is evident that the unfortunate side-effect of this 'analogy, plus' representation of property development is that it only succeeds in drawing attention to the complex nature of the process and even greater need for a simplified model of such activities. It is perhaps with this need in mind that a number of academics have sought to model the property development process. This is a matter Cadman and Topping (1995) have been the first to address and model through the adoption of a 'stage-event' analogy of the process: the stage being the site of some activities required for a development to take place, and the events being the sequence of acts leading from its initial stages to eventual completion. It is this 'stage-event/activities analogy' that provides perhaps the most simplified model of property development and one which Dubben and Sayce (1991), Fraser (1993), Greed (1993), and Isaac (1996) have all, to a greater or lesser degree, also adopted to represent the process.

In addition to this particular representation of urban property development, a further distinction is often drawn between the property market analysis, valuation investment appraisal, production and post-production stages of the process. Here the terms analysis, valuation, appraisal, production and post-production are taken to mean the following:

- *Property market analysis*: survey of market values including income, rents, yields, land acquisition, etc.
- *Valuation*: financial evaluation of the urban property development, undertaken via residual valuation (traditional) methods on a freehold or leasehold basis.
- *Investment appraisal*: consideration of funding agreements (on a ground rent, partnership, or equity sharing basis) and use of cash flows to calculate the rate of return from the urban property development.
- *Production*: design, and construction stages.
- *Post-production*: the letting management, or disposal of the completed project.

TRANSFORMING URBAN PROPERTY DEVELOPMENT

In reviewing traditional models of the urban development process, Guy and Heneberry (2002) provide a fourfold classification of the property market analysis, valuation and investment appraisal underpinning their representations. These are as follows:

- The event-sequence models, otherwise referred to as sequential, or descriptive models, depicting the development process as a series of stages during which certain events take place (Healey 1991).

- The agency model, or the behaviourist and decision-making models that draw particular attention to the different actors promoting the development process (Gore and Nicholson 1991).
- Production-based approaches focusing on the forces and relations organising the development process (Harvey 1996).
- Institutional models emphasising the organisations involved in the development process (Ball 1998).

Reflecting on the 'part, stage-event activities' model set out in the previous section, it is evident that this particular representation of the development process is firmly rooted in the event-sequence model, linked to an agency model and loosely connected to the production-based approach. However, it is clear that the said model is not currently linked to the institutional model, or the connection this in turn provides to the property development process. As Guy and Heneberry (2002) point out, this is unfortunate because this categorisation of the development process is broader, overlapping with the others and including them as specific techniques of analysis. As the authors go on to suggest, the advantages of the so-called institutional approach lie in the fact that being conjunctural in nature, it opens up the possibility of transforming what is known and understood about urban property development, by linking the technical analysis of property markets, valuation and investment appraisal together and connecting them with the environmental, economic and social content of the development process, which has previously not been possible.

Exploring the question of environmental innovation and the (economic and) social organisation of the development process, Guy (1998, 2002) explores the value of taking an institutional approach to urban property development. Here the assumption that the degree of environmental innovation in the development process is something which can be explained by the agents' (planners, architects, engineers and surveyors) attitudes towards green building is questioned and re-examined in terms of how property market analysis, valuation and investment appraisal are just as much, if not more, influential in the production of urban spaces. That is to say, influential in not only transmitting the degree of user demand for green buildings to the market and on further to the producer, but also in signalling the type, range and extent of the economic and social reorganisation which institutions need to undergo in order to cultivate the practices capable of realising such environmental values. As Guy (2002) goes on to suggest, what the institutional approach to property development teaches us is that we can no longer view buildings simply as technical structures, the design quality of which can be simply related to the external definition of either accepted environmental standards, or economic and social benchmarks, but instead need to see them as complex cultural phenomena, formally inscribing the commercial logic of the market into the environmental, economic and social content of the development process. As Guy and Heneberry (2002: 295) go on to point out:

> Here the 'market' is interpreted not simply in economic terms, but rather as a cultural entity shaped by dynamic organisational, economic, social, legal, regulatory and ecological factors.

The institutional factors, it might be added, influence the production of urban property and behaviour of the agents responsible for the sequence of events depicting the development process. If we are able to learn this lesson and accept that buildings are not simply technical in nature, then it is important to approach property market analysis, valuation and investment appraisal as a more inclusive cultural entity, whose institutions – organisational, economic, social, legal, regulatory and ecological factors – structure the development process (see D'Arcy and Keogh 2002, Ball 2002). This, the authors suggest, is also an important lesson to learn because the legal and regulatory factors in turn provide a direct link to public policy and the connection this also has to the discourse on sustainable development (Guy 2002, Guy and Heneberry 2002).

BEQUEST

It is just this type of link and connection that BEQUEST has sought to provide for the urban property development process. They form the framework and protocol to act upon, guide and check the environmental, economic and social content by subjecting the institutions of the urban property market – as complex cultural entities – to assessments which evaluate the sustainability of the development process. This requires the following:

- adopting the PICABUE model, with its emphasis on the principles of environment, equity, participation and futurity as key components of sustainable development;
- viewing urban property as a particular development activity;
- seeing the actors in the urban property development process as the main agents of change;
- using the BEQUEST framework setting out the vision and methodology of an integrated – environmental, economic and social – SUD as the main terms of reference for such agencies;
- listing the property-related actions needing to be taken in order to guide decision makers through the process and to check on the sustainability of urban development;
- detailing the spatial levels and time scales of urban property development;

- setting out the property-related assessment methods it is possible to enlist and make use of in evaluating the sustainability of the urban development under examination.

In terms of how this transforms our knowledge and understanding of the urban property development process, the adoption of the PICABUE model starts by connecting urban property to the discourse on sustainable development and linking this to the market as a complex cultural entity, made up of organisational, economic, social, legal, regulatory institutions and ecological factors. Within this institutional milieu, it in turn becomes possible to examine the multidisciplinary team of experts (real estate surveyors, financial advisers and economists) representing the agents of the urban property development – the team of experts whose framework of analysis, vision and methodology provide the said agencies with the scope required to balance the technical requirements of the property market with the environmental, economic and social dimensions of the urban development process. It is this framework for analysis, vision and methodology, whose agencies of real estate surveyors, financial advisers and economists are valuable for the fact they provide the scope required to balance the technical requirements of the property market with the environmental, economic and social dimensions of the urban development process, which integrates them sufficiently for the actions taken by decision makers to be effective in targeting sustainable urban development.

It is because the actions taken by decision makers need to be reflexive, integrated, balanced and adequately scoped, that a protocol for urban property development is required. This is because without the protocol the framework for analysis, vision and methodology would not have the agencies needed to scope urban property development, or balance the technical requirements of the property market with the environmental, economic and social dimensions of the urban development process – not to mention integrate them. It is this integration, balancing and scoping that the protocol for urban property development focuses on, by detailing the guidelines and checklists decision makers need to follow in making urban property development sustainable.

In many respects the very absence of such a protocol goes a long way to explain the lack of success of previous attempts to transform urban property development and make it sustainable over the past decade. This is because under the hegemony of the urban property market, existing stakeholders have tended to promote solutions of a technical 'end-of-pipeline' nature and have failed to see the challenge sustainable urban development poses in more fundamental terms, i.e. as one requiring a radical rethink, framework for analysis, vision and methodology capable of transforming the institutional structure of the property market, strengthening its environmental, economic and social content (Deakin 1997, 1999, 2003a, 2003b, Deakin and Curwell 2003).

THE SUSTAINABLE URBAN PROPERTY DEVELOPMENT PROTOCOL

Table 4.1 sets out the guidelines decision makers need to follow in ensuring that the transformation of the property market meets the challenge sustainable urban development poses. The considerations decision makers need to bear in mind at this stage are relatively generic, represented by way of: preliminary activities, planning, property market analysis, valuation, investment appraisal, assessment, consultation, reporting and monitoring. The left-hand column of the table sets out what the protocol seeks to provide guidance on, and the type of action prescribed for such purposes is shown on the right as a set of checklists. At this stage there is no requirement to define the protocol in terms of the hard (legal and regulatory) and soft (organisational, environmental, economic, social and ecological) gates needing to be passed through, en route to – and as part of the 'step-wise' journey down a path leading towards – sustainable urban property development. This will be examined later on in the chapter.

Perhaps one of the main observations to draw from Table 4.1 is the strong interface urban property development has with the planning stage of SUD. This reflects the switch in the United Kingdom, and other neo-conservative-dominated states of Europe, towards legislation on resource conservation and environmental protection as part of a transition to a plan-led system that seeks to realign the relationship between the market and environment, putting a stop to the former dominating the latter in the process of local economic development and growth management. However, the degree to which this transformation of the urban property market has met with limited success has already been reflected on. The rest of this chapter intends to illustrate the formal classification of the protocol in terms of the hard and soft gates of sustainable urban property development. The way this will be done is as follows:

- Taking the hard gates (legal and regulatory matters) as those set out in Table 4.1.
- Approaching the soft gates (the organisational, economic, social and ecological factors) through the technological transformation of the urban property market and representation of the said techniques of analysis in turn in terms of the environmental, economic and social dimensions of sustainable urban development.

While this emphasis on the technological transformation of the relationship between the market, environment, economy and society may at first sight appear a little defeatist, focusing attention on the market for environmental, economic and social technology at the expense of the institutional issues surrounding culturally specific responses to the challenge sustainable urban development poses, such a reading of the situation would be misplaced. This is because it is this said technology which they all share in

Table 4.1 Guidelines and checklists for the sustainable urban property development protocol

Guidelines	Checklists
Preliminary activities	• Clarify what statutory requirements need to be met and what regulations are in place • Clarify what institutional norms urban property needs to satisfy in international, national and local contexts • Identify what actors will participate in the urban property development under consideration • Consider the agencies promoting the said development
Planning	• Consider statutory documents prepared by the said urban property development agencies and any regulations connected with them • Examine the relevant statutory planning documents, policies towards resource conservation, environmental protection, economic growth and any relevant sustainability strategy on land use, transport and related infrastructure provision • Relate these to the urban property development under consideration and the sustainability objectives it proposes to meet • Allow the urban property development team to consider the objectives in consultation with the statutory bodies regulating such actions • Consider the need for the public to participate in the development and agree a suitable strategy of consultation
Property market analysis	• Collect data on the performance of the property market relating to the urban development under question • Analyse the information obtained in terms of rents, capital transfer prices, market yields and returns on investment
Valuation	• Carry out financial evaluation of the urban development using the said indicators of property market performance • Use the simple residual method, profit evaluation and detailed calculations of site value available for such purposes
Appraisal	• Consider the alternative partnership structures to fund the urban development • Structure an equity sharing agreement for the urban development, using cash flows to support sensitivity analysis, risk assessments and their effect on the internal rate of return
Assessment	• Consider and decide upon the need for an environmental impact assessment and the methods able to assist in evaluating the sustainability of the development
Consultation	• Consult with the relevant statutory regulators about the assessment and advise all relevant stakeholders on the outcome of the evaluation and give due consideration to relevant feedback
Reporting	• Report on the aforesaid and provide appropriate statements on the sustainability of the urban property development in question
Monitoring	• Monitor movements in the planning regime, market, valuation and appraisal of urban property development and any additional requirement with regard to an environmental impact assessment

common and which not only links the market to the environment and to the economy and society, but also connects them to one another. Given that it is also this technology that does more than anything else to single them out as distinctive dimensions of sustainable urban development, it would seem appropriate to use it as a means to direct the protocol from the rather generic considerations of Table 4.1 on towards a more specific set of guidelines and checklists to support actions taken by decision makers. This is the object of Table 4.2. Under the heading 'Guidelines', the left-hand column of this table singles out the technologies of the urban property market. As can be seen, this column takes the guidelines of the previous table and the checklists set out under the relevant headings as its reference point. The right-hand column goes on to list their specific expression as techniques of analysis, available to check the actions of decision makers on the environmental, economic and social dimensions of sustainable urban development.

It should be noted that Table 4.2 does not simply try to reproduce the step-wise logic of the previous table; it dispenses with the guidelines needed to be listed in

Table 4.2 Guidelines and checklists for environmental, economic and social factors

Guidelines	Checklists		
	Environmental	Economic	Social
Property market analysis			
• Collect data on the performance of the property market relating to the urban development under question • Analyse the information obtained in terms of rents, capital transfer prices, market yields and returns on investment	• Examine property market performance in relation to environmental quality via analysis of natural habitat bio-diversity, energy consumption, waste, emissions and contamination • Consider the aforesaid in terms of their effects on rents, capital transfer prices, etc.	• Examine the relationship between environmental quality and economic growth, the competitiveness and efficiency of the urban development under consideration • Consider the pressure economic growth, competitiveness and efficiencies put on the demand for land, related infrastructure provision of public services • Establish if the urban settlement pattern is able to accommodate such growth without placing undue pressure on the environment	• Examine if the urban settlement pattern can accommodate economic growth, efficiency and competitiveness in a land use proposal capable of supporting a mix of income groups drawn from a diverse range of social backgrounds

Valuation

• Carry out financial evaluation of the urban development using the said indicators of property market performance • Use the simple residual method, profit evaluation and detailed calculations of site value available for such purposes	• Examine the significance of environmental quality on the said performance • Consider the cost of meeting environmental standards on natural habitat bio-diversity, energy consumption, waste, emissions and contamination	• Examine the significance of environmental quality, economic growth, competitiveness and efficiency on the said performance • Consider how the said environmental standards can consolidate the feasibility of the urban development under consideration	• Examine the equity of the environmental quality, economic growth, competitiveness and efficiency across income groups and the social backgrounds they are drawn from • Consider ways to be socially cohesive and distribute the costs and benefits of the urban development evenly

Investment appraisal

• Consider the alternative partnership structures to fund the urban development • Structure an equity-sharing agreement for the urban development, using cash flows to support sensitivity analysis, risk assessments and their effect on the internal rate of return	• Examine how the possible partnerships affect environmental quality and consolidate the said standards • Consider the equity sharing agreement's effect on resource conservation, natural habitat, bio-diversity and energy consumption and subject the proposal to the said analysis' assessments	• Examine the same on economic growth, competitiveness, etc. • Consider the same in relation to the growth, competitiveness and efficiency of the labour market and demands this places on infrastructure provision	• As previously, but in regard to social cohesion and equity • Consider the pressure this places on the public sector to draw upon limited funds available for such expenditures and the equity of the said spending

Assessment

• Consider and decide upon the need for an environmental impact assessment and the methods able to assist in evaluating the sustainability of the development	• Examine the appropriate statement on environmental impact assessment • Consider and select the assessment methods available to evaluate the sustainability of the urban development proposal	• Examine the same, but with reference to growth, competitiveness and efficiency	• Examine the same, but with reference to the public participation exercises specific to the urban development under consideration and social equity of the proposal

order to check actions in the preliminary and planning stages, so as to allow this reiteration to home in on the property market analysis, valuation, appraisal and assessment stages of the urban development process. It should perhaps also be recognised that this is done in the interests of directing decision makers towards the environmental, economic and social dimensions of sustainable urban development, guiding and checking their actions in this respect (see Table 4.2).

The following provides an example of 'cutting edge' attempts by stakeholders in the urban property market to support the switch towards plan-led development and follow the type of sustainable urban property development protocol set out above. The example is of the new settlement phenomenon in the UK, its settlement model and design solution for the development of sustainable communities. After discussing the issues behind the development of sustainable communities, the protocol's settlement model, design solution and criticism thereof, the examination will go on to look at the matter of environmental assessment. The examination should go some way to show the challenge any attempt to break free of tradition and represent the property market in cultural terms – as an environmental, economic and social structure – faces, not only in terms of the protocol to follow, but in the matter of environmental assessment and methods to select in evaluating the development of – in this instance – sustainable communities.

THE NEW SETTLEMENTS

As Ward's (1992) review of new settlements in the United Kingdom establishes, with the privatisation of the New Towns Commission, private consortia have sought to develop new settlements as an alternative to peripheral expansion and urban sprawl. It is a development Glasson et al. (1994) also examine. Their research shows that during the review of structure plans, carried out between 1988 and 1993, forty-six new settlement proposals had been submitted to planning authorities throughout England and Wales, and out of these only two developments were successful in receiving outline planning consent. As Ratcliffe and Stubbs (1996) also note, while the tight fiscal regime local governments operated during this period made the development of new settlements by private consortia attractive, they were too speculative, not supported by the planning system and unable to allay fears the public had about their impact on the environment.

The search for a pattern of settlement that is sustainable is a matter which the urban property development protocol puts forward as a settlement model and design solution for the formation of 'sustainable communities'.

THE DEVELOPMENT OF SUSTAINABLE COMMUNITIES

Modelling the development of sustainable communities, it is proposed that such experiments in managing growth through plan-led, environmentally friendly patterns of settlement, should be based on the following:

* a distinctive urban culture;
* a spatially compact form;
* a strong landscape framework in a countryside setting;
* a set of neighbourhoods;
* a high density of population;
* a balance of land use, economic and social structures;
* an energy-conscious public transport network;
* high levels of infrastructure and shared service provision;
* a pattern of settlement that is able to integrate existing communities with those emerging from the development;
* a financial structure that is viable in the short-, medium- and long-term horizon.

These design features reflect the findings of Breheny (1992a, 1992b, 1995), Breheny and Rookwood (1993) and Breheny et al.'s (1993) study of settlement models in the UK. The settlement model and design solution also draw attention to the experiences of sustainable developments from a number of UK cities. The experiences of Cambridge, Portsmouth and Swindon are reported on by Selman (1996) and Brown (1998). Hall and Ward's (1998) examination of such developments draws particular attention to the fiscal regimes regulating the infrastructures needed to service the settlements' high-quality living and working environments. Similar examinations are also provided by Roberts et al. (1999) and the Urban Task Force (1999). This type of development has also recently been championed by the Urban Villages Forum (2003). What these examinations all have in common is their tendency to represent their settlement models and design solutions as prototypes for the development of sustainable communities.

CRITICISMS OF THE SUSTAINABLE COMMUNITIES MODEL

In its current form the model and design solution it puts forward are vulnerable to many of the criticisms Glasson et al. (1994) and Ratcliffe and Stubbs (1996) have previously made about the new settlement phenomena and the sometimes less than friendly way in which plan-led developments of this kind treat the environment. These criticisms are also echoed by Lichfield (1996). The criticisms suggest that little has been learnt about the environmental values of the urban culture, spatially compact forms, strong landscape framework and countryside setting the model sets out, or how this in turn leads to a position where the population densities, socio-economic structures, energy-conscious public transport, and high levels of both infrastructure and service provision advance a design solution which is efficient in greening economic development (see also Beatley 1995, Campbell 1996, Gibbs et al. 1996, Cosgriff and Steinmann 1998).

Set against the said criticism of such models and the design solutions they advance, the environmentally friendly nature of the settlement pattern might be seen to add up to little more than an aesthetic – an aesthetic about the value of distinctive urban cultures, spatially compact forms and strong landscape frameworks in country-side settings. About – in this instance – the value of distinctive urban cultures, spatially compact forms and strong landscape frameworks, whose countryside settings have the population densities, land uses, socio-economic structures and public transportation systems which form the infrastructures needed to service high-quality living and working environments.

The value of this aesthetic may be seen to lie in the abilities it has to develop high-quality living environments which are 'friendly'. If this is where the value of the aesthetic is seen to lie, then both its limitations and shortcomings need to be recognised. This is because in its current form it is not possible to say whether the high-quality environments appearing in the model are friendly because they are ecologically sound, or because the design solution allows the land market to produce the level of planning gain needed to be efficient in greening economic development.

Asking whether the high-quality living environments are friendly because they are ecologically sound or efficient in greening economic development is instructive because it exposes the limitations of the model and shortcomings of the design solution the aesthetic rests upon. It reveals that the limitations of the model rest with the inability of the design solution to illustrate whether the high-quality living environments are friendly because they are ecologically sound. It also goes a long way to contrast this shortcoming with the considerable lengths the model goes to allow the design solution to show how the land market produces the level of planning gain needed to efficiently green the economic development in question.

The question that remains unanswered is where the true value of the aesthetic lies. Whether it is with the value of models that are ecologically sound, or with the ability of design solutions to efficiently green economic development. Ultimately, the question that remains unanswered is whether it is the former, or the latter, that has the right to make claims about the environmentally friendly nature of the settlement pattern and sustainability of the communities which the model and design solution propose to develop. With the former – even though the model does not raise them

– the questions are to do with the site's ecological footprint, bio-diversity and environmental loading (Barton *et al.* 1995). They are to do with environmental values and matters concerning bio-mass, the levels of energy consumption, waste and emissions. They are questions about levels of energy consumption, waste and emissions, whether the high-quality living and working environments are friendly and if this is because they are ecologically sound (Barton 1997, Breheny and Archer 1998, Stead 2000, Barton and Kleiner 2000, Guy and Marvin 2001). With the latter, the questions concern the land market and level of planning gain needed to be efficient in greening economic development and make it financially viable.

If such concerns about energy consumption, waste and emissions are seen to be key, then it shows there is a pressing need for these matters to be integrated into such models. It also illustrates that there is a critical requirement for the designs which follow to demonstrate whether they are ecologically sound – and because of this able to use land markets (and the levels of planning gain they in turn produce) in a manner that is not only efficient in greening economic development, but which also has the effect of making it financially viable to produce an environmentally friendly pattern of settlement. These needs and requirements are pressing, because as soon as a critical distinction is drawn between the environmental values of ecologically sound designs or land markets and the levels of planning gain needed not only to be efficient in greening economic development but also to make it financially viable, questions arise about:

- the science and technologies needed to make the energy consumption, waste and emissions of the high-quality living and working environments friendly;
- how the said technologies provide the infrastructures required for the high-quality living and working environments to be friendly because they are ecologically sound;
- the degree to which it is the science and technologies of the infrastructures and ecologically sound designs, rather than articulation of the said land markets and planning gain, that efficiently greens economic development;
- how the science, technologies, infrastructures and ecologically sound designs in turn use the said market and levels of planning gain to efficiently green economic development and make it financially viable;
- how this particular, ecologically sound use of land markets and planning gain is efficient in greening economic development and making it financially viable for experiments of this type to produce environmentally friendly patterns of settlement;
- how this environmentally friendly pattern of settlement is sustainable in terms of the communities that develop from plan-led experiments of this type;

- how the said settlement pattern is sustainable in terms of the relationship the communities in turn have to the city and its surrounding region (Deakin 2000, 2002).

Against the science and technology of ecologically sound designs, it can be seen that matters concerning the articulation of land markets and planning gain reveal little about where the real issues associated with the transformation of the new settlement phenomenon currently lie. This is because by effectively reducing the environmental values of the settlement model to an aesthetic about the virtues of good design it is simply not possible to say whether the solution advanced is friendly because of its ecological footprint, bio-diversity, or natural capital. Nor is it possible to say so in terms of the environmental loading, levels of energy consumption, waste and emissions the settlement pattern produces. As a result, and as ridiculous as it may seem, it is currently not possible to say whether the plan-led experiment is an environmental good or not. This is because in line with the conventions and traditions built up since the 1980s (under the policy of privatisation, resulting 'boosterism' of civic privatism and drive towards the all-pervasive marketisation of the public sector), the main point of concern lies elsewhere (Deakin 1996, 1997, 1999). Not so much with plan-led experiments aimed at assessing the ecology, bio-diversity, natural capital and environmental loading of distinctive urban cultures, having spatially compact forms and strong landscaping frameworks in countryside settings, as with the need to provide accountability, value for money, economic, efficiency and effectiveness disclosures (Deakin 1999) – the accountability, value for money, economic, efficiency and effectiveness disclosures needed for the land market to release the level of planning gain required from the neighbourhoods, population densities, land uses, socio-economic structures and public transportation networks forming the high level of infrastructure and service provision the settlement model puts forward as the design solution.

THE MATTER OF ENVIRONMENTAL ASSESSMENT

The matter still outstanding is that of assessing whether plan-led experiments of this kind are environmentally friendly and able to produce a pattern of settlement which is sustainable because the model and design solution are both ecologically sound and efficient in greening economic development. In meeting this challenge there are the following matters to consider:

- the terms of reference adopted as a framework to develop the settlement model and design solution it advances as sustainable communities (Deakin *et al.* 2001);

- how this framework structures the relationship between the environmental values of the settlement model and the design solution advanced to efficiently green economic development (Bentivegna *et al.* 2002);
- the protocol(s) adopted to assess the sustainability of the communities undergoing development and to evaluate how ecologically sound the settlement model is (Deakin 2002);
- the environmental assessment methods needed to evaluate the sustainability of the communities and to model whether the ecology of the design solution is not only sound, but efficient in greening economic development (Deakin 2000, 2002);
- if this in turn makes it financially viable for plan-led experiments of this kind to produce environmentally friendly patterns of settlement (Deakin *et al.* 2002a, 2002b);
- the question of what methods should be used in undertaking such an environmental assessment (Deakin *et al.* 2002a, 2002b).

To a large degree the first three bullet points have been dealt with while looking at the BEQUEST framework and protocols for sustainable urban property development. As a consequence, the following discussion will focus attention on the questions surrounding the use of environmental assessment methods for evaluating the sustainability of such developments. It should be noted that such considerations are particularly challenging because they demand a shift of attention away from understanding the environment as an aesthetic and towards a knowledge of its status as an ecological system – an ecological system which has a set of values that in turn make it possible to measure the environmental loading, levels of energy consumption, waste and emissions, as opposed to the land markets and levels of planning gain needed to be efficient in greening economic development.

In recognising this, the problem that surfaces is over the methods adopted to carry out such an environmental assessment. This task is particularly difficult because there are two classes of environmental assessment methods: those providing environmental valuations and those assessing the sustainability of development. With the former it is important to recognise that this class of methods provides an index of the problems that have been experienced when the environment is reduced to little more than an aesthetic and is not represented as an ecological system (Deakin *et al.* 2002a, 2002b). With the latter the emphasis is firmly upon assessing the environment as an ecosystem logically connected to the economy. This requires a systematic modelling of the relationship between the ecology of design solutions and their economic structures. This in turn requires that the models and design solutions advanced are themselves subjected to an environmental assessment, capable in this instance of evaluating whether the ecology of the model is sound and if the resulting design solution is efficient in greening economic development.

THE ASSESSMENT METHODS

At present very few such models exist and their design solutions tend to be city-wide rather than district-, or neighbourhood-based. However, those that can be made use of include the following:

* the NAR (Net Annual Return) model
* the eco-neigbourhood model
* the transit-orientated settlement model.

These models illustrate a strong environmental inheritance and constitute serious attempts to assess the sustainability of communities in terms of their eco-systems and underlying economic structures (see Table 4.3).

The NAR model provides a critique of the discounting mechanism underlying the greening of economic development (Deakin 1996, 1997, 1999). It offers an environmental assessment of the impact this has upon the eco-system and provides a settlement model of how the discounting mechanism can be rehabilitated to provide a design solution producing the levels of planning gain needed to make any greening of economic development financially viable (Deakin 2000, 2002). The eco-neighbourhood model focuses on assessing the ecological footprint, bio-diversity and natural capital in terms of the environmental loading, levels of energy consumption, waste and emissions this greening of economic development produces (Stead 2000, Barton and Kleiner 2000, Deakin, et al. 2002a, 2002b). The transit-orientated settle-ment model provides a design solution which assesses whether eco-neighbourhoods have environmental loading, levels of energy consumption, waste and emissions which are friendly because the infrastructures required to service such high-quality living and working environments have the land markets and levels of planning gain needed to be efficient in greening economic development and make such a course of action financially viable (Calthorpe 2001).

The value of approaching the matter as a question of assessment rests with the potential such exercises have to evaluate the environmentally friendly nature of settlement patterns in terms of whether their sustainability develops in terms of the ecological, economic and financial qualities needed to guard communities against changes which are seen to threaten them – in particular, the coalescence of settle-ments, loss of identity and break-up of communities resulting from the type of infill development traditionally associated with peripheral expansion. While going a long

Table 4.3 The environmental assessment methods, models and attributes

Model	Attributes		
	Ecological	Economic	Financial
NAR	Critique of discounting mechanism underlying CBA-type models and rehabilitation of this particular environmental assessment technique	Use of land market to release planning gain as a means of supporting major infrastructure expenditures required to green economic development	Analysis of return on capital investment in terms of a discounting mechanism adjusted to fund high-quality living and working environments
Eco-neighbourhood model	Assessment of ecological footprint, bio-diversity and natural capital as an evaluation of environmental loading, levels of energy consumption, waste and emissions of settlements	Resource consumption analysis, costing of infrastructure expenditures	Consideration of funding mechanisms for repair and maintenance of design solutions as part of a total cost analysis
Transit-orientated settlement model	Assessment of transport and mobility requirements, interaction with land uses, environmental loading, levels of energy consumption, waste and emissions of settlements	Growth management strategy for greening economic environment through regulation of transport and mobility and use of design solutions to raise environmental standards	Effect of increased revenues on local budgets and expenditure of tax revenues on public services

Sources: Deakin (2000, 2002); Stead (2000); Barton and Kleiner (2000) and Calthorpe (2001)

way to rehabilitate CBA-based environmental assessment methods and meet the ecological, economic and financial demands of sustainable development, it would be wrong to suggest that the class of methods which are outlined here – the NAR, eco-neighbourhood and transit-orientated settlement models – can be easily applied to evaluate the communities in question. This is because the assessment of the environmental loading, levels of energy consumption, waste and emissions, greening of economic development and financial viability is a highly complex matter and is contingent upon the terms of reference adopted for the development of sustainable communities. This is a contingency which cannot be overlooked because, without the vision needed to scope the right terms of reference, it is not possible for the framework, or – in this instance – the property development protocol's settlement model and design solution, to integrate the ecological, economic and financial qualities needed to be environmentally friendly, let alone produce patterns of settlement which are sustainable in terms of the communities that in turn develop.

CONCLUSIONS

The protocol for sustainable urban property development provides a tool linking the technical requirements of property market analysis, valuation and investment appraisal with the more substantial environmental, economic and social issues and the connection this in turn has to the assessment and evaluation of sustainable urban development. The instrument provides a tool to guide actions taken by decision makers aiming to link the technical analysis and substantive issues of the aforesaid and check the connection they have with the assessment and evaluation of sustainable urban development. In this respect the protocol is a valuable tool because the linkages and connections which it makes have the potential not only to guide actions aimed at overcoming the prevailing hegemony of the urban property market, but also to check if the actions taken, guidelines adopted and checklists drawn up – to transform urban property development and make it sustainable – are sufficiently targeted. That is to say, sufficiently targeted so as not only to balance the formal requirements of property market analysis with the environmental, economic and social content of sustainable urban development, but also to direct decision makers to the assessment methods currently available to evaluate the sustainability of urban development. In taking this form, the value of the protocol can be seen as lying in the potential that it has not only to overcome the hegemony of the urban property market and strengthen the environmental, economic and social structure of the said development process, but also to provide a gateway – set of actions, guidelines and checklists – to pass through, en route and a path which leads directly towards sustainable urban property development.

The examination of the protocol has also shown how the hegemony of the urban property market can be overcome and the way in which this in turn strengthens the environmental, economic and social dimensions of sustainable urban development. This has been done by providing a technological representation of the urban property market and setting out the gateways that need to be passed through as part of a step-wise journey – a journey which not only beats a path towards sustainable urban property development, but also points us in the direction of the best practices the assessment process should follow in evaluating the sustainability of urban development. It should be noted that in the case of developing sustainable communities it has been seen that the balance of environmental, economic and social criteria has not been sufficiently integrated and has tended to work against environmental criteria in favour of the economic and financial. The examination has gone some way to show how this balance can be restored in the interests of ensuring that the transformation of urban property development is based on the modelling, design and layout of communities which are sustainable in environmental, economic and financial terms. From the account of the assessment methods currently available to help with this, it is evident that this transformation of urban property development is not yet complete and further steps need to be taken before they can be said to hold out the possibility of making communities sustainable in terms of their environmental, economic and social development.

REFERENCES

Ball, M. (1998) Institutional approaches to British property research: a review, *Urban Studies* 35: 1501–1518.

Ball, M. (2002) The organisation of property development, professions and practices. In Guy, S. and Heneberry, J. (eds) *Development and Developers*, Blackwell Publishing, Oxford.

Barton, H. (1997) Environmental capacity and sustainable urban form. In Farthing, S. (ed.) *Evaluating Local Environmental Policy*, Avebury, Andover.

Barton, H. and Kleiner, D. (2000) Innovative eco-neighbourhood projects. In Barton, H. (ed.) *Sustainable Communities*, Earthscan, London.

Barton, H., Davies, G. and Guise, R. (1995) *Sustainable Settlements – A Guide for Planners, Designers and Developers*, Local Government Management Board, Luton.

Beatley, T. (1995) Planning and sustainability: the elements of a new (improved?) paradigm, *Journal of Planning Literature* 9(4): 383–395.

Bentivegna, V., Curwell, S., Deakin, M., Lombardi, P., Mitchell, G. and Nijkamp, P. (2002) A vision and methodology for integrated sustainable urban development: BEQUEST, *Building Research and Information* 30(2): 83–94.

Breheny, M. (1992a) The compact city, *Built Environment* 18(4): 241–246.

Breheny, M. (1992b) *Sustainable Development and Urban Forms*, Pion, London.

Breheny, M. (1995) Counter-urbanisation and sustainable urban forms. In: Brotchie, J. (ed.) *Cities in Competition*, Longman, Melbourne.

Breheny, M. and Archer, S. (1998) Urban densities, local policies and sustainable development, *International Journal of Environment and Pollution* 10(1): 126–150.

Breheny, M. and Rookwood R. (1993) Planning the sustainable city-region. In: Blowers, A. (ed.) *Planning for a Sustainable Environment*, Earthscan, London.

Breheny, M., Gent, T. and Lock, D. (1993) *Alternative Development Patterns: New Settlements*, HMSO, London.

Brown, F. (1998) Modelling urban growth, *Town and Country Planning*, November, 334–337.

Cadman, D. and Topping, R. (1995) *Property Development*, E&FN Spon, London.

Calthorpe, P. (2001) *The Regional-City*, Island Press, New York.

Campbell, S. (1996) Green cities, growing cities, just cities? *Journal of the American Planning Association* 62(4): 296–312.

Cosgriff, B. and Steinemann, A. (1998) Industrial ecology for sustainable communities, *Journal of Environmental Planning and Management* 41(6): 661–672.

D'Arcy, A. and Keogh, G. (2002) The market context of property market activity. In Guy, S. and Heneberry, J. (ed.) *Development and Developers*, Blackwell Publishing, Oxford.

Deakin, M. (1996) Discounting, obsolescence, depreciation and their effects on the environment of cities, *Journal of Financial Management of Property and Construction* 1(2): 39–57.

Deakin, M. (1997) An economic evaluation and appraisal of the effects land use, building obsolescence and depreciation have on the environment of cities. In: Brandon, P., Lombardi, P. and Bentivegna, V. (ed.) *Evaluation of the Built Environment for Sustainability*, Chapman and Hall, London.

Deakin, M. (1999) Valuation, appraisal, discounting, obsolescence and depreciation: towards a life cycle analysis and impact assessment of their effects on the environment of cities, *International Journal of Life Cycle Assessment* 4(2): 87–94.

Deakin, M. (2000) Developing sustainable communities in Edinburgh's South East Wedge, *Journal of Property Management* 4(2): 72–88.

Deakin, M. (2002) Modelling the development of sustainable communities in Edinburgh's South East Wedge, *Planning Practice and Research* 17(3): 331–336.

Deakin, M. (2003a) Developing sustainable communities: the settlement model and design solution, *Journal of Urban Design* 8(2): 138–149.

Deakin, M. (2003b) The New Deal for Transport: the BEQUEST protocol for assessing the sustainability of urban development. In Hine, J. and Preston, J. (ed.) *Integrated Futures and Transport Choices, Ashgate*, Aldershot.

Deakin, M. and Curwell, S. (2003) Sustainable urban development: the BEQUEST framework for analysis and directory of assessment methods, *Open House International* 28(1).

Deakin, M., Curwell, S. and Lombardi, P. (2001): BEQUEST: the framework and directory of methods, *International Journal of Life Cycle Assessment* 6(6).

Deakin, M., Curwell, S. and Lombardi, P. (2002a) Sustainable urban development: the framework and directory of assessment methods, *Journal of Environmental Assessment Policy and Management* 4(2): 171–91.

Deakin, M., Huovila, P., Rao, S., Sunikka, M. and Vrekeer, R. (2002b) The assessment of sustainable urban development, *Building Research and Information* 30(2).

Dubben, N. and Sayce, S. (1991) *Property Portfolio Management*, Routledge, London.

Fraser, W. (1993) *Principles of Property Investment and Pricing*, Macmillan, London.

Gibbs, D., Longhurst, J. and Braithwaite, C. (1996) Moving towards sustainable development: integrating economic development and the environment in local authorities, *Journal of Environmental Planning and Management*, 39(3): 317–332.

Glasson, J., Therival, R. and Chadwick, A. (1994) *Environmental Impact Assessment*, University College London, London.

Gore, T. and Nicholson, D. (1991) Models of the land development process: a critical review, *Environment and Planning* 23: 705–730.

Greed, S. (1993) *Introducing Town Planning*, Routledge, London.

Guy, S. (1998) Developing alternatives; energy, offices and the environment, *International Journal of Urban and Regional Research* 22(2): 264–282.

Guy, S. (2002) Developing interests; environmental innovation and social organisation in the property business. In Guy, S. and Heneberry, J. (ed.) *Development and Developers*, Blackwell Publishing, Oxford.

Guy, S. and Heneberry, J. (2002) Approaching development. In Guy, S. and Heneberry, J. (ed.) *Development and Developers*, Blackwell Publishing, Oxford.

Guy, S. and Marvin, S. (2001) Urban environmental flows: towards a new way of seeing. In Guy, S. and Marvin, S. (ed.) *Urban Infrastructure in Transition*, Earthscan, London.

Hall, P. and Ward, C. (1998) *Sociable Cities*, John Wiley, London.

Harvey, J. (1996) *Urban Land Economics*, Macmillan, Basingstoke.

Healey, P. (1991) Models of the urban development process: a review, *Journal of Property Research* 8: 210–238.

Isaac, D. (1996) *Property Development: Appraisal and Finance*, Macmillan, Basingstoke.

Lichfield, N. (1996) *Community Impact Evaluation*, University College London, London.

Ratcliffe, J. and Stubbs, M. (1996) *Urban Planning and Real Estate Development*, University College London, London.

Roberts, M., Lloyd-Jones, T., Erickson, B. and Nice, S. (1999) Place and space in the networked city: concepualising the networked metropolis, *Journal of Urban Design* 4(1): 51–65.

Selman, P. (1996) *Local Sustainability*, St. Martin's Press, New York.

Stead, D. (2000) Unsustainable settlements. In Barton, H. (ed.) *Sustainable Communities*, Earthscan, London.

Urban Task Force (1999) *Towards an Urban Renaissance*, E&FN Spon, London.

Urban Villages Forum (2003) *Urban Villages and the Making of Communities*, E&FN Spon, London.

Ward, S. (1992) *Garden Cities, Past, Present and Future*, E&FN Spon, London.

5

Urban Design
Martin Symes

Creating the urban design is a vital stage in any urban development process. From the point of view of sustainable urban development, it is through the design of urban space that many of the intentions of sustainability will be realised. However, design is a notoriously difficult activity to understand, and assessing design is fraught with problems. The design of urban space is a major output of modern economies and has significant impacts on the environment. If the results of urban design decisions are not understood and controlled more effectively than they have been so far, the quality of life available to citizens will continue to deteriorate. Having adopted the PICABUE objectives, environmentalism, futurity, equity and participation (which are considered in more detail in Chapters 1 and 2), and when developing the BEQUEST framework, members of the network have also had to think carefully about the actors who are involved in urban design processes (outlined in the ATEQUE model also discussed in other chapters) and about the criteria they could use in addressing design decisions. These considerations are being carried forward by the members of the network, and the work of proposing detailed protocols for use by urban designers has begun. This chapter presents the state of the art for urban design, and readers should understand that the ideas reported here remain under review. Later volumes in this series of books will no doubt give them further consideration.

THE URBAN DESIGN PROCESS

It is arguable that the process of design has never been properly described. This could be because it is partly intuitive, or because there is no one general process, or because various different types of design can be carried out at one and the same time. Brandon (1999) (drawing on Lawson 1993) takes this last view:

> Most of the research on design suggests that the [designer] ... is wrestling in his mind with complex scenarios at various levels of detail and with several parallel lines of thought.

These lines of thought often follow more conventional patterns of problem-solving: working sequentially from general questions to detail, or in reverse, from the detail to the overall form; working iteratively, returning to partly solved problems when new facts or interpretations come to light; using analogy, applying metaphors, or metonymy; thinking 'outside the box' or just plain brainstorming. It is probably not true that no two designers think alike – they are not, in the final analysis, artists, free to speculate without responsibility for the results, but must take account of some, at least, of the constraints of 'reality'. Urban designers are a case in point: they are expected to make novel or unexpected suggestions which will expand conventional thinking about the possibilities for shaping urban space, but they must also show how such suggestions can be applied to real situations. They are able to influence the quality of life, but they must do it for other people, not just for themselves. To help improve their performance, assessment methods have to be incorporated in their patterns of problem-solving.

Assessing urban design can be about assessing a process, but it can also be about assessing products: both designs for realisation in stages and designs for complete projects. Urban design processes may be private, although probably not as secretive as when a design team works on an architectural design competition. Urban design processes can also be very public, as when a group of designers 'sets up shop' in a local community and invites participation by interested residents. Urban designs for realisation in stages can be schemes for the physical changes which will be made to a neighbourhood over a period of time (masterplans) or they can be policies for the types of design solution which will be introduced in an area when change becomes possible (design guides). Complete urban design projects may consist of area developments created by a variety of builders over a number of years (typical of the New Towns around London and Paris). More commonly they are either very large building programmes carried out as if they were a single project (the Barbican in London) (Figure 5.1), or a linked series of smaller interventions which alter the character of an area (as in Manchester in the 1990s) (Figure 5.2).

Protocols for including sustainability assessment in urban design processes have therefore to meet a number of very different practical requirements. But they can have some characteristics in common. They must deal with physical as well as socio-economic aspects of development; they must cover a geographical scale larger than a single building but smaller than a complete city; they must seek to extend consideration to long-term as well as to short-term outcomes. They will certainly be of interest to a number of different types of social actor.

The remainder of this chapter uses the BEQUEST framework to help define this common ground.

THE SYSTEM OF ACTORS IN URBAN DESIGN

Who is proposing action, for whom this work is to be undertaken, whose interests are to be taken into account, by whom it will be assessed, to whom the results will

5.1 The Barbican Centre, London

be reported and by whom action will then follow: these are fundamental questions and all apply to each of the development activities discussed in this group of chapters. It is important to point out, however, that the practical expression of the system of actors affecting and affected by sustainable development is not the same for each level of activity. The planning system (Chapter 3), the development industry

5.2 Smithfield Buildings, Manchester (Urban Splash)

(Chapter 4), the construction industry (Chapter 6) and the management teams for urban built space (Chapter 7) have different structures. The set of actors varies, as do the protocols they should use.

Discussions leading up to the establishment of the BEQUEST framework made reference to a number of ways of listing the social actors influencing the built environment (see Chapter 2). One of the more general was the French ATEQUE system which classifies various groups of actors by *poles*:

the *pole* of collective interest
the *pole* of operational decision making
the *pole* of design
the *pole* of project carry-through
the *pole* of use

– each pole being subdivided into officially recognised professional or semi-professional groups, with the third pole including those involved in urban design.

To ensure full consideration of the factors considered essential for increasing the sustainability of development at the urban design scale, the ATEQUE view of the range of participants involved is too limited and its conception of the design process as being carried out by a group of professional actors must be expanded. Discussion of this third pole must take account of the view that more people are involved and that their activities are not all easily codified. The following paragraphs therefore divide a larger group of actors into 'insiders', who can expect to be closely involved with official decisions, and 'outsiders' who are affected by these decisions, but must make their case for inclusion within any particular design process. The ways these types of actor work will differ, so design processes can have a variety of structures and include different kinds of decision. The following paragraphs therefore also discuss different types of decision-making 'gate'.

Designers need to undertake assessments as they progress their work, to inform themselves of their success in meeting the objectives set for their design, or to persuade those for whom, or with whom, the design is being produced, of its virtues. The pole of design may be quite broad. ATEQUE lists only five actors: designers (architects and engineers), technical consultants, town planners, landscapers and economists (in the United Kingdom these would usually be surveyors). But this list is too restrictive. The poles certainly overlap in Britain, for example. Whatever the composition of the urban design team assembled (and this will vary in different parts of Europe), its members will normally find themselves collaborating both with actors inside other poles, and also with groups who are outside the list of poles altogether. They have to be able to express their ideas in ways that these others can understand, and come to terms with the need to establish confidence in their way of working. Using a common language and adopting a common protocol for the assessments which are needed can be steps in this direction.

Urban design is a flexible process and has a variety of outcomes. Who are 'insiders' and who 'outsiders' will vary according to the context. As a generalisation, however, those listed in the design pole will interact regularly with some of those listed in the operational decision-making pole (such as development companies and infrastructure owners, whose approach is discussed in Chapter 4). Together these actors form an 'insider' group, and for them a process of negotiation will seem the everyday way of working. We can think about passing through 'soft' gates, where provisional agreements are reached on the appropriate strategy to be adopted, before the team proceeds to considering the succeeding stages of design development.

'Outside' this group will be two other groups. The first group of 'outsiders' is formed by representatives of the pole of collective interest (government agencies, regional and local authorities, elected representatives, consumer associations, etc., including those mentioned in Chapter 3). In some types of administrative or financial partnership, actors concerned with the pole of project carry-through (development control and building control officers, cost accountants, construction managers and component manufacturers, such as those whose evaluation criteria are discussed in Chapter 6) will also be involved. This group will expect formal presentations of progress in the design team's thinking, and may wish to, or have to, operate 'hard' gates, where formal approval is required before the design team can continue developing an urban design concept.

The second group of 'outsiders' is formed by social actors in the pole of use (users of buildings, users of transport and utility services, the managers of buildings and services, and insurers, whose interests are mentioned in Chapter 7). Even if they can be identified during the design process (and this is a question in situations like town expansion on newly developed land) they may not be in a position to control any 'gates' at all. Their only reaction may be that of 'voting with their feet' if, when implemented, the scheme fails to meet their expectations. Much of the academic and practical concern currently being expressed about the need to reform urban governance, such as in the suggestion by Oestereich (undated) which is noted below, focuses on the possibility of altering the position of this second outsider group. Some commentators would have them join the other 'outside' group, and become active participants in the control function. Others would have them join the 'insiders' and be fully consulted at all stages of the work of the design team. British examples of experiments in making this happen can be found in community design workshops and 'Planning for Real' events. In France, Germany, Italy, Denmark and so on, best practice differs.

URBAN DESIGN AS A DEVELOPMENT ACTIVITY

An interest in the design of cities began at the turn of the nineteenth century, with the City Beautiful movement in America, the publication of Camillo Sitte's treatise on the Continent and the enthusiasm for garden cities generated in Britain by Ebenezer Howard. This interest in large-scale neighbourhood design was given a major impetus in the 1930s by le Corbusier and other members of CIAM with the 'Charter of Athens'. However, the origin of urban design as it is thought of today, that is to say as more of a process than a product, can be found in Gropius's 1956 discussions at Harvard and in Llewellyn-Davies's teaching at University College London in the 1960s. In the Kassler Memorial Lecture at Princeton in 1980, the latter answered the question: 'Urban Design: what is it?' as follows:

> An essentially practical subject, concerned with that negotiation between long- and short-term interests which occurs as the built environment is developed.

The first step in a process of physical development, identifying possible uses for a plot of land, is often carried out by planners, as described in the previous chapter, and can require negotiation between officials at various levels in the planning hierarchy. There is little doubt about the importance of such negotiations if sustainable development is to be achieved. Money may not always be at stake directly at this stage, as the issues are likely to be geographical and aesthetic, but behind these may well lie financial questions. They may include the need for new infrastructure or the desirability of inward investment, and such questions may not always be simply answered by adding up direct costs and calculating expected rental returns. There may be a decision which is 'hard' in the sense that a proposed allocation must either be allowed or refused, and some of the arguments which will provide evidence to influence the negotiation should come from a multidimensional assessment process, as discussed in Chapters 8 and 9. Innovative urban design will often stimulate a great deal of public interest, as was the case at the time proposals were made for developing the Festival of Britain on London's South Bank (Figure 5.3).

The second step in the development process is the assembly of land under a single ownership, and this can also involve numerous parties in a complex negotiation process. Each party has to decide what they are prepared to pay, or accept, as a price for their interest. To do this they need quite accurate estimates of the short- and long-term costs and benefits of being party to the development of a consolidated site. This is exactly the situation described by Llewellyn-Davies and often depends on three-dimensional sketches of the built environment which might be created being available. These sketches have to be sufficiently accurate for the types of space use and quality

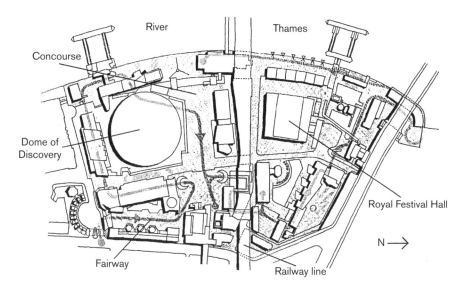

Concourse

River Thames

Dome of Discovery

Royal Festival Hall

N →

Fairway

Railway line

5.3 The Festival of Britain

of construction and services possible to be clearly understood. An element of the competition which comes into the financial negotiation could be 'imperfect knowledge' on one side or the other, as the skill and imagination of the design team responsible for exploring the potential of a particular site will probably give the buyer or the seller a hidden advantage. The architect Richard Siefert made himself an enviable reputation for being able to assess the architectural possibilities of particular sites better than any other practitioner during the London office-building boom of the 1960s and negotiating highly favourable 'hard' permissions.

In the third step in a development process, the detailed design of large development projects or area-wide development schemes, it is increasingly clear that urban designers are able to play an important part in building confidence about the future quality of the places which will eventually be created. Mixed-use development is now looked for in many inner-city areas, such as the Millennium Village currently rising beside the Thames at Greenwich. Village-like designs are now de rigueur for inner-city developments and assumptions are, perhaps too readily, made that all aspects of such 'compact city' solutions are essential if sustainable development is to be achieved. Brindley (2003) discusses this point in some detail. Certainly, the availability of a high level of urban design skill must be demonstrated if investors are to be convinced that residents will come forward in sufficient numbers to make such schemes a financial success in the long term. In this situation, the potential developers are usually negotiating 'soft' gates with various kinds of planning authority when

making their decisions. In other situations masterplanning has proved especially contentious and urban designers may prefer to work directly with local citizens groups
(see Figure 5.4). In design for sustainability the quality of the urban design process
will be as important for acceptability as the form of the scheme being drawn. Symes
et al. (1993) show how some practitioners specialise in this approach to practice.

The emergence of the sustainability agenda, with its concern for life-cycle
costing, has renewed interest in the implications of the reuse of existing buildings and
in the resources embedded in building materials. Notable examples are seen in areas
which were first developed at the time of the Industrial Revolution and suffered a
severe economic decline in the 1960s and 70s (see Eley and Worthington 1984, and
Figure 5.5). Designers can consider these factors at an early stage in the decision-
making process and, depending on the problem-solving methods they employ, return
to them again as the design progresses. Decisions here are more likely to be 'soft' in
that they become adopted as the project moves forward, than 'hard', as are those
described above which are made when proposals need to obtain official approval.
The protocol for urban design assessment must address the information needs of
negotiations concerning both these kinds of decision.

A drawing may communicate more easily than the written
word in a collaborative event

Planning for Real helps
residents determine their own
priorities

5.4 'Planning for Real'

5.5 Aerial view of Little Germany, Bradford

ENVIRONMENTAL AND SOCIETAL ISSUES IN SUSTAINABLE URBAN DESIGN

Although urban design is fundamentally concerned with the physical form taken by an environmental project, it is both the result of a socio-economic process and the stimulus for social and economic effects. There is a growing body of research evidence to support this point of view (see, for example, Neary *et al.* 1994 and Moser *et al.* 2003) and any protocol for sustainability assessment must show how it can be taken into account in urban design processes.

The strongest theoretical tradition of research in human–environment interaction is based on the economic factors: these will be discussed again in more detail in other chapters and in the second volume of this series. At the level of discussion in this chapter, it is useful nonetheless to note that urban design qualities affect not only the supply of space for work, of housing, of public and private open space, of transport facilities, but also the demand. Often left out of the calculations made in the market-place concerning the optimum price for these economic goods are the less tangible externality costs of the services provided by urban space: a clean environment, without pollution, a natural landscape and the experience of bio-diversity. Appropriate assessment methods should be able to demonstrate the consequences of urban design choices for the full cost of access to these elements, and influence negotiations (see, for example, Barton *et al.* 2003).

Social and psychological studies of human interactions with the environment have a more complex theoretical basis, as the economist's assumption that individuals are able to make choices and that the role of institutions is to regulate them, is not always accepted. The research referred to by Neary *et al.* and Moser *et al.* discusses such aspects as: the constraints on behaviour of a cultural context; the social structures which influence the attitudes which people hold; the learning processes which are prerequisites for particular modes of perception to develop. Historical studies show that these patterns of thought and behaviour have changed over both long and short periods of time, partly as a result of changes to the urban physical environment (the removal of the Berlin Wall being a recent example of this), and the desire for sustainability can sometimes seem an essentially conservative point of view. Imposing change on emerging societies which would have good reasons to resist them is a frequent focus for criticism of modern urban design.

Nonetheless, today's European society, largely urbanised and increasingly living in self-consciously designed environments, probably expects urban design to provide for certain basic standards, of health, of safety, of access to services and of a sense of belonging to a place. Oestereich (undated) refers to the concept of property rights, extending it to suggest that any claim on resources can be treated 'as part of a "bundle of rights" connected with a piece of land or territory', and that a new kind of certificate could be issued permitting the exploitation of rare resources or the use of the limited absorption capacity of eco-systems. These could be introduced at the local level and allow communities to help determine the sustainability of their own 'habitat'. At present the negotiation of such commitments is clearly part of the 'soft' gates to project acceptance, but if a binding certificate of rights were introduced it could become a 'hard' gate.

Urban design as product, and as process, is deeply implicated in Local Agenda 21 (LA 21) processes. These have been very widely implemented in the years since the Rio conference. They seek to ensure that sustainability is given a high priority in decision making and administration of the local environment, and provide for community participation at local government level. Indeed LA 21 can be seen as emblematic of a more general attempt to alter the shape of 'governance' by introducing collaboration and partnership between central and local government, the private sector and voluntary non-governmental organisations (NGOs). These attempts to generate a more collaborative culture have not always been successful: they can increase transaction costs, and depend on the sharing of risk and the creation of new relationships of trust. Cushman *et al.* (2002) have studied these problems in construction industry partnerships. Their work suggests that collaborations in urban development are likely to bring together organisations with imperfectly aligned interests and incompatible information systems. Symes (2002) has argued that the additional barriers which there are to collaboration with the design professions include their educational experience and 'incomplete' professional status. As the strength of these factors in the production of urban design varies between member states of the European Union, the successful integration with them of a protocol for assessing the environmental sustainability of urban design will require both sensitivity and flexibility.

SPATIAL LEVELS OF URBAN DESIGN

Urban designers often focus professionally on the physical elements of the city and their relationships with each other. Madanipour (1996) quotes the DoE (1992) as proposing that planners should concentrate on: 'broad matters of scale, density, height, massing, layout, landscape and access, [avoiding] excessive prescription and detail'. But Madanipour goes on to argue that urban design is a social practice and that designers should understand how the physical elements with which they are concerned are informed by, and in turn inform, the social and economic context. Sustainable urban design clearly must involve a strong emphasis on this interpretation of the topic.

The definitions of urban design activity given earlier in this chapter suggest that the spatial scale at which assessment should be introduced is essentially that of the urban neighbourhood. Neighbourhoods are, however, rarely independent of the city of which they are a part. So assessing urban design means assessing the contribution a neighbourhood-scale design will make to a larger whole, the city. While focusing on action taken at the neighbourhood scale, an urban design assessment protocol must take account of the relationship with those possible only at larger, or smaller, geographical scales (some of the latter are shown in Thomas 2003).

TIME SCALES FOR URBAN DESIGN

Time is an important dimension of urban design. A seminal text by Lynch (1972) dealt with the evidence of time *past* which is embodied in the built environment and in our perceptions of the quality of urban space. But Lynch also introduced innovative thinking about development *for the future* by discussing 'the crucial issues of environmental change management [as well as the problem of] managing transitions'.

Sustainable urban design puts a premium on these questions, and the evaluation methods chosen by designers must be appropriate for their assessment. In this respect the BEQUEST framework suggests that the time scale to be covered in sustainability assessment could be short (up to five years), medium (from five to twenty years) or long (above this). Aspects of urban design can have consequences over all these periods. The implications of change over time should be considered in 'soft' gates to design decision making and contribute to the establishment of appropriate 'hard' gates.

Why time matters can be illustrated with reference to a presentation on 'Factor 20' made at one of the BEQUEST discussions (Bureau of Sustainable Building 1998). The Factor 20 project is intended to motivate and inspire policy-makers, research institutes, the business community and environmental organisations to collaborate in providing the knowledge base for reducing the environmental pollution produced by the building industry and to increase the quality and comfort of the residential environment.

Factor 20 is described as a metaphor. The presentation quoted the American environmentalist, Barry Commoner, who defined environmental pollution (EP) as a product of three factors: the world population (Po), prosperity per person (Pr) and metabolism (M), the environmental pollution per unit of prosperity. His formula, $EP = Po \times Pr \times M$, can be used to calculate the level of M which must be attained if EP were to be reduced to some desirable level. The Factor 20 team estimate that Po will rise by a factor of 2 and Pr by a factor of 5 over the coming fifty years. For EP (already at an undesirable level) to be reduced by a factor of 2 over the same period, M would have to fall by a factor of 20. At the end of this period the change would have been $EP (-2) = Po (+2) \times Pr (+5) \times M (-20)$.

This calculation is concerned with global figures, but area statistics of all kinds contribute naturally to these totals. If urban design decisions contribute to changes in population, prosperity and 'metabolism' (environmental pollution per unit of prosperity) at a small area scale, they contribute to the global improvements required. According to this interpretation of the time perspective, it would be suggested that different components of urban design decisions will have differing levels of impact over a variety of time scales. The same design proposal might have an effect, for example, on population over ten years, on prosperity over five years, and on 'metabolism' immediately. The effects on pollution will be noticeable over a short period of time, but only partial in terms of the stated objective, whereas over the longer term, the effects will be much greater, and the objective may be fully achieved. Assessors of urban design need information on the likely development over time of the effects they seek to measure.

A PROTOCOL FOR URBAN DESIGN ASSESSMENTS

The protocol for urban design assessments which follows is intended to support decision makers who wish to find a clear role for environmental sustainability assessment in this complex set of needs and possibilities. It follows the outline protocol process produced by the BEQUEST team, and adapts it for urban design.

Preparation

*   Determine whether there are legal requirements for assessment ('hard' gates).
*   Establish the national and local norms which apply ('soft' gates).
*   Clarify the set of actors with an interest in the design and their responsibilities.
*   Clarify the time and resources available for an assessment to be implemented.

Planning an assessment

*   List the sustainability objectives which will be covered by the assessment.
*   Assemble the assessment team.
*   Establish procedures for collaboration with 'insiders' in the design group.
*   Establish a communication process with 'outsiders' in the approval group.
*   Determine the role of the user group (whether 'outsiders or insiders').
*   Produce a timetable for meeting 'hard' and 'soft' gates in the approval process.
*   Check the availability of data.
*   Make provision for collecting new information.

The content of the assessment

*   Determine whether to assess the process of urban design.
*   Determine the scale of urban design proposals to be covered.
*   Determine the time period over which effects are to be estimated.

The assessment process

*   Obtain the design documents.
*   Collect all the information needed to assess the agreed aspects.
*   Select the evaluation methods which will be used.
*   Assess the situation before any changes are implemented.
*   Determine the probable impact of the design proposals at an agreed future date.
*   Determine acceptability of the design as currently conceived (if a 'hard' gate).
*   Consider and review alternatives to the given design.

Consultation

- Discuss findings with the design team (insiders).
- Discuss findings with the approval group (outsiders).
- Discuss findings with the user group (usually outsiders).
- Repeat the process if major changes to the design are required.

Reporting

- Draw up a final assessment report and pass to design team.
- Make a formal submission to the approval group (if a 'hard' gate).

Providing information

- Provide information for the user group.
- Agree and implement publicity.

Monitoring

- Meet insider and outsider groups to agree a follow-up strategy.

ASSESSMENT METHODS FOR URBAN DESIGN

The use of the protocol will result in the selection of assessment methods (as described in the second volume in this series) for use in urban design processes. The brief discussion which follows is intended to give readers an idea of the range of possibilities that will emerge.

Methods specially geared to the urban design scale include those being produced by the team working on another European Research and Development project (HQE2R, discussed in more detail in the following case study). This team is proposing three evaluation models for use in neighbourhood planning which aims to increase sustainability. When complete, and fully tested, these models should be of considerable value to urban designers. One will estimate global costs (including externalities) for large development projects, and should have a facility for taking account of returns over a number of different time periods. A second will calculate the environmental impact of local investments or regulatory programmes. It will seek to make provision for the inherent difficulty of determining the exact geographical areas on which the impacts will fall. The third will be based on the full range of qualitative indicators assembled by the research team and give a sense of the quality of life which should result from a neighbourhood development programme. Again the model will allow users to select the time period of the projections they wish to study.

More general methods considered appropriate for urban design assessment by the BEQUEST team, and described in detail in the second volume of this series, include five generic methods:

Analytic hierarchy process
Contingent valuation method
Impact matrix techniques
Social cost-benefit analysis
System dynamic approach.

The BEQUEST directory of assessment methods also identifies sixteen specific techniques which could be of use to designers. These include proprietary methods such as BREEAM (the Building Research Establishment Environmental Assessment Method) and GBC (Green Building Challenge), which take a wide variety of factors into account and produce overall evaluations of design proposals. In addition, a selection of tightly defined methods for evaluating particular components can be found in the directory. Examples include PIMWAQ which defines ecological levels of residential buildings, various methodologies for assessing office buildings, MASTER for managing the speed of road traffic, and BRE Environmental Profiles, which supports the evaluation of building materials.

CONCLUSION

Urban design is a complex process and its results are crucial for the success of attempts to improve the sustainability of urban development. The key change required to urban design practice is for a greater emphasis now to be placed on improving its processes. These must allow interested parties to give careful consideration to the long-term consequences of those environmental, economic and social changes which will follow from urban design decisions. The BEQUEST directory of assessment methods indicates the types of decision-aid tools which they will need. Using the directory, actors in an urban design process will be able to select and include one or more of these neighbourhood-scale, building-scale or component-scale methods in their assessment activity. The discussion in this chapter, and the protocol suggestions made in its closing sections, are intended to assist these actors in making their choice.

CASE STUDY OF EUROPEAN URBAN DESIGN CRITERIA

HQE2R Sustainable Renovation of Buildings for Sustainable Neighbourhoods

This European research and demonstration project is producing a methodology for sustainable neighbourhood regeneration. The project team includes ten European research organisations, and demonstration projects are being carried out in fourteen cities from seven different member states. The term HQE refers to well-established French guidelines for sustainability in building (Haute Qualité Environnementale), but it is argued that at the neighbourhood level it is important to add consideration of the Economic and other social factors implicated in Regeneration projects (hence the acronym HQ*E2R*). The factors are then regrouped to express objectives which are important for increasing sustainability at the neighbourhood scale (see Box 5.1) and can be translated into design terms. Two of these are physical (the Heritage and the

---

BOX 5.1

HQE2R: objectives for neighbourhood sustainability

The sustainable development approach requires **prior consideration of the objectives of sustainability for that city**. It is not a question of diachronic sustainability (in this sense, any city is sustainable). It is a question of broad options which, at the present time, render the city desirable and liveable for its residents and users without compromising the abilities and quality of life of future generations.

The HQE2R project proposes the use of **five global objectives of sustainable development** for European cities as a point of departure for a thought process which does not, however, prejudge the specific and particular forms of each city, defined by its history, geography and the men and women who live and die there. These five global objectives of sustainable development for the city are as follows:

- **To preserve and enhance heritage and to conserve resources**, i.e. human resources, constructed or natural heritage, natural resources (energy, water, space), whether local or global, bio-diversity, etc.
- **To improve the quality of the local environment**, for the residents and users of the city.

- **To ensure diversity**: diversity of the population, the habitat, human activities, space.
- **To improve integration**: integration of the inhabitants in the city, in order that everyone feels they are both an inhabitant of and have a role to play in the city; integration of neighbourhoods in the city, with reference to the multi-centre city.
- **To reinforce social life** through local governance, and relations of social cohesion and actions of social equity.

These five objectives (heritage and resources, quality of local environment, diversity, integration, social life) must serve as the foundation for regeneration projects, development, and construction, whether for a city or for a neighbourhood as well as for buildings. According to the scale and characteristics of the area, the concrete form of these objectives will change. They will also vary according to the project to be handled, as the aforementioned principles do not apply in exactly the same terms to all projects. It is, in fact, a question of an analysis or **grid**, which allows an overview of all the problems to be tackled in an approach to sustainable development.

Environment) (see Box 5.2), two are geographical (Diversity and Integration) (see Box 5.3) and the fifth is social (see Box 5.4). The objectives are quoted at length as they give a good example of how more general considerations of sustainability can be focused on the elements of urban design at a neighbourhood scale.

The project team have set out a four-stage process for project design:

Decision
Analysis
Assessment
Action

In each stage a number of procedures are recommended (see also Figure 5.6). In the first stage, it is necessary to identify the problems of the neighbourhood which require action: these can be social, environmental and technical. A strategic decision must be made that sustainable regeneration should be attempted. In the second stage an inventory must be made, various targets are identified and a list of essential indicators established. At this stage it is possible to carry out a diagnosis (including studies of neighbourhood potential as well as of dysfunctions), priorities can be agreed and

BOX 5.2

HQE2R: objectives for environmental sustainability

➤ *To preserve and enhance heritage and to conserve resources*

Building on the notion and principles of sustainability as laid down in the 'Charter of European Cities and Towns towards Sustainability' ('Aalborg Charter', Aalborg, Denmark, May 1994), one of the baselines of sustainable development is defined as environmental sustainability: 'Environmental sustainability means maintaining the natural capital. It demands from us:

- that the rate at which we consume renewable material . . . does not exceed the rate at which the natural systems can replenish it,
- that the rate at which we consume non-renewable resources does not exceed the rate at which they are replaced by sustainable renewable resources, and
- that the rate of emitted pollutants does not exceed the capacity of the air, water and soil to absorb and process them.'

Above that, the overall question is how to develop towards a sustainable society, taking into account the restrictions of nature together with the economic and social dimensions of behaviour, within a global context. The development of new structures, organisations and technologies is as important as the inclusion of all people and of communication between them. People have to learn to change their attitudes, show initiative and interact to ensure a viable future for themselves and the following generations. Therefore living conditions (e.g. within an urban neighbourhood) have to be organised in such a way that these changes are supported.

As regards the common heritage, this embraces, in a twofold meaning of the term, both **the present and the future**:

- by considering energy, material, water and space resources, and also built assets as a stock that must be **preserved** for future generations;
- by building on the wealth of the land as formed by humans currently living on it: this involves enhancing the potential of the material and human resources available to us to **develop** a heritage which can be handed on to the future generations.

These two dimensions highlight not only the economic and natural heritage but also the **cultural** heritage which current generations wish to pass on to their successors.

> ➤ *To improve the quality of the local environment*

Sustainable development must enable citizens to gain the benefit of a better standard of living, both now and in the future, and must direct actions which place residents at the focus of development. Our standard of living lies at the very heart of European policy, the aim of which is 'to improve the quality of the life in cities and conurbations whilst facing the problems of the quality of air, noise, traffic congestion, waste, economic competition, employment, security and improving the infrastructure and built environment so as to enhance social inclusion and promote sustainable development' (European Commission, objective of 5th Framework Programme of the European Community for Research, Technological Development and Demonstration Activities).

The reduction of nuisance (noise, waste, quality of the air and water) and natural and technological risks lies at the heart of all these problems.

The neighbourhood and the city are not simply territories, but complex systems of networks, activities, users and human experience, with similarities and differences that are constantly changing. To allow for the increasingly dynamic aspect of urban flows, one must reconcile within the different time scales of the city,[1] life at work and life outside work, and offer the possibility of access to the different services of the region, modulated to suit the requirements of its inhabitants.

BOX 5.3

HQE2R: objectives for economic sustainability

> ➤ *To ensure diversity*

A district must be capable of offering **a variety of economic, social, cultural and natural functions** and of ensuring the greatest possible degree of adaptability **in the long term**. Diversity must reflect the complexity of these systems, and can increase the information content and quality of exchanges.

A varied supply of the functional opportunities as well as of human and material resources underlies the concept of diversity, the aim of which is to guarantee **social and urban mix**, to fight social exclusion, to support the development of economic and cultural activities, and to define the continuity of a system where although heterogeneous elements interact they form, together, a homogenous region.

Supporting sustainable development of a neighbourhood and region also means promoting diversity and cultural vitality whilst fostering human resources (gender, ethnic origins, social strata, etc.) and material resources (variety of functions, spaces and activities).

Diversity must also take into account all the functions available at the boundaries of the district, and they must be easily accessible.

➤ *To improve integration*

A neighbourhood continuously interacts with contiguous areas and all those surrounding it (city, conurbation, sub-region, region, state and planet). This relation with its neighbours, as also with the global environment, is necessary, so that each feels as an inhabitant of their city or their agglomeration, as of the planet, and conversely, so that no territory is excluded from development.

To guarantee continuous exchange of resources and information, the neighbourhood, and the city and the neighbourhood must hence form **open and permeable systems**. This opening-up is a **denial of 'neighbourhood Balkanisation'** and fundamental both to upholding the life of the neighbourhood, which cannot itself possess all the means to develop comprehensively and independently, and to ensuring real social and economic integration.

The concept of integration also refers to that of **equilibrium** between neighbourhoods. However, we focus on the concept of integration since this highlights the interdependence of residents, districts and cultures in a SD dynamic process, at the neighbourhood scale.

specific objectives defined. The third stage is a very important one from the point of view of urban design, for it is now that alternative scenarios must be established and their evaluation undertaken. In the fourth stage a complex set of processes must be set in motion: the drawing up of an action plan, proposing changes to planning regulations (where they exist), writing specifications for building projects and for neighbourhood elements, ensuring that monitoring procedures are put in place. These

---

BOX 5.4

HQE2R: objectives for social sustainability

➢ *To reinforce social life*

The creation of relations of exchange and **respect between individuals** and **participation** in the life of the town are fundamental objectives for ensuring the perennial nature or sustainability of neighbourhoods. One of the objectives of the Treaty of the European Union is to achieve balanced and sustainable development, in particular by strengthening economic and social cohesion.[2] **Social cohesion is absolutely vital** to the development of neighbourhoods: Wilson (1996) argues that a neighbourhood in which social organisation, or social capital, is strong will offer a better quality of life. He points out that neighbourhoods which suffer from poverty and exclusion are also likely to lack social capital. One of the key questions facing regeneration at present is the extent to which excluded neighbourhoods have the capacity to use their social capital to bring about improvement. There is a growing consensus that regeneration programmes initiated by external organisations will only succeed if they work in partnership with local people and utilise local social resources.

As the primary urban forum in which residents can share a common identity and **common values**, the neighbourhood represents a scale of analysis at which all issues and sustainable development objectives can be fully expressed, particularly with respect to the social dimensions.

To ensure a process of social participation, each inhabitant must develop a feeling of belonging to the district in which they live: this can be strengthened by a policy of information and of stimulating greater awareness, particularly concerning sustainable development issues of interest to the neighbourhood concerned.

Accordingly, the common values of **civics, solidarity and citizenship** must be expressed by social bonds, situating the citizen in relation to the sustainable development of their neighbourhood.

---

will incorporate both 'hard' and 'soft' decision-making gates, depending on the national and regional, legal and economic contexts in which they are set.

A major component of the work has been the creation of a special set of indicators to measure aspects of sustainability at the neighbourhood scale and it has

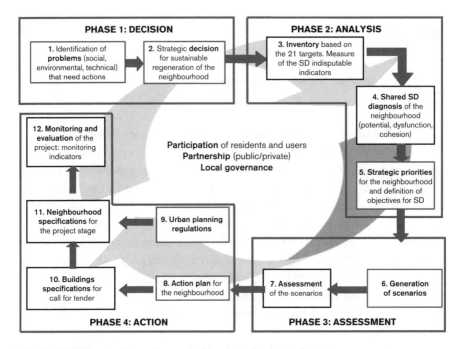

PHASE 1: DECISION

1. Identification of **problems** (social, environmental, technical) that need actions

2. Strategic **decision** for sustainable regeneration of the neighbourhood

PHASE 2: ANALYSIS

3. **Inventory** based on the 21 targets. Measure of the SD indisputable indicators

4. **Shared SD diagnosis** of the neighbourhood (potential, dysfunction, cohesion)

5. **Strategic priorities** for the neighbourhood and definition of objectives for SD

12. **Monitoring and evaluation** of the project: monitoring indicators

11. **Neighbourhood specifications** for the project stage

9. **Urban planning regulations**

10. **Buildings specifications** for call for tender

8. **Action plan** for the neighbourhood

7. **Assessment** of the scenarios

6. **Generation of scenarios**

Participation of residents and users **Partnership** (public/private) **Local governance**

PHASE 4: ACTION

PHASE 3: ASSESSMENT

5.6 The HQE2R methodology for sustainable urban planning projects

proposed twenty-one such measures. A substantial proportion of the indicators are composite indicators which relate data available for the neighbourhood scale to the data available for the city in which it is set. These are organised under the five objectives and should all be measurable in each member state, but they can be supplemented in any particular case by locally generated indicators covering factors of particular interest to the community there. It is recommended that urban designers apply these measurements to four physical urban design elements:

Residential space
Non-residential space
Non-built space
Infrastructure

Figure 5.7 gives a graphic representation of the system.

5.7 Sustainable renovation of buildings for sustainable neighbourhoods

Source: in progress table done by Foment de Ciutat Vella and CAATB (Spain) for Raval neighbourhood case study from an original concept of the HQE²R Project (http://hqe2r.cstb.fr)

NOTES

1 HQE2R Sustainable Renovation of Buildings for Sustainable Neighbourhoods, EVK4-CT-2000-00025
2 Article 2 of the European Union Treaty.

REFERENCES

Barton, H., Grant, M. and Guise, R. (2003) *Shaping Neighbourhoods: A Guide for Health, Sustainability and Vitality*, London, Spon.

Brandon, P. (1999) Sustainability in management and organisation: the key issues? *Building Research and Information* 27(6): 391–397.

Brindley, T. (2003) Village and community: social models for sustainable urban development. In Moser, G., Pol, E., Bernard, Y., Bonnes, M., Corraliza, J.A. and Giuliani, M.V. (eds) *People, Places and Sutainability*, Goettingen, Hogrefe and Huber.

Bureau of Sustainable Building (1998) *Building up to Factor 20: Towards a 20-fold Reduction in Environmental Pollution Per Unit of Prosperity*, The Hague, Ministry of Housing, Spatial Planning and the Environment.

Cushman, M., Franco, L.A. and Rosenhead, J. (2002) Problem Structuring Methods for Cross-Organisational Learning. In Purdue, D. and Stewart, M. (eds) *Understanding Collaboration: International Perspectives on Theory, Method and Practice*, Bristol, University of the West of England, pp. 45–51.

DoE (Department of Environment) (1992) *Planning Policy Guidance: Development Plans and Regional Planning Guidance, PPG 1*, London, HMSO.

Eley, P. and Worthington, J. (1984) *Industrial Rehabilitation: The Use of Redundant Buildings for Small Enterprises*, London, The Architectural Press.

Lawson, B. (1993) *Parallel Lines of Thought, Languages of Design, vol. 1*, Amsterdam, Elsevier.

Lynch, K. (1972) *What Time Is This Place?* Cambridge, Mass., MIT Press.

Madanipour, A. (1996) *Design of Urban Space*, Chichester, Wiley.

Moser, G., Pol, E., Bernard, Y., Bonnes, M., Corraliza, J.A. and Giuliani, M.V. (eds) (2003) *People, Places and Sustainability*, Goettingen, Hogrefe and Huber.

Neary, S.J., Symes, M.S. and Brown, F.E. (eds) (1994) *The Urban Experience: A People-Environment Perspective*, London, Spon.

Oestereich, J. (undated) From Communal Use of Natural Resources to the Local Agenda 21, European Science Foundation Workshop on Concepts and Paradigms of Urban Management, mimeo, 8 pp.

Symes, M. (2002) Why designers find it difficult to collaborate. In Purdue, D. and Stewart, M. (eds) *Understanding Collaboration: International Perspectives on Theory, Method and Practice*, Bristol, University of West England, pp. 109–114.

Symes, M., Eley, J. and Seidel, A.D. (1993) *Architects and their Practices: A Changing Profession*, Oxford, Butterworth Architecture.

Thomas, R. (ed.) (2003) *Sustainable Neighbourhoods: An Environmental Approach*, London, Spon.

Wilson, W.J. (1996) *When Work Disappears: The World of the New Urban Poor*, New York, Knopf.

6

Construction of the Urban Environment
Steven Curwell

The purpose of this chapter is to explore how construction can and should be made more sustainable. It addresses two main areas of good practice. The first is the design of more sustainable buildings and urban landscapes, which have become known as 'sustainable architecture'. The other is the construction activity itself, which includes procurement of materials and components, the process of assembly and/or refurbishment of a building or element of the infrastructure and/or landscape in a more sustainable manner, now known as 'sustainable construction'. As these two areas are closely interdependent, the terms do not have clear definition and are used interchangeably both locally and internationally. Thus the chapter attempts to embrace them both through exploration of the environmental, economic, social and institutional issues involved in achieving a more sustainable built 'product' in terms of individual buildings, civil structures and the urban landscape. All form part of the broad agenda to be addressed. Civil structures include the utility service systems, gas, electricity, water, drainage, telecommunications and the associated infrastructure, as well as the fixed elements of urban transport such as roads, railway track, bridges and tunnels, etc. The urban landscape includes the space between buildings and civil structures, i.e. all urban fixtures such as paving, signage and seating collectively described as hard landscape as well as the provision of parks, gardens and other green spaces known as soft landscape.

Clearly all these aspects form a broad definition for 'construction of the urban environment' which in turn implies a very wide range of actors and stakeholders. This includes, on the one hand, the developers – those who are the clients or users, or those that represent them, who commission construction projects (the demand side) – and on the other, the various designers, architects, engineers, constructors, demolition contractors, materials and component manufacturers and suppliers (the supply side or supply chain) who collectively offer design and construction services. It should not be forgotten that this complex web of construction services has evolved to satisfy the fundamental human need for shelter and security – to be warmer or cooler than nature provides depending on the season, for privacy to perform a range of bodily functions, for protection of family and belongings from the elements and predation and to provide a conducive working environment or to house a productive process. Together these factors cohere to form the underlying core demand for buildings and their associated infrastructure as well as for repair and maintenance to ensure continued functionality. Beyond the basic requirements, the form, nature and content of modern buildings continue to be variously shaped by a complex set of social and economic factors and higher-level human aspirations or values. Understanding these is one of the main functions of design where, for example, the needs of individual users or citizens have to be balanced against corporate objectives and wider community interests. Such a balance has to be struck within a context of free consumer lifestyle choices, influenced by a combination of interrelated factors more or less symbolically expressed through architecture, including:

- wealth and affluence influencing ability or willingness to pay (for goods and services);
- fashion;
- perception of individual and corporate status;
- societal values (of which sustainable development is one);
- systems of belief or religion (or lack of same?).

Thus it is recognised that the neo-liberal, free-market model inadequately represents the complexity of interactions necessary for the creation of a high-quality 'sustainable' built environment, which attempts to address the wider socio-economic dimensions of the sustainability principles outlined in Chapter 2, particularly those of ecological integrity, equity and participation in decision making. Another weakness relates to the principle of futurity (the time dimension). Buildings and associated infrastructure are very long-lived artefacts which contain community activities and over time, individually and/or collectively, become part of the cultural heritage, and so preservation of the built cultural heritage has become an additional sustainability principle (UNCHS 1996). This creates a clear tension with the *current* and ongoing requirement to satisfy immediate consumer needs, which has serious implications as current choices predetermine options for future generations, as the problem with CFCs (freons) and ozone depletion indicates. This provides a clear example of how the futurity principle can be contravened (Chapter 2).

There are alternative socio-economic paradigms for the nature of construction that are related to, or are drawn from, the traditional or vernacular examples present in so-called primitive societies. An example is the construction co-operative, where a group of individuals collectively pool their resources (human, financial, physical) to self-build their homes and possibly other community buildings, rather than purchasing building as a product or associated design and construction services from others. Such alternatives support all four of the PICABUE sustainability principles of ecological integrity, participation, equity and futurity (explored in Chapter 2), although sustainable construction may not have been the primary purpose of their establishment. Some have clearly demonstrated the application of lower impact technologies which could contribute to greater environmental sustainability if more widely applied (Centre for Alternative Technology (CAT) 2004, see also Von Weizsaker et al. 1997). Although other hybrids exist (Homes for Change 2004, Peabody Trust Housing Association 2004) wider application in the affluent countries has been limited so that to date such alternatives lie very much at the margin in relation to the total volume of construction work necessary to support modern urban society. The Peabody Trust perhaps comes closest to a mass market high-volume breakthrough.

The market-orientated supply–demand model continues to be used within the affluent countries to describe the nature of mainstream construction, i.e. as a manufacturing industry producing a 'product' for purchase and consumption. In fact recent reviews of construction in the UK have further reinforced this narrow view (Latham 1994, Egan 1998, Fairclough 2002), by concentrating on the corporate client requirement for higher quality at a lower cost, delivered on time and within budget using a combination of advancing technological development and more effective, efficient and productive construction processes. Hence the use of the descriptor 'product' for the output of the design and construction process in the opening paragraph of this chapter, and, despite all the inadequacies of the model, the chapter seeks to relate sustainability actions and targets to mainstream industry. Therefore a construction process perspective is adopted. This chapter identifies the main sustainability issues and factors that could and should be borne in mind in each of the main steps in producing the 'built' product, from inception through to occupation.

REDUCING ENVIRONMENTAL IMPACTS – THE CHALLENGE FOR CONSTRUCTION

The manufacture, use, demolition and disposal of buildings, building materials and components contribute to a wide range of global, regional and local environmental impacts. Very large quantities of resources are used to support the construction, use and maintenance of the built environment. It has been estimated that 6 tonnes of construction materials are used per person per annum in the UK (BRE 1996), where 10 per cent of energy consumption is used in the production and transport of construction materials (DETR 1998), and that 70 per cent of UK CO_2 emissions are associated with the construction and use of buildings. As well as the pollution impacts occurring directly to land, water and air as a direct consequence of construction activities, on-site impacts on the environment also accrue due to the extraction of raw materials including quarrying, dredging, mining, forestry, water reservoirs, etc. These activities cause damage, sometimes irreversible, to landscapes and natural habitats, flora and fauna, either directly in the area of the site or in the region where raw materials are extracted. The implementation of a wide range of 'end of pipe' pollution control measures in the affluent nations in the period from the 1970s has served to control or curtail the pollution from the majority of extraction and manufacturing processes in western countries. However, improvements in other manufacturing sectors means that pollution from the construction site has grown in proportion, so that construction has been cited as the UK's most frequent polluter (Addis and Talbot 2001). UK construction generates approximately 7 million tonnes of waste per annum, which forms 17 per cent of the total UK waste arising (DETR 1998), the majority of which goes to landfill. The best way to minimise all these impacts is to avoid them. This can be done through significant material and energy utilisation efficiency gains and recycling in the construction process itself and whole life-cycle of buildings and components, through refurbishment and rehabilitation, in other words by doing much more with less. There is no clear agreement over the targets that need to be set, except that performance above the minimum required by regulations should be sought. Although a number of demonstration projects show examples where 70 per cent savings have been achieved the author believes that a minimum resource reduction of 50 per cent below current levels forms an achievable target for mainstream construction, without incurring excessive costs or recourse to advanced and unproven technologies (DETR 2000, DTI 2003).

TOWARDS A SUSTAINABLE DESIGN AND CONSTRUCTION PROCESS

Attempts to address the inadequacies of the 'construction industry' (Latham 1994, White House Construction Industry Workshop 1994, Egan 1998, Fairclough 2002) are motivated by the perceived decline in competitiveness of the industry in relation to the increasingly global market for design and construction services. An underlying objective is to make the industry 'leaner and fitter' and thus ensure the long-term sustainability of the industry as a whole and the construction companies in particular. This has emphasised the requirement to meet clients' business needs more effectively, through a stronger customer satisfaction focus, better briefing and project management. The fact that design and construction is a complex activity involving a very wide range of stakeholders[1] has already been mentioned above. As explained in Chapters 3 and 5, the French 'ATEQUE' classification of the roles of the range of actors involved in design, construction and maintenance of the built environment shows that each stakeholder may play multiple roles in decision making in a project. In addition to the main design and construction roles there are various management roles as well as quality, supervisory, health and safety and other regulatory functions, a reality that is much more complicated than that represented by process models used in the past, e.g. the RIBA Plan of Work in the UK (RIBA 1973).

The complexity of interaction is one factor that makes establishing the project brief and its effective delivery in the project, on time and within budget constraints, a very difficult management and logistics task. The problems of effective project briefing at the inception stages and co-ordination of all those involved during design and construction have led to the evolution of more sophisticated process models for design and construction, such as the Process Protocol (Kagioglou et al. 1998) developed as part of the UK's Integrated Manufacturing Initiative (IMI).

The process protocol provides 'a framework for carrying-out any construction project' via an integrated teamwork approach proven in manufacturing and founded on the concept of continuous improvement. It addresses the full life cycle of a project's evolution, not just the design and construction. In this the client becomes an integral member of the team to enable more effective briefing and project control. The importance of this type of integration between actors has also been identified by BEQUEST (Bentivegna et al. 2002, BEQUEST 2001) in the context of SUD, especially as the client can play a crucial role in achieving more sustainable outcomes. The supply and demand model discussed earlier implies that without demand for more sustainable goods and services the market will not respond. On the other hand there is clear evidence that, through purchasing strategies, clients can drive good practice down their supply chain and thus stimulate the market (Addis and Talbot 2001). If the client is unaware of best practice in SUD or sustainable construction s/he is unlikely to provide leadership in the quest for more sustainable outcomes. In this circumstance it is much more difficult, if not impossible, for the professional actors to instigate sustainability measures on their own, particularly in construction, which is characterised by a predominance of lowest capital cost decision making (Wong et al. 2000). With the process protocol the client and professionals are completely integrated in the development process, which enables various options and their sustainability impacts to be more fully explained and evaluated so that decision making can be better informed in terms of a balance between quality factors, life-cycle costs and the potential return on investment. This all emphasises why this new view on process management where the client is more empowered through the process protocol is extremely valuable in the context of more sustainable construction. In fact the client can establish with the help of all the members of the project team a project protocol to follow that sets standards for the sustainability improvements to be delivered through design and construction.

THE PROCESS PROTOCOL

The process protocol identifies objectives, briefing and management actions for the wide range of management roles through a matrix of eight activity zones and ten distinct process steps grouped into four main process phases – see Table 6.1. The activity zones consider the whole spectrum of an activity beyond a simple functional task, e.g. architectural design, to include inputs from others such as suppliers, production, health and safety, and the client. Another key feature is the concept of critical success factors for the project and process. These can be directly related to building performance targets or indicators and thus to those for socio-economic and environmental improvement. They provide points of reference at 'phase reviews', which may form soft or hard gates. Soft gates enable the team to understand the concurrency in the project whereas hard gates form the main stop/go decision-making points. Taken together this presents a rich picture of the teamwork interactions – for further details and how to operate the process protocol see www.salford.ac.uk/gdcpp/ and Kagioglou *et al.* (1998). Research continues to develop the protocol in terms of 'sustainable construction', i.e. to understand all the additional sustainability actions to be undertaken in each of the management activity zones and phases. In the interim this chapter will summarise the wide range of good practice advice on sustainable construction that has emerged from recent EU projects such as BEQUEST (2001), Practical Recommendations for Sustainable Construction (PRESCO 2004) and the European Green Building Forum (EGBF 2004). This will be addressed through three of the four high-level phases of the process protocol, i.e. pre-project, pre-construction and construction phases. The final post-construction phase, which is concerned with operation and maintenance during use, is explored subsequently in Chapter 7. In order to provide a direct link to both the BEQUEST framework and the UN Indicator set each of the project phases in this chapter is structured using the UNCSD four-sided EESI model: environmental, economic, social and institutional (UNCSD 1996).

THE PRE-PROJECT PHASES

During the **pre-project phases** the various and collective needs of the client are progressively established, defined and assessed to determine the need for a construction project solution and to secure outline financial authority to proceed to the later phases. The pre-project phases are the most important, because many of the decisions taken in this phase largely determine or lock-in many options in later phases (DTI 2003). They relate directly to a client's or developer's[2] need to build and the strategic business case for 'a project' and whether these comply, or at least can

Table 6.1 Design and construction process protocol

Phases	Pre-project phases			
Activities	0. Demonstrating the need	1. Conception of need	2. Outline feasibility	3. Substantive feasibility + outline financial authority
Development management				
Project management				
Resource management				
Design management				
Production management				
Facilities management				
Health and safety, statutory and legal management				
Process management				

be reconciled, with the wider community interest. They examine the feasibility of the project in all its aspects, which has a direct interconnection with the urban planning and property development and design activities explored in the previous chapters. In most jurisdictions the design and erection of new, or refurbishment of existing, buildings, transport and utility infrastructure and associated facilities has normally to be carried out within the context of a local plan and sometimes within a more specific and detailed urban design master plan, which together guide the development control process. Increasingly these local plans respond to or incorporate Local Agenda 21

Pre-construction phases			Construction phases		Post-construction phase
4. Outline conceptual design	5. Full conceptual design	6. Coordinated design, procurement + full financial authority	7. Production information	8. Construction	9. Operation and maintenance

Outline planning approval

Detailed planning approval

criteria (see a description of this in Chapter 2). Plans are created to direct, in physical, social and economic terms, the nature of the various human activities that take place within a district and/or the whole city. In most cases these plans are made to support and stimulate further 'growth' in human activity aimed at the enhancement, or, at the very least, maintenance, of the prosperity of the community. As such, access to public funds and other regeneration grants important to support the business case, for example, to clean-up contaminated land, may be conditional or dependent on the need to work within, or comply with, public planning proposals. Therefore the hard gate at the end of the pre-project phases is formed by the essential requirement to secure outline planning approval and access to project funding including various forms of grant aid.

Environmental issues in the pre-project phases

Demonstrating need in Phase 0 is a central sustainability criterion because it underlies the justification of the key 'decision to build' and the rational use of resources. Putting aside the motivational complexities for a moment and addressing the issue of resource efficiency from a simple standpoint, the most effective way to reduce the consumption of both energy and construction materials and thus to avoid the associated environmental impacts explored earlier, the most sustainable option, is not to build at all, or at least to minimise the need for new buildings. Therefore it is vital to explore with the client or developer(s) whether their requirements can be met by using their existing accommodation more efficiently. Some architectural firms specialising in space planning (e.g. DEGW) have shown that new forms of office space more suited to the new ways of working emerging in an age of rapid development of information and communication technology can increase occupational efficiency (Bordass and Leaman 1997). Similarly, if the need for some form of physical change is established, then the option of refurbishment of an existing building should also be considered before deciding on new build.

Refurbishment is a particular sector of construction that deals with the renovation of existing buildings, urban landscape and city infrastructure in order to extend service-life and/or adapt for a new use, and as such is increasingly relevant, particularly in the cities of the developed world most of which contain a significant proportion of redundant and underutilised buildings. In fact it has become commonplace to consider that refurbishment of buildings or infrastructure can provide a more sustainable solution than to build anew, an assumption which requires fuller examination.[3] This assumption has evolved because, in principle, refurbishment has the combined advantages of concentrating development within existing urban areas, thus minimising land-take and urban sprawl, as well as reducing overall consumption of material resources through prolonged use of the existing building fabric. Whether the decision is for new build or refurbishment, in all cases clear resource efficiency targets for energy, materials and water consumption should be set for all members of the design team to address in the following pre-construction phase. As mentioned previously, 50 per cent savings should be considered as a minimum.

As already mentioned, refurbishment can also support continuity of communities and preservation of the built cultural heritage, which have been identified as key SUD criteria (UNCHS 1996). Similarly if the need to build anew is established then it is better to select a brown-field site in preference to a green-field site, because this will have the dual advantage of minimising the need for new infrastructure and reducing loss of green space and habitat for flora and fauna.

Feasibility studies (Phase 2) need to predict and manage potential environmental protection requirements and/or problems. Larger development projects will require a full environmental impact analysis or assessment (EIA) (CEC 1985, 1997). The basic principle of EIA is that the assessment is made early enough, before major decisions on the project are made. The assessment should cover the whole life cycle of the activity, facility or infrastructure, although normally the focus is on construction and operation. There may be a requirement to monitor after the construction phase to ensure compliance with requirements, for example in terms of traffic noise, identified in the Environmental Permit and/or Building Permit. Development proposed near or within areas of special scientific interest or outstanding natural beauty and in national parks will require special measures, but additionally, due to the changing expectations of society, site owners, developers, designers and contractors now find that they are expected to protect the flora and fauna on all construction sites. For example, ignorance of a tree protection order is no defence. Thus it is important to audit flora and fauna before commencing re/development, particularly to identify endangered and/or protected species and then to put in place a protection strategy throughout construction (Phase 8). In protected areas approval for development is likely to require the replacement of flora and habitat for fauna destroyed or displaced by development, which is good practice on all larger developments. Together these requirements and expectations may add to the cost of development and so the location of the proposed development and the influence of environmental protection measures can form a key determinant that may 'make or break' a project proposal.

Economic issues in the pre-project phases

From a client's perspective the core economic consideration is the role the project plays in his or her business development plans. Therefore the briefing phase (Phase 1) needs to identify key client satisfaction and design and construction service expectations as measured against existing national norms, such as the M4I construction indicators in the UK (Constructing Excellence 2004). This could include key economic sustainability targets for the project, aimed at:

- improved design and construction quality;
- reduced design and construction costs;
- reduced construction time;
- reduced (zero?) defects at handover.

Clearly, at a time when the profitability of construction companies is very low, these aims cannot be achieved at the expense of the economic sustainability of the design and construction firms engaged in the project, so a considerate client will recognise that the target of these companies is to improve, or at least protect, profitability and will collaborate with designers and contractors to seek to achieve targets through continuous productivity improvements (Fairclough 2002).

Clearly design services and construction activities contribute to the local and national economy (Bon and Hutchinson 2000). Construction contributes directly in terms of the employment that will be created on-site, plus that in material and component manufacturing and indirectly in terms of the range of other services employed or used by all those involved in the process. From a long-term perspective the building or infrastructure will be important to support the economic base. However, the design and execution of large building and infrastructure projects can have negative effects over the short to medium term. The period from inception to completion can extend, in some cases, up to ten years and possibly more. During the pre-project phases this can blight the locale (see the discussion of planning in Chapter 3), and subsequently construction activities have the potential to cause considerable dislocation to normal commerce in the immediate vicinity. Therefore the pre-project phases should consider these negative influences on the economic sustainability of neighbouring areas. In fact negotiation over a range of these issues in terms of minimising damage to disadvantaged businesses may be essential to secure planning approval. With very large projects a wider social impact analysis may be required, which is explored further below.

With larger projects the provision of transport and mobility in terms of access to, and movement within, the development may also influence decision making over the feasibility of the project. Public planning policies generally provide disincentives to private car use and promote various 'greener' modes of transport, and if this is mirrored in the project it is likely to facilitate granting of planning permission. In fact as part of the planning negotiations over the project it is sensible to involve service providers and to consider new public transport routes. Authorities may seek 'planning gains', i.e. the provision of new stations, stops and shelters as well as new cyclist and pedestrian routes.

Social issues in the pre-project phases

With larger projects EIA is increasingly extended to include social impact analysis (SIA), which is aimed at assessing the impact of the project on people (Finsterbush et al. 1983, Juslen 1995). Such forms of analysis should be seen as important to fulfil the equity principle of SD and to support social cohesion. SIA like EIA intends to predict and evaluate impacts before the project is implemented so that a rational assessment of 'who benefits and who loses' can be made. The pre-project phases should consider this through a set of social indicators such as the following:

- *socio-economic status*: median family income, employment, school attainment level, etc.
- *health and safety*: overall mortality, infant mortality, crime incidence, etc.
- *family status*: proportion of children living with both parents, ratio of males to females in the labour force, percentage of families with female heads, etc.

In connection with this the client and their design and construction team should also be concerned with issues of fair employment and trade. Policy should be established in the briefing phase in terms of requirements on design team members and contractors to implement:

- an Equal Opportunities Plan (for women, ethnic minorities, disabled, etc.);
- targets to reduce the rate of fatal and non-fatal accidents during manufacture and assembly;
- job creation in the project for the locally unemployed.

This could also consider staff share-save schemes and possibly relevant donations (staff time or percentage profits before tax and interest) to local charities.

In all but the smallest projects a key requirement in the pre-project phases is to establish provision for local community participation in decision making, when the client can set important policy requirements for the project team to fulfil in later phases. This should include effective dissemination of information in order to advise the community of the aims and objectives of the project, how it will impact on the human development aspects of Local Agenda 21 (from the EIA and SIA analyses) and on progress in each of the phases. The means of consultation, tailored to different stakeholder groups, needs to be established, e.g. through citizens' advisory committees or action groups, business holders' email discussion forums, etc.

Institutional issues in the pre-project phases

The client should ensure that all the companies involved in the project have in place, or develop, a corporate social responsibility policy and/or one is developed for the project as a whole. It should include many of the provisions already outlined but three additional institutional requirements are necessary. The first and most important is a requirement to establish an environmental management process for the project based on ISO 14001 principles (International Standards of the ISO 14000 1992). This should include resource reduction and pollution minimisation targets so that the whole team can audit and justify all the resource inputs and waste outputs to and from the proposed building and throughout its development process, including energy, materials and water management. The second requirement is to ensure that all team member organisations, including the client and suppliers, publish independently validated annual reports including environmental, sustainable development and social responsibility issues. Finally, firms involved in the project should have a staff consultative committee and team members should be regularly surveyed regarding their satisfaction with the way they are treated by their company.

THE PRE-CONSTRUCTION PHASES

Once the feasibility of the project is confirmed, including outline planning approval, and financial authority to proceed is granted, an appropriate design solution, to meet the client's needs, is developed during the pre-construction phases. During the conceptual design phase (4) the creative architectural and engineering development of the design takes place. Here most of the design decisions are taken and increasingly the main design elements – orientation, shape, size, access and egress, materials and servicing – are progressively fixed. In Phase 5 the architectural or engineering design begins to take full shape within the developing understanding emerging from the cost and project implementation plans. The outcome of this phase is a design realised in sufficient detail for submission for detailed planning permission (hard gate). Decisions through these phases are taken more or less objectively, either consciously or subconsciously, and they predetermine and/or close-off options and possibilities in the later phases. For example, the shape of the building may determine whether natural or mechanical ventilation has to be used, which can also influence and be influenced by the layout of the fenestration, window to wall ratio and whether shading devices are necessary. Alternatively a decision on these aspects may be taken entirely on aesthetic grounds or to satisfy planning requirements. Selection of the heating and ventilation system will also be influenced by the type of structural and cladding material options, heavyweight concrete or lightweight steel, and how thermally responsive the fabric is to diurnal temperature changes. This illustrates the iterative process of design – gradually working towards the solution (as already described in Chapter 5). In the process protocol, the outcome of Phase 6 is a fully co-ordinated design including a detailed product model, cost plan, maintenance plan, project execution and communication plans and a health and safety plan, upon which full financial authority to proceed to construction is based.

Environmental issues in the pre-construction phases

For buildings, conceptual building design should seek to maximise utilisation of available solar, wind and water energy resources from the site, and to minimise fossil fuel consumption during the life of the building, by creative exploration of alternative building forms and servicing technologies. Passive techniques use:

- relatively narrow plan forms that permit natural daylighting and ventilation;
- the thermal mass in the structure to reduce temperature fluctuations;
- well-proportioned and orientated windows and shading that reduce the risk of summer overheating;
- a super-insulated fabric.

Together these can reduce energy consumption requirements by around 70 per cent below current norms and meet the targets already recommended earlier and set in the briefing (Phases 1 and 2).

Reducing the physical footprint within functional considerations through efficient spatial planning can also help reduce the resources needed for the building or civil structure and in the case of buildings reduce the energy subsequently required to run it. Reduced footprint will also minimise the need for aggregates and other raw materials that cause impacts associated with 'quarrying'. Where deep plan building forms are necessary, well-designed and optimised mechanically ventilated buildings have demonstrated well below average energy consumption performance.

More rational decision making over minimising environmental impacts can be achieved through life-cycle analysis of the whole building and sub-components (ISO 1997, Curwell *et al*. 2002, Edwards and Bennett 2003). This enables exploration and minimisation of pollution and other environmental outputs to air, land and water in three stages. First, the upstream impacts resulting from the extraction of raw materials and manufacture of components, second, at the assembly and/or refurbishment stage, and third, at end of life. Here the downstream impacts resulting from demolition and disposal can be evaluated against better options developed through design for disassembly, reuse and recycling. Although buildings are very long-lived (sixty years plus is common), strategies that seek to extend the whole building and sub-component life through reused and/or recycled materials and components from demolition will reduce resource consumption and reduce pressures on landfill, e.g. the BRE Environment Office, which achieved 90 per cent recycled content (BRE 2004).

Creating additional planting, soft landscape and habitat for fauna in confined urban areas is important. Provision of adequate green space, in relation to the building and urban location, is known to be very beneficial to human health and well-being, and needs fuller attention in the design process. Careful design that responds to the local climate in terms of optimising plant species selection with regard to maintenance budget considerations is vital. It is worthwhile anticipating trends in climate change and re/introducing locally relevant species, such as drought-resistant species in water-stressed areas – for example, in East Anglia in the UK and in southern Spain and Portugal. Increasing the area of soft landscape and reducing the area of impermeable hard landscape to the minimum required for various human and transport needs can significantly decrease excesses in local summer temperatures in cities. Provision of roof gardens and grass roofs can assist in this endeavour, as proposed by Ken Yeang (1999) in his book *The Green Skyscraper.*

Economic issues in the pre-construction phases

In pursuit of a better balance between resource efficiency and economy of provision of utility service infrastructure to the site and building(s) designers might beneficially consider rainwater harvesting, local waste and sewage treatment, provision of local wind power or combined heat and power plants (Sustainable Building Sourcebook 2004). In order to promote 'greener', more energy-efficient, less polluting modes of travel to and from the site, it is inadequate just to constrain motor commuting by traffic-calming and reduced provision of on-site parking without improving accessibility via public transport (as identified in the previous section). This may require developers to discuss potential travel-cost barriers with users and possibly to offer start-up incentives to transport service providers. Provision of secure cycle storage and changing and showering facilities is important to promote cycling, and this can be done collectively, rather than in every building, through, for example, the 'cycling café'. Here cycle commuters can leave their bikes, change, shower and get breakfast! It is also recognised that offering employees an ex gratia payment to change, for example to cycling, is often cheaper than providing car parking with all the associated ongoing security, automatic payment and entry control systems necessary to protect the car in inner urban areas. Consideration of these options will be greatly influenced by economies of scale and the size of the development and may be more appropriately addressed at the scale of the urban design master plan (Chapters 3, 4 and 5).

In order to maximise the contribution that the development can make to the local economy, construction materials should be sourced locally. Before demolition commences, a strategy for dismantling in order to maximise salvage, recycling or reuse of materials and components from building(s) and civil structures to be demolished should be developed. Continuously rising landfill costs provide a strong financial incentive to recycle. Older buildings often contain features, e.g. carved stone, which are of high value as well as materials that are now scarce and therefore valuable resources, such as copper and slates. Established markets for architectural salvage and some construction materials mean that the strategy should seek to engage local specialist demolition and consolidation[4] contractors in order to maximise returns from demolition and recycling through a balance of economic and resource efficiency considerations. In turn, demolition contractors need to make modest investment in inventory information systems so that one of the main barriers to selecting recycled materials at the design phase can be eliminated, i.e. access to accurate information on the quantities of recycled material and salvaged components which are available.

Social issues in the pre-construction phases

In addition to the ongoing need to engage in consultation with the local community over the overall nature of the development, as identified in the pre-project phases, the main consideration in the pre-construction phases is design to promote health, safety and well-being, both of the users of the building or civil structure as well as of members of the local community. The importance of green space to overall health and well-being has already been addressed. An important additional consideration is design against crime. Internal building layouts, building relationships, pedestrian routes and the form of planting are important in order to improve the sense of security and help reduce crime. Consultation should take place with the police and other security concerns over the proposed layout, illumination and possibly the provision of surveillance, e.g. via CCTV.

A key equity consideration in design is accessibility. Consideration of access to all areas – buildings, transport facilities and open space – by all sectors of the community, including the young, disabled and elderly, is a very relevant sustainability criterion.

Also from a health and safety perspective provisions to avoid 'sick' building problems in buildings[5] are also important as is selection of building materials and components of low toxicity with minimum hazard to health and to reduce the incidence of allergic reactions. It is also important to remind designers of a number of health and safety regulations that need to be addressed, including:

- road safety;
- fire protection within and around the buildings;
- proper exhaust of combustion products;
- human and solid waste disposal;
- the construction design and management (CDM) provisions;
- asbestos removal during demolition and refurbishment;
- minimum air change rates to the interior of buildings;
- Legionnaire's disease control measures.

Institutional issues in the pre-construction phases

All design team members should receive structured training in the concepts and delivery of sustainable urban development and be familiar with the general concepts outlined in this book. Individual knowledge and/or skill levels should be audited before this phase and appropriate staff development action set in place.

As an alternative strategy to the extensive research that is necessary to undertake life-cycle analysis of materials and components it is possible to select them, and to select design and other services, from suppliers who have demonstrated sound sustainable development policies and practice (Curwell *et al.* 2002). This should include implementation both of environmental management schemes within their organisation and of 'triple bottom line' reporting (e.g. Carillion 2004).

THE CONSTRUCTION PHASES

The construction phases are solely concerned with production of the project solution, in terms of the supply of production information (7), logistics, procurement of materials, fabrication of components and the actual assembly (8), including all the management roles and contractual relationships necessary to facilitate these activities.

Environmental issues in the construction phases

Measures to minimise environmental impacts and resource consumption in the construction phase relate mainly to waste minimisation in manufacture and in on-site assembly, and to reducing energy consumption. Although designers are responsible for the initial selection of materials, this is typically communicated to construction contractors through performance specifications, which leaves them free to source materials and components. Thus, the decision on the actual supplier of many materials, e.g. whose cement, softwood windows or radiators are used, is often taken by a construction contractor. Therefore most of the factors mentioned in the pre-production phase concerning materials selection are also relevant here, such as maximising reuse and/or recycling, controlled dismantling of existing buildings or infrastructure that have to be demolished, selecting materials and components with high renewable material, renewable energy and/or high recycled material content, etc.

Contractors should aim to reduce construction solid waste by a minimum well below current practice (75 per cent?) and, as far as possible, dispose of the unavoidable waste remaining by recycling the inorganic and/or composting the organic material for use in soft landscaping (RICS 2002). Component manufacturers can assist by reducing the amount of packaging, consistent with adequate protection in transit and prior to installation in buildings. Some construction processes are water-intensive. Selecting dry construction techniques such as gypsum board linings instead of plaster will reduce site consumption. Fuel efficiency in construction plant and in transport to and from site is also worth attention, particularly where this is hired-in. Part-load inefficiencies can be reduced through collaboration between suppliers.

In the construction phases unnecessary damage to flora and fauna during construction can be avoided by:

- Minimising the area required for temporary works and accommodation.
- Compact construction process plant designs and technologies.

- Minimising excavation, earth movement and destruction of landscape and natural habitats.
- Reinstatement of habitat disturbed by temporary works and accommodation on completion.
- Where necessary arranging for temporary support for flora and fauna during the construction process and their reintroduction to reinstated habitat on completion.

Economic issues in the construction phases

The primary economic consideration in the construction phase is to deliver the client's key economic sustainability targets for the project identified in the brief (Phases 1 and 2), in terms of construction with improved quality at lower cost, delivered on time and within budget. Economic equity can be supported through purchase of materials, components and services from local sources and the use of local trade contractors and local labour for construction and dismantling works. During demolition and dismantling efficient stock control and adequate stock records are necessary for the information of designers and specifiers and/or to facilitate onward sale to local recycling and architectural heritage companies.

It is important to avoid unnecessary costs such as planning landfill levies and pollution penalties arising from poor environmental management or environmental practice. A common problem is escape of fuel oil stored on site for use by plant and machinery. Similarly it will be important to protect trees, landscape features and heritage buildings during the construction phase.

Impacts from transport can be reduced by providing incentives for car-sharing, public transport and cycling for all members of the construction workforce and management personnel. Main contractors can use their position of leverage over suppliers and sub-contractors in order to seek co-operation over site and personnel transportation movements. For example, tipper-lorries delivering materials to site could also be used to remove excavated spoil and waste rather than the normal case where separate vehicles are used for these tasks with 50 per cent of their journeys made empty. In very large infrastructure projects, rail or water-based transport may be very competitive for bulk material supplies.

Social issues in the construction phases

As mentioned in previous sections, consultation with the local community is important. Considerate contractors will view establishment of good relations with 'the locals' as essential. For this it is important to consult the community over the nature of the works, the time scale and phasing of operations, in order to minimise disruption and disturbance, and to establish an effective communication system, such as a project newsletter delivered free of charge to homes and local schools. A single-point 'rapid response' procedure for handling complaints from local inhabitants is essential in all projects. Construction can be a dirty business and so measures to control dust and fumes, to eliminate casual incineration of waste materials and to regularly clean streets and pedestrian walkways soiled by construction activities is vital to public relations. Similarly consultation with transport agencies, local community groups and local associations for the disabled, blind and the elderly about the anticipated disruption to transport and utility services during the progress of the works can help avoid upsetting local inhabitants. Provision of temporary, safe viewing areas so that members of the community can follow the progress of the works can foster good community relations as well as helping to reduce unauthorised access by adolescents out of working hours.

It is very important to minimise the risk of accidents to site personnel engaged directly on the works, to the management personnel in supervisory roles and also to the general public around the perimeter of the works. This includes:

- Compliance with all regulations concerning safe working practice, materials handling and site and structural safety.
- Ensuring material, components and equipment conform to regulations on safety and fire protection requirements.
- Ensuring the works are adequately protected (with security fencing?) to prevent unauthorised entry, particularly by children and adolescents.
- Providing adequate illumination at the perimeter and in other appropriate places to ensure the safety of members of the public at night.
- Ensuring access for fire and other emergency services can be maintained during the progress of the works.
- Consulting adjoining owners, police and other highways and traffic agencies over the protection of public safety during the construction works, transport and crane operations.

In large projects of long duration contractors should consider providing facilities on site for local employment agencies to enable small local trade contractors and local labour to secure employment on the construction works.

Institutional issues in the construction phases

Contractors must set up environmental management processes and procedures, e.g. ISO 14001 (ISO 1997), with clear sustainable development objectives and lines of responsibility for all those involved in the project within the main contracting and all sub-contracting organisations. This responsibility should embrace the social and economic development objectives as well as the environmental resource minimisation and efficiency objectives in terms of energy, materials and water management strategies. Partnering between various specialist trade contractors and suppliers is seen as an important element in achieving the construction targets mentioned above as well as the economic, time and cost targets identified at the conception stage. In addition to the improvement of supply chain efficiency, partnering has the benefit of dispersing good practice in environmental management as well as corporate social responsibility and sustainable development (Addis and Talbot 2001).

In a number of countries groups of contractors have come together to set standards of behaviour for site construction and operation which seek to minimise local nuisance, e.g. national equivalents of the UK Considerate Contractor Scheme (Addis and Talbot 2001 and e.g. Carillion 2004). This could be extended to embrace other aspects such as fair employment practices, ensuring fair reward for effort for all employees involved in the works, and to include equipment and material suppliers, component manufacturers and designers in order to help co-ordinate sound sustainable development policies and practice across the whole industry sector and supply chain.

CONCLUSION

This chapter has placed the extensive range of advice on environmental protection and good practice over sustainable development in the construction sector that has emerged in the last five years in close juxtaposition with the current concerns over the efficiency of the construction industry. This has provided an additional layer of detailed advice for design and construction activities to that presented in the BEQUEST toolkit. It brings the protocol section included in the toolkit more up to date with current thinking. This sees the SD challenge as part of the overall issue of providing a good-quality built environment and of the role that design and construction can play in delivering this for clients and users. In this it has tended towards a corporate industry perspective, and while this overlooks other approaches to construction, including those prevalent in the less developed world, it is important to address and communicate with the key decision makers in the affluent countries where the majority of construction takes place.

While designers and constructors can and should seek to provide leadership over the issue of SD in their projects, their influence will be ineffective without the support of their client. Thus the attitude of the client to SUD and their leadership role is crucial. The integrated manufacturing initiative process protocol has been selected for presentation in this context because it foregrounds the importance of the client in the project team and his or her role in the inception phases of the project. The BEQUEST project identified the overall lack of demand for more sustainable goods and services in society as one of the main barriers to more sustainable urban development. Thus a key question is the underlying value system of the client or client organisation and whether this contains or embraces the concept of sustainability. The importance of the 'lead from the client' has been reinforced in a recent survey of young construction professionals (Sponge 2004). Thus, one of the principal foundations implicit in all the advice and recommendations in this chapter is that the client and all professional actors – the designers, managers, constructors, material suppliers – should see themselves as agents for change with a corporate and individual responsibility.

The chapter has condensed into a compact space a very large range of relevant sustainability considerations, which stem from an even broader range of more detailed recommendations. However, it is important to keep in mind the main underlying goals of sustainable architecture and construction, which are summarised here as:

- Use less resources – seek to reuse and recycle, minimise fossil fuel energy consumption.
- Respect the physical and cultural context – place the re/development in the continuum of history.
- Minimise damage to the environmental systems (air, land, water, plants and animals).
- Ensure participation of stakeholders in the decision-making process.

AND, considering the point made immediately above:

- Seek to persuade the client that they care! (DTI 2003)

In this latter endeavour the pre-project phases are crucial. Here a range of more or less sustainable options can be evaluated, for example using cost-benefit analysis or decision-weighting techniques, in a non-threatening environment, i.e. a situation where project resources are not yet committed, thus avoiding the usual negative response – 'if it costs more forget it'. Thus it is possible to consider the financial viability of the project in the context of a wider, longer-term life-cycle perspective and gain the commitment from the client to fund the project within a business plan and budget which has considered all the SD factors.

However, these forms of analysis are not easy. Many still lie in the research domain. In the pre-project phases the very large amount of resources used in construction and the various forms of environmental damage that result have to be balanced against the human development advantages that flow from the resource expenditure. For example, the balance sheet for a manufacturing enterprise might include:

- A new building's role in expansion plans which are necessary to sustain the business financially in the medium term.
- The expansion may create additional employment and so help sustain the wider community into the medium term.
- Alternatively if the development means a new robotic manufacturing process the loss of employment will have entirely the opposite effect in the short term.
- The construction project itself will offer additional employment in the short term.
- A modern building should be much more efficient than an older one, in both energy and functional performance, and thus save money in the medium to long term.

Thus the decision to build may have complex and conflicting sustainability implications for both the organisation and wider society. Establishing the evidence base, with any degree of confidence, for this type of complex predictive trade-off analysis is extremely difficult if not impossible to undertake. At present we do not have tools that can give unequivocal answers to the range of questions raised by consideration of these difficult trade-offs (Bentivegna *et al.* 2002). Many of the techniques for this task are to be explored further in Volume 2 of this series. The use of an individual 'sustainability index' measure for the project as a whole, which can be directly related to local and/or national sustainability indicators and targets, provides a concise way to represent the outcomes of the analysis in a form that is more readily understood by all stakeholders.

NOTES

1   The professional actors involved include clients, investors, funding agencies, property developers, architects, civil, structural, services and utility engineers, surveyors, construction managers, production managers, safety managers, construction process planners, process engineers, materials manufacturers and suppliers, cost consultants and surveyors and the various construction tradespeople.

2   This raises the perennial problem of who is in fact the client. In terms of a large client organisation a project team is faced with a number of 'clients'. Three classes are commonly recognised. The first is the 'real' client, i.e. the person(s) who engages the design team and pays the fees, the second is the user client and the third society in general. Whilst the positive benefits to owner and user may be clear, those to wider society are less clear. As a consequence of any particular development the local community may receive improvements, such as replacement of an unsightly disused lot by a beautiful building beneficial to townscape, or degradations such as additional road traffic noise.

3   The degree to which any particular refurbished building can contribute to resource reduction is related to the extent of reconstruction that is necessary, the useful life extension that is achieved and whether energy efficiency is raised to a level comparable to that for a new building.

4   Consolidation refers to the role of bringing together smaller quantities of recovered materials from various individual building sources to create sufficient quantities for use in larger re/developments.

5   Sick building control measures include provision of adequate daylight, protection from glare, good indoor air quality, good-quality physical and aural environment, personal control of the interior environment, e.g. through opening windows, individualised temperature control, task lighting, etc.

REFERENCES

Addis, B. and Talbot, R. (2001) *Sustainable Construction Procurement – a Guide to Delivering Environmentally Responsible Projects*, CIRIA, London.

Bentivegna, V., Curwell, S., Deakin, M., Lombardi, P., Mitchell, G. and Nijkamp, P. (2002) A vision and methodology for integrated sustainable urban development: BEQUEST, *Building Research and Information* 30(2).

BEQUEST (2001) http://research.scpm.salford.ac.uk/bqextra/

Bon, R. and Hutchinson, K. (2000) Sustainable construction: some economic challenges, *Building Research and Information* 28(5/6): 310–314.

Bordass, W. and Leaman, A. (1997) Future buildings and their services: strategic considerations for designers and clients, *Building Research and Information* 25(4): 190–195.

BRE (Building Research Establishment) (1996) *Buildings and Sustainable Development*, Information Sheet 1A, BRE, Garston, Watford, UK.

BRE (Building Research Establishment) (2004) http://projects.bre.co.uk/envbuild/

Carillion (2004) http://www.carillionplc.com/sustain/pol_012.htm

CEC (1985) (1997) EU Directives on EIA (On the assessment of the effects of certain public and private projects on the environment), http://europa.eu.int/comm/environment/eia/eia-legalcontext.htm

CAT (Centre for Alternative Technology) (2004) http://www.cat.org.uk/index.tmpl?refer= index&init=1

Constructing Excellence (2004) Construction KPIs: http://www.constructingexcellence.org.uk/ productivity/kpis/kpis.jsp

Curwell, S., Fox, B., Greenberg, M. and March, C. (2002) *Hazardous Building Materials: A Guide to Environmentally Responsible Alternatives*, 2nd edition, E&FN Spon, London.

DETR (Department of the Environment, Transport and the Regions) (1998) *Sustainable Development Opportunities for Change – Sustainable Construction*, DETR, London.

DETR (Department of the Environment, Transport and the Regions) (2000) Building a Better Quality of Life: A Strategy for More Sustainable Construction, http://www.dti.gov.uk/construction/sustain/bql/pdf/sus_cons.pdf

DTI (Department of Trade and Industry) (2003) Sustainable Construction Brief, DTI, London, http://www.dti.gov.uk/construction/sustain/scb.pdf

Edwards, S. and Bennett, P. (2003) Construction products and life-cycle thinking, *Industry and Environment* (joint edition combining *Sustainable Building and Construction*), UNEP, 26(2–3).

Egan, Sir John (1998) *Rethinking Construction*, Department of the Environment, Transport and the Regions.

EGBF (European Green Building Forum) (2004) http://www.egbf.org/

Fairclough, Sir John (2002) Rethinking Construction Innovation and Research – a Review of Government R&D Policies and Practices.

Finsterbush, K., Llewellyn, L.G. and Wolf, C.P. (1983) *Social Impact Assessment Methods*, Sage Publications, London.

Homes for Change (2004) http://www.lookingatbuildings.org.uk/default.asp?document=3.T.2.5

International Standards of the ISO 14000 (1992) Environmental Management Systems – Specifications with Guidance for Use, British Standards Institute.

ISO (1997) International Standards Organization: Life Cycle Assessment – Principles and Guidelines, ISO CD 14 040.2.

Juslen, J. (1995) Social impact assessment: a look at Finnish experiences, *Project Appraisal*10(3).

Kagioglou, M., Cooper, R., Aouad, G., Hinks, J., Sexton, M. and Sheath, D.M. (1998) *A Generic Guide to the Design and Construction Process Protocol*, University of Salford.

Latham, Sir Michael (1994) *Constructing the Team – Joint Review of Procurement and Contractual Arrangement*, London, HMSO.

Peabody Trust Housing Association (2004) http://www.peabody.org.uk/main/index.htm

PRESCO (Practical Recommendations for Sustainable Construction) (2004) http://www.etn-presco.net/

RIBA (1973) *Architectural Practice and Management*, RIBA, London.

RICS (2002) *Recycling through Demolition*, RICS, London.

Sponge (2004) Sponge Survey 03–04: http://www.dti.gov.uk/construction/sustain/sponge_survey_03_04.pdf

Sustainable Building Sourcebook (2004) http://www.greenbuilder.com/sourcebook/

UNCHS (United Nations Conference for Human Settlement) (1996), Habitat II, Istanbul, United Nations.

UNCSD (United Nations Commission for Sustainable Development) (1996) Working List of Indicators: http://earthwatch.unep.net/about/docs/indicat.htm

Von Weizsaker, E., Lovins, A.B. and Lovins, L.H. (1997) *Factor Four: Doubling Wealth – Halving Resource Use*, Earthscan, London.

White House Construction Industry Workshop (1994) National Construction Goals: Construction Industry Perspective, Civil Engineering Research Foundation, Washington, USA.

Wong, C.H., Holt, G.D. and Cooper, P.A. (2000) Lowest price or value? Investigation of UK construction clients tender selection process, *Construction Management and Economics* 18.

Yeang, K. (1999) *The Green Skyscraper: The Basis for Designing Sustainable Intensive Buildings*, Prestel Verlag, Munich.

7

The Sustainable Operation and Use of Buildings
Mark Deakin, John Hudson and Martin Symes

The preceding chapters in this part of the book have looked at protocols for the planning, property development, design and construction of sustainable urban development (SUD). This chapter aims to study the sustainability issues underlying the operation and use of buildings. Studying the sustainability issues underlying the operation and use of buildings takes this section full circle, from the 'upstream' concerns of planning, property development, design and construction, towards more 'downstream' activities concerning the operation and use of buildings as products and infrastructure services.

As a distinct stage of the urban development process, the sustainability issues underlying the operation and use of buildings are complex. Understanding them in itself is challenging, so any proposal to turn this into a set of guidelines for property and construction managers to follow in making the operation and use of buildings sustainable, is particularly so. This chapter aims to meet this challenge and outline a protocol to follow in making developments surrounding the operation and use of buildings sustainable. With this aim, the chapter begins by setting out the organisational context of the study and in that sense the legacy of how the operation and use of buildings has previously been dealt with by property and construction managers. Critical of the limited developments that have previously taken place in this field, this section of the chapter takes the opportunity to set out recent changes which point managers towards the sustainable development agenda and how to address it.

From here the chapter develops its framework for understanding *the sustainable operation and use of buildings*. Here six criteria are set out for property and construction managers to take account of in ensuring the sustainable operation and use of buildings. From here the chapter draws attention to the procurement and evaluation of building products and their infrastructure services and goes on to set out how post-occupancy methods of assessment can be made use of to evaluate the sustainability of such products and their services.

CONTEXT

The organisational context for property and construction management has changed considerably in recent years. In the public sector the trend towards what is sometimes known as the New Public Management (NPM) has seen a greater emphasis on competition in the provision of services, and more explicit and measurable standards of performance, including value for money, with clearly identifiable cost centres and greater accountability (Hood 1991, 1995, Deakin 1999a, b). In the private sector such measures are increasingly expected to be 'business-like', with a clear set of corporate strategies, financial instruments and commercial standards (then 1999, Langston and Lauge-Kristensen 2002, Deakin 2002, 2004). The frameworks for property and construction management have led to buildings operating in a largely market- (or quasi-market-) based context. It is common practice for building and infrastructure services, such as facilities management, to be partially or totally sourced from specialist suppliers. Even where such services are carried out 'in-house' within an organisation they are usually identified as a cost centre, are benchmarked against external contractors and have a 'customer–client' relationship with those who use their services (Hui and Tsang 2004, Barrett and Baldry 2003, Deakin 2004).

Atkin and Brooks (2000) describe the range of contractual options that exist in this context. Within this market structure there are clear demand and supply sides. On the demand side there is a:

- Client role – ensuring

    - user requirements for a functional, supportive environment are met
    - corporate policies, including those for sustainability, are translated into targets, service level agreements, etc. that can be used to:

        - manage an 'in-house' workforce
        - manage contracts, partnerships, etc. with external suppliers.

On the supply side there are:

- External service providers: these can range from small local suppliers to FTSE100-quoted companies. Increasingly the management of the built environment is offered as one facet of more general business support services.
- Internal service providers: usually identifiable as a cost centre to enable comparison with external suppliers and transparency of management.

Within this demand and supply framework a number of actors can be identified:

- **Strategic level managers** (owners, directors, etc.)
    - Those who set strategic organisational objectives, including corporate social responsibility, sustainability, etc.

- **Operational level managers**
  - Those who manage day-to-day operations in the context of strategic objectives including those for sustainability etc. Procure operational services setting performance specifications (including those for sustainability).

- **Suppliers**
  - Those who deliver operational services to specifications set by operational level managers (including specifications for sustainability):
    - in-house
    - outsourced
  - A range of professional actors whose services may be required during operations and use, e.g. space planners, building services engineers, property managers, surveyors, architects, interior designers, utilities managers.

- **Users**
  - Occupants/users of buildings/facilities – various levels of empowerment/control over local environment.

- **Institutional/government**
  - Those who set the legal framework for occupation/use, e.g. health and safety, accessibility, etc.
  - Those who provide tools/benchmarks etc., e.g. ISO 14000, sustainability indices.

This context of relatively tight control over the management of the built environment and the requirement to deliver corporate objectives may seem to limit the extent to which property and construction managers can work towards sustainable development. Fortunately, however, the corporate context is itself widening in both public and private sectors to address sustainability issues. In the public sector there is the adoption of Agenda 21 and Quality of Life issues (Sustainable Development in Government 2004). In the private sector there is a move away from a narrow focus on the delivery of shareholder value and towards a wider programme of corporate social responsibility (Association of British Insurers 2001). These include developments such as:

- Integrated visions and methodologies of property and construction management, based on the environment, equity, participation and futurity principles of sustainable urban development (Deakin *et al.* 2001, 2002, Bentivenga *et al.* 2002, Deakin and Curwell 2004).

- Triple bottom line reporting, in which the narrow financial criteria of traditional company reporting are supplemented by broader environmental, economic, social measures (Elkington 1999).
- Stakeholder theory in which the traditional focus on shareholder value is broadened to encompass value to all individuals and groups with an interest in the company. This has been distilled into the 'Clarkson principles' of stakeholder management (Donaldson 2002).
- Benchmarking of sustainability performance through indices such as FTSE4Good and the various Dow Jones sustainability indices (FTSE4Good 2004, Dow Jones 2004).

Developments of this type suggest that corporate strategies in both the public and private sectors are now based on sustainability principles, and both property and construction managers need to be aware of these principles and the new standards of measurement they set for the operation and use of the built environment. They also suggest that the said managers need to know how they can be drawn upon to evaluate the sustainability of developments taking place to the operation and use of buildings.

SUSTAINABLE OPERATION AND USE

Given the organisational context of property and construction management, the operation and use of buildings takes place largely through a series of procurement processes. Procurement may be for products, e.g. replacement building services equipment, or it may be for services, e.g. cleaning or security. Increasing adoption of sustainability principles will therefore come, in part, due to the need for a proper consideration of environmental, economic and social criteria within the procurement process. These considerations are not fundamentally different from those of the procurement cycle for property/design/construction considered in the earlier chapters of this book and many of the principles expounded there are relevant. Perhaps the main difference is that building services such as fabric maintenance are increasingly being bundled with other 'non-core' activities such as catering and office supplies as part of a general 'business support' function (Fitzsimmons *et al.* 1998).

Some idea of the range of functions of the manager at operations and use level can be obtained from considering competencies that must be demonstrated by candidates for membership of the British Institute of Facilities Management (BIFM). These competencies are grouped into six key management areas that broadly define the scope of facilities management. These are: understanding business organisation;

managing people; managing premises; managing services; managing the working environment; and managing resources (BIFM 2004). Using these areas as a framework we can begin to explore how sustainable urban development issues might be addressed by the practising facilities manager (Hudson and Curwell 2004).

Understanding business organisation

Facilities management provides support services to organisations and is therefore driven by the goals and policies of those organisations. As organisations increasingly adopt policies of social corporate responsibility, so the drivers for sustainability within the practice of facilities management will increase. As a result, facilities managers will need to be able to understand, and to demonstrate, how they can contribute to the general sustainability of the organisation. This will require:

1   that the organisation as a whole can chart its progress towards sustainability, perhaps using key performance indicators;
2   that facilities management set its own performance targets in support of those of the organisation.

Managing people

Facilities management, as a service industry, can be labour-intensive with an often low-skilled and low-paid workforce, sometimes employed using complex outsourcing contracts. The social dimension of sustainability is very important in this context. The facilities manager needs to be able to develop ethical employment polices and working practices and to monitor their implementation. In the UK the TUPE (Transfer of Undertakings (Protection of Employment) Regulations) provide an institutional framework for protecting, in some measure, the rights of employees where services are outsourced.

As more sustainable practices are introduced into facilities management, training will become an increasingly important issue. Staff will need to be updated on new working practices, not just in terms of tools and techniques but also on the broader issues of progress towards more sustainable practices.

The prevalence of outsourcing in facilities management can lead to complex supply chains. It is important that suppliers, particularly small businesses, are treated responsibly in such arrangements. The facilities manager should be able to develop and implement clear policies for the ethical treatment of suppliers.

Individuals and groups within organisations may have competing claims for facilities resources so that facilities management may often involve conflict with management. Conflict may also arise between the aspirations of users and corporate policy. Campbell and Finch (2004) have discussed the concept of organisational justice in relation to facilities management and the strengths and weaknesses of approaches such as participatory decision making in this context. A further source of conflict can be between the user and the technology of the building or facility. For example, Beggs and Moodley (1997) have discussed how passively controlled low-energy buildings can sometimes conflict with user and facilities management requirements, particularly in the organisational context of outsourcing. This is an important issue to be resolved for more sustainable operations and use.

Communication with building users is also of great importance as measures to improve sustainability will often prove ineffective without their active co-operation. For example, efficient use of heating and ventilation systems can be difficult to achieve if users do not feel actively involved in their management.

Managing premises

The BIFM include property portfolio management, understanding building design and building fabric maintenance within this key management area. In as far as the facilities manager is involved within the property development and construction procurement processes, reference should be made to the principles set out in Chapters 4 and 6 of this book. It should be noted that evaluation tools such as BREEAM (2004), used for new projects, can often also be used effectively for the evaluation of buildings in use.

Building fabric maintenance is important for sustaining the financial value, safety and usability of buildings. An effective maintenance plan with an appropriate balance between reactive and preventative maintenance will be key to this. The general principles of maintenance planning are well established (Chanter and Swallow 1996, Wordsworth 2001). Keeping and Shiers (1996) have highlighted the importance of a planned preventative maintenance programme in reducing energy use and increasing the lifespan of fabric and service in buildings. Fabric maintenance will often involve an element of upgrading and this presents possibilities for specification of materials and components with low environmental impact.

There is also an important social element to the management of premises. Steps need to be taken to ensure accessibility of all potential users regardless of disability, age or other factors that may affect mobility. This is increasingly required by statute, as in the Disability Discrimination Act in the UK (Department of Work and Pensions 2004). Premises can also adversely affect the neighbouring community through local pollution, unsociable operating hours, noise levels, visual intrusion, traffic generation and other factors. The facilities manager needs to plan to keep these adverse local effects to a minimum. Local traffic generation can be a particular problem and effective policies on car use and parking, public transport and the provision of adequate cycling facilities are necessary (Dabson 2000).

Managing services

In addition to the provision of building fabric maintenance, facilities management often has responsibility for a wide range of other support services. These will vary somewhat from organisation to organisation.

Building services management is an area in which facilities management can have a significant effect on sustainability. Services are replaced on a much shorter cycle than structure so that there is scope for considerable environmental improvement within the lifetime of a building through upgrading. Much can also be achieved through energy-efficient use of existing systems; in the UK the government-funded Action Energy (2004) programme can provide a wide range of advice on this issue. Good building services management can also have an important impact on the well-being of users, not only through providing a comfortable environment, but also by preventing environmental health problems such as Legionnaire's disease which has been associated with poorly maintained air-conditioning systems (Cowles 2001, Brundrett 2003).

Other facilities services can include cleaning, security, reception, waste management, catering, grounds maintenance and office management. Each of these will present particular opportunities for the introduction of more sustainable practices (Wastebusters 2000). Cleaning, for example, presents issues of the specification of cleaning materials with low environmental impact, their disposal subsequent to use and the health and safety of operatives.

Managing the working environment

The BIFM divide this key management area into two sections: environmental issues and space management. The case being presented in this chapter is that environmental (and social) issues should not be compartmentalised but rather understood as an integral part of professional practice.

Space management has a very important influence on the quality of working life of building users and the effectiveness of an organisation (McGregor and Then 1999). Well-designed and managed space can enhance productivity and reduce workplace stress, and the opportunity for active user participation in the processes that affect them can be critical in achieving this.

Workplace management can also have significant effects on transport requirements. Flexible working hours, opportunities for teleworking, car sharing and the provision of facilities for cycling can smooth out peaks of traffic and lessen overall levels (Dabson 2000).

Managing resources

Resource management is key to improving the sustainability of facilities management. This has been recognised by the Managing Buildings Sustainably (2003) project which has developed detailed guidance for the procurement of more sustainable facilities management services (Edwards 2004). In the environment of complex outsourcing relationships that characterises facilities management, the ability to promote sustainability within the supply chain is critical. Briefing, specification and the development of service-level agreements need to make specific reference to sustainability issues, e.g. through setting key performance indicators. This should be followed through by the measurement of performance against the targets specified. Risk management also needs to be extended from standard business risk to environmental and social risk (Association of British Insurers 2001, Turner *et al.* 1994).

Within these broad categories of competence it is useful to distinguish again between issues of **procurement**, i.e. obtaining the goods and services necessary to ensure effective operations throughout the life cycle of a building or infrastructure, and issues of **evaluation**, i.e. appraising the effectiveness of a building or infrastructure in supporting its users. Taken together, procurement and evaluation can be considered as a cycle in which built products and their infrastructures are evaluated and necessary action taken in response to any shortcomings that may be detected. If sustainability issues are to be incorporated into this cycle they need to be considered both as part of procurement, e.g. in writing specifications for services, and as part of evaluation, e.g. in measuring the effectiveness of an energy efficiency programme.

Procurement

A comprehensive methodology for procurement at the operations and use level has been developed by the Managing Buildings Sustainably project (2003) (Edwards 2004). This contains both guidance on procurement and detailed checklists of sustainability issues to be considered. Procurement is through a six-step process that 'aims to bridge the gap that often exists between policy aspiration and day-to-day operation and management (O&M)'. At present three guides exist:

How to procure More Sustainable Property and Construction Management is targeted at those looking to appoint managing agents or equivalent (including in-house) managers.

How to procure More Sustainable Facilities Management is for those looking to outsource (or set internal guidelines for in-house) assurance of one or more elements of non-'core-business' building services (e.g. cleaning, security, catering, maintenance, etc.)

How to procure More Sustainable Service Contracts is for those looking to outsource (or set internal guidelines of in-house) delivery of specific services (e.g. cleaning, security, catering, mechanical, electrical and fabric maintenance).

Table 7.1 Matrix of facilities management competencies against the SUD model

BEQUEST SUD model	BIFM competencies: key management areas					
	Understanding business organisation	Managing people	Managing premises	Managing services	Managing the working environment	Managing resources
Environmental	FM strategy to support corporate environmental policy	Effective staff training in environmental issues	Local/global environmental impact – bio-diversity, CO_2 emissions	Energy efficiency Local/global environmental impact	Waste management Transport	Green procurement Risk management
Economic	FM strategy to support corporate economic policy	Manpower planning Sourcing strategy	Life-cycle planning Maintenance and operational costs	Energy costs Maintenance and operational costs	Productivity	Value for money Procurement Risk management
Social	FM strategy to support corporate social responsibility policy	Fair and safe employment policies Responsible dealing with suppliers Community impact of employment policy Conflict management	Usability Accessibility User participation Security	Usability Accessibility User control	Quality of life	Socially responsible procurement Risk management
Institutional	Companies Act Benchmarks	Transfer of Undertakings (Protection Of Employment) Regulations 1981 (TUPE)	Disability Discrimination Act (DDA) Environmental management systems (EMS) Building regulations	EMS Climate change levy	Health and safety	

Detailed guidance identifies property-specific issues coupled with specific guidance and forms of action classified broadly under Facilities Management, Hard Services, Soft Services and Consultants.

Evaluation

A number of tools and methodologies are available for evaluating sustainability at the operations and use stage (Deakin 1999b, 2002). Some approaches that can be used in the design and construction stages are also appropriate for the evaluation of completed buildings. An example of this is the UK BREEAM method and its derivatives (BREEAM 2004). Another example can be found with the NAR model (Deakin 2004). Most of these methods are primarily concerned with the physical fabric of buildings and infrastructure.

There is another group of methods that are focused on the experience of a building from the point of view of the user; these have the general name of Post-Occupancy Evaluation (POE) (Preiser *et al.* 1988). POE has a long and somewhat chequered history (Cooper 2001). Although not specifically about sustainability issues, the potential for POE to make an important contribution to sustainability in building operations and use has been noted by a number of writers (Cooper 2001, Fisk 2001, Bordass *et al.* 2002). There are three main uses of POE:

- Feedback on the design process – this is the loop back to the design and construction stages. Although often promoted, it has been difficult to implement, partly because of threats of litigation and partly because time between design and evaluation lessens the value of findings.
- 'Tuning' of facilities to user preferences – this is to ensure that the building is as effective as possible in supporting its users.
- Briefing for new projects – using the experience of an existing building to guide the procurement of a new building.

A distinction is often drawn between hard and soft measures in POE:

- Hard – measures that can be made through instrumentation, e.g. temperature, humidity, light levels, etc. These affect users but can be measured independently of them.
- Soft – user experience of the environment. This information is usually gathered by asking users directly for their opinions.

Most POEs will incorporate both hard and soft measures. For example, the PROBE study, one of the most widely known publicly available POEs carried out in recent years, involved both an energy survey and an occupant survey (Cohen *et al.* 2001).

POST-OCCUPANCY EVALUATION USING INDICATORS

The case study that follows illustrates the implementation of a post-occupancy evaluation using the IANUS system, a POE method developed with funding from the European Union and having as its aim the improvement of municipal decision making in relation to public investment in buildings and services. Its authors argued that by learning from the past it is possible to improve the future: clearly this is a fundamental belief if public service providers are to achieve any form of sustainable development through local investment and service delivery programmes. The specific objective of the project was to develop a methodology to evaluate the performance of different types of public buildings and related services. It was intended to be both politically relevant and user oriented. As a result some common issues emerged which illustrate the implications of emphasising 'soft' evaluation objectives at the same time as attempting to generate 'hard' information concerning the perception of building performance.

During the course of the IANUS project, the project partners completed a total of twenty building evaluations in four different countries. The case studies include examples of the following types of facility:

- Sports
- Civic centre
- Library
- Museum
- School
- Social centre
- Administrative centre.

The main issues emerging from the first stage of the model application can be summarised as:

- Achievement of quite disparate results regarding each evaluation project.
- Average or low level of data requirements, fulfilment and form completion.
- Difficulties of incorporating qualitative data.
- Categories represented by hard quantitative data are the most answered.
- The environment dimension appears to be suffering the most.
- Difficulties in applying user satisfaction measurement.
- Low success rate in constructing core indicators.

In terms of data, information about environmental quality was the most difficult to obtain, while activity building adaptation data is relatively easy to get if the evaluator has access to updated building plans. The difficulty with the environmental data is partly explained by the relatively new incorporation of a sustainability rationale in the design and management of buildings. At the same time there seem to be significant differences at national level regarding the environment legal framework and the state-of-the-art in environmental audits. Economic viability measurements also proved to be somewhat problematic, and it is suggested that the evaluator should obtain the definitive construction budget as well as annual budget and financial provisions to undertake building operations and service delivery. The pilot case studies also revealed the additional difficulty of evaluating large and complex facilities and services.

Experience from the IANUS project suggests that there are a number of practical issues that need to be considered very carefully in POE in connection with the politically relevant assessments which are inevitable when sustainable development is being sought.

The first is the difficulty that the work team may have in collecting certain pieces of information. In some cases, data may not be available, or it may be in an inappropriate format for use with IANUS. In other situations the cost and time involved in obtaining particular pieces of information may not be worthwhile. IANUS partners reported difficulties in obtaining economic data and some environmental information.

The second issue concerns the role of other partners (client, building manager, etc.) in the evaluation. A good working relationship between the work team and other partners will assist the evaluation process considerably. Feedback from the IANUS partners indicates that there were few problems with participation in the evaluation as people were interested in the process (and presumably its results). Staff in particular responded well to the evaluation interviews and questionnaires. However, the pressure of other work may compromise the ability of the building manager and/or client to assist with the data-gathering process. It is suggested that, where possible, a single individual on the client/facility side is given the responsibility of collating the relevant information.

Finally, a recurring theme for the project partners in the early stages of an evaluation is the need to explain the exact methodology and approach to the client and other stakeholders. This is not necessarily straightforward, but is essential, and might be achieved through workshops and other training sessions. Training thus needs to be considered as part of the evaluation process.

PROTOCOL

One of the objectives of BEQUEST was to develop a protocol for assessment in pursuit of SUD (Deakin *et al.* 2001). A generic protocol was developed following the structure proposed in the EU Directive on the 'assessment of the effects of certain plans and programmes on the environment'. For certain development activities within the BEQUEST framework more specific protocols have been drawn up which can be consulted via the BEQUEST toolkit (BEQUEST 2004). However, no detailed protocol has yet been developed for assessment at the operations and use level. It is useful to consider the generic protocol in relation to the implementation of a post-occupancy evaluation using the IANUS system given in the case study below (generic protocol headings given in italics).

a. *Preliminary activities*

- determine hard (legal) and soft gates (norms) making assessment necessary

b. *Planning your assessment activity*
c. *What to do for assessing.*
d. *Carrying out the environmental assessment*
e. *Carrying out consultations*
f. *Taking into account the environmental report and the results of the consultations*
g. *Provide information on the decisions*
h. *Monitoring.*

CASE STUDY: THE IANUS SYSTEM

The IANUS framework evaluation model

IANUS is an integrated evaluation methodology dealing with both the physical fabric of a building and the services it provides. As such the method aims to evaluate social and institutional factors associated with the provision of services, as well as economic and other performance-related evaluation methods associated with the construction and operation of buildings.

The IANUS framework model for evaluation is built around three premises. The first is that the full range of actors influenced by the building and service should be represented and involved in the evaluation. The second is that sustainable development can be seen as the interface of policies for environmental, economic and social development of the stakeholder community.

For each building that is evaluated, the IANUS framework thus incorporates four dimensions:

- activity building adaptation (ABA)
- environmental quality (ENQ)

- economic viability (ECO)
- user satisfaction (USR)

The third premise of the IANUS model is that each of these four dimensions has a number of aspects – or categories – which need to be understood.

Dimensions

The dimensions of the IANUS framework relate to the dimensions of sustainable building. Much has been written about the meaning of sustainability in construction, and these debates will not be repeated here. The IANUS approach takes account of the economic, social and environmental elements of sustainability in the four dimensions that it defines.

Activity building adaptation represents the technical characteristics of a building – the spaces, their accessibility and use, materials, dimensions, lighting and temperature control. The key issue here is about the suitability of the building for its uses, the quality of the services provided and the flexibility of the building to adapt to future changes.

Environmental quality concentrates on resource consumption, use of materials, pollution and other environmental variables. It has to do with the use of natural and technological solutions in the design of the building, including energy saving, ventilation, natural lighting, etc. Since the environmental quality of individual buildings is affected by the wider environment, IANUS incorporates evaluation of both the building and its urban context.

Economic viability represents the concern with economic efficiency and the use of resources.

To contribute to community development, IANUS considers it important to record and monitor the views of building and service users. The expectations and perceptions of users can be contrasted with objective data in a way that not only takes into account how things are, but also how things are experienced and lived.

Categories

Each of the four dimensions of the IANUS framework (listed above) has multiple aspects that need to be considered as part of the evaluation. These aspects – or categories – are as follows.

Activity building adaptation:

- building suitability
- accessibility
- users and function
- technical.

Environmental quality:

- urban structure
- noise
- electromagnetic pollution
- air
- water
- energy
- waste
- mobility.

Economic viability:

- investment cost (past)
- operational efficiency (short-term)
- maintenance of system (medium-term)
- life-cycle costs (long-term).

User satisfaction:

- safety and security
- health
- durability
- efficiency
- utility
- design.

Modular approach

In addition to the characteristics of the IANUS model outlined above, the IANUS methodology is also notable for its modular approach. This means that evaluators are able to choose between basic or complete evaluations and provide summary or detailed results according to the time, resources and motives of the evaluation team.

The process of evaluation is divided into a number of stages as illustrated in Figure 7.1.

As the diagram illustrates, the IANUS evaluation model can be applied in a basic mode or in a more complete mode where additional consultation and reporting is included. Similarly the IANUS indicators (discussed further below) are organised in two categories: core and complementary indicators. Core indicators are obligatory, and represent the minimum information required for an evaluation to take place.

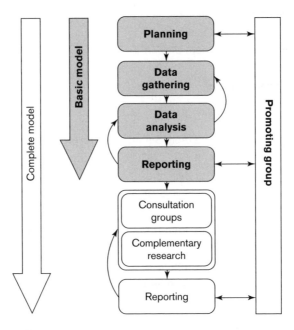

7.1 Modular approach

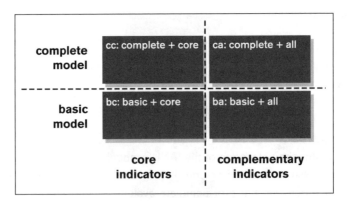

7.2 Evaluation model

Complementary indicators are optional, allowing more detailed analysis and interpretation of results. Some or all of these indicators may be selected by the evaluation team to meet the specific requirements of the evaluation project.

Given the structure of the IANUS evaluation framework – as a basic and a complete model, and with core and complementary sets of indicators – there are four different ways of carrying out an evaluation, as illustrated in Figure 7.2.

The choice of an application mode depends on the motives and requirements of the evaluation project representatives,[1] the resources available and the type of results required by the evaluation. Moving from the basic model and from the core indicators requires: a greater degree of technical detail; a higher level of participation; and more time and more money, as illustrated in Figures 7.3 and 7.4.

IANUS indicators

Another key characteristic of the IANUS framework revolves around the use of indicators. An indicator is a parameter, or a value derived from parameters, which points to, provides information about, or describes the state of a phenomenon, environment or area, with a significance extending beyond that directly associated with a parameter value.

At the heart of the IANUS framework is a hierarchical structure of data, as illustrated in Figure 7.3. Data about individual characteristics or parameters of the

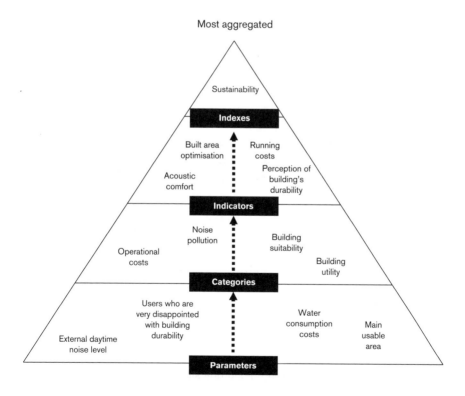

7.3 Hierarchical structure of data

building form the basic building blocks of the evaluation. These data are combined to describe categories and indicators – and ultimately an index (or indices) – of sustainability.

The IANUS indicators cover a diverse range of subjects. Some of these are derived from easily measured scientific data, others from data involving personal judgements. This combination raises questions about objectivity. The results of an indicator relating to energy efficiency, for example, will be largely objective. However, interpreting whether the result represents good or bad performance may be a subjective process, and may have a political dimension.

IANUS classifies indicators in the following way:

- Objective or subjective indicators: objective when reflecting a given condition and subjective when trying to measure people's perceptions.
- Descriptive or performance indicators: initially all indicators will be descriptive, unless there is a target fixed for some of them. In that case, deviation from target will be considered as a performance indicator.
- Core or secondary indicators: core indicators will be a limited set of indicators covering all dimensions that will constitute the minimum recommended to evaluate a certain facility. Secondary indicators will allow deeper penetration into a given matter of concern.
- Base and specific indicators: base indicators will be the ones universally applicable to all facilities. Specific indicators will only be applicable in certain cases. Two kinds of specificity have been foreseen: geographical and typological. Geography-specific indicators will only be applicable in certain countries. Typological indicators will be formulated for different building/facility types.

Participatory approach

The IANUS approach to evaluation revolves around user experiences. As a result, the success of the evaluation process will rely on the organisation and involvement of different groups of people at different stages of the evaluation. A number of key actors will need to be involved throughout the process, and should work in partnership with the work team carrying out the evaluation.

It is suggested that before the evaluation process begins, the key actors are organised into three groups:

- the promoting and supervising group (the steering group);
- the consultation group;
- the work team.

The steering group should include a representative for the building – usually somebody who has been elected and/or a technical manager – and someone involved in the management organisation, represented by the site manager. The main function of the group will be to co-ordinate and supervise the work, and give approval for the resulting documentation. A member of this group will act as assessment co-ordinator. Their role will be to:

- co-ordinate the different services of the property (technical services, economic services, etc.) and the work team;
- plan the different stages of the procedure – interviews, work meetings and visits, etc. – with the work team;
- gather the necessary documentary information and data;
- supervise the writing of documents;
- take part in the work meetings.

The consultation group should include representatives of users and those groups or organisations affected by the assessment. The role of this group will depend on the degree of participation required for the evaluation. The group will assist the work team in forming a critical view of the site, and help with the analysis and evaluation of the building. The membership of the consultation group will be agreed by the work team and the steering group.

The work team will carry out all of the assessment work, i.e. gathering information, synthesising, diagnosing, writing up and presenting the findings. The work team should include a number of professionals, bringing together expertise in the following areas:

- site programming;
- architectural and technical building design;
- organisation of participation;
- management.

Evaluation process

Once the relevant personnel have been assembled and organised, work can begin on the process of evaluation. The IANUS evaluation process is divided into six stages, as follows:

Stage 1   Planning the work
Stage 2   Information gathering, the participative process
Stage 3   Information analysis

Stage 4a   Reporting
Stage 4b   Participation and complementary research (optional stage)
Stage 5   Assessment dissemination

The quantitative data to be collected and the collection mechanisms may be categorised as shown in Table 7.2.

The work team should make a complete and detailed visit to the facility (all different spaces must be visited) in order to make observations and measurements. This process should be complemented by detailed interviews to clarify any areas of uncertainty and to allow those responsible for the facility to offer additional information.

Areas to be covered include:

- access to the building
- visibility and signing (within the building and its vicinity)
- the real functioning of the building (access, operation and services)
- dimensions of the spaces and their functions
- possible modifications from the original project
- technical performance of the building installations
- state of maintenance
- possible visible identifiable defects (cracks, fissures, malfunctions, signs of degradation, etc.)
- comfort of the inner spaces
- level of flexibility.

The work team should carry out a photographic report to be included in the final report.

The visit may be completed with informative meetings with technicians responsible for the maintenance of the facility.

Table 7.2 Collection of qualitative data related to the building

Type of data	Collection method	
	Basic	Complete
1 Data related to the building itself	Interview and request to general manager and owner	Basic + personal contact with maintenance and personnel managers and original designer
2 Data related to the municipality	Desk-based research (internet + publications)	Basic + personal contact with technicians
3 Data for comparison	Desk-based research (internet + publications)	Basic + personal contact with experts

Collection of qualitative data required may be possible by inspection and survey by trained personnel. It is advisable that this work be complemented by some interviews with key people involved in the building (management, municipal department, urbanism or planning department) in order to check or corroborate the results. These data may also be complemented by some of the data collected regarding users' point of view.

The point of view of the users is extremely important as it provides:

- the main source of information for evaluating user satisfaction;
- information for indicators relating to the other dimensions of the evaluation;
- information that contrasts with the quantitative data obtained in other sections.

However, when approaching the study of people's perceptions it is important to remember that people's opinions, feelings and perceptions are essentially subjective, changeable and volatile. This means that there is a risk of gathering unrepresentative or misleading results.

IANUS foresees different methodologies for obtaining user satisfaction data. In most cases the choice of method will rely on the size of the population under investigation. For small groups (owners, managers, architects involved in the construction project and other individuals), discussion is best managed through interviews and, if time and money allow, panels and workshops. For large groups (staff, clients, stakeholders and other groups), opinions are best gathered through surveys/questionnaires and, if time and money allow, interviews, panels and workshops. If, however, the evaluation is for external use and will affect future policy decisions, questionnaires offer a more scientifically rigorous result.

Analysis of the information

This stage of the evaluation focuses on the analysis of the information gathered and the elaboration of the diagnosis of the current situation. It is structured into three separate steps:

- Processing of indicators
- Interpretation and analysis of results
- Preparation of results.

Processing of indicators

Data must be manipulated so that it is homogeneous and comparable before the indicators can be processed. The analysis to be undertaken is as follows:

- the application of the formula or the value rating detailed in relation to each indicator;
- monitoring and checking the results to establish that sufficient data have been collected;
- checking for errors.

This review may reveal the need to undertake new information gathering. If this is the case, two routes may be taken:

- Obtain the missing information by other means.
- Obtain alternative data to fill in the information gaps.

Interpretation and analysis of results

The result of the previous step is an ordered set of indicators, classified into four dimensions (environmental quality, economic viability, etc.). These data are the starting point for an objective evaluation. Two key questions arise to frame interpretation, as shown in Figure 7.4.

Comparison has been determined as the most appropriate means of evaluating a given indicator. To know if the result is satisfactory or not, three forms of comparison are proposed, as shown in Figure 7.4.

Preparation of results

The evaluation and analysis must give sufficient information about each of the four dimensions to allow the preparation of a report in clear and concise language for the

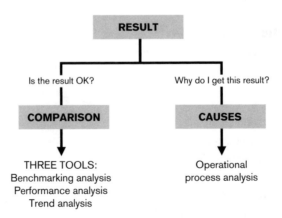

7.4 Comparison of results

benefit of non-specialists. The information must also be organised so as to give a complete image of the building and to emphasise the pertinent results of the analysis.

The results to be presented must be objective and complete, reporting both the satisfactory and unsatisfactory points of the building in relation to the appropriate context. The strong and weak points of the analysis should also be included in the results.

Reporting

Once the results of the analysis have been prepared, the work team should prepare a full assessment report. The report will consist of two documents:

- A detailed description of the assessment containing numerical analysis and background information to allow future implementation of the results.
- A presentation document. This is an executive summary of results with emphasis on graphic representation of the results to ease comprehension.

These reports should be presented to the client by the work team at a meeting. The reports should also be presented to the consultation group, once the amendments and observations of the client have been taken into consideration.

The final version of the document is then edited and sent to the client's representatives for final approval.

Benchmarking and comparative analysis

Once the indicators have been calculated and weighted (following agreement with the client) a comparative analysis should be undertaken. There are three elements to this:

1   Trend analysis: a comparison with past results from the same facility using data from previous audits or evaluation studies. This type of comparative analysis gives an idea about the trajectory of different parameters of the facility: evolution of the users' perception, operative costs fluctuations, etc.
2   Performance analysis: comparison with the stated objectives or performance targets of the facility (as set out in maintenance policies, services programmes, strategic plans, and other documents).
3   Benchmarking analysis: comparison with results from other facilities recorded in the IANUS database.[2]

While carrying out the comparative analysis, it is important to remember that there are many factors that influence public buildings and services. These factors include:

- the type of facility being studied (school, museum, sports centre, etc.);
- the background (sociocultural context, public or private management, previous facility functions, period of construction, etc.);
- the urban context;
- the country (normative context, climatology, specific location, etc.).

CONCLUSIONS

The sustainable operation and use of buildings is an important but relatively undeveloped area of research. Although many parameters for sustainable operation and use are set by property and construction managers for procurement and design decisions, there is still considerable scope for increasing sustainability in the management of building products and infrastructures. The structure of the facilities management industry with its reliance on outsourcing of services has an impact on how this can be done and highlights the importance of supply chain issues. Furthermore, as sustainability issues increasingly become a focus of mainstream business management they are likely to become integrated into the corporate goals that the facilities management industry will be required to meet. Although management of the built environment has traditionally concerned itself with physical and technical issues – such as building maintenance – there is an increasing amount of evidence to suggest it has now widened its scope to a range of softer issues such as change management and quality of life. By mapping the BEQUEST environmental, economic, social and institutional issues against professional facilities management competencies, it is possible to explore how the sustainability agenda is likely to impinge on practice.

Procurement and evaluation are the two broad areas of management action where sustainability issues can be addressed. Procurement obtains the goods or services necessary to improve performance. Although there are a number of evaluation methods that have been applied to operations and use, most of these have been developed primarily for decision making during the property development, design and construction stages. There is scope for developing evaluation tools specifically for operations and use. Procurement issues during this stage are not essentially different from those involved in the design and construction of new buildings (e.g. in taking account of the environmental impact of materials during specification), although as the industry moves towards a general business support service, the range of issues is likely to broaden considerably.

One group of evaluation techniques that is of particular interest for the management and operation of the built environment is Post-Occupancy Evaluation. Although POE has been available for some time it is only in recent years that it has begun to specifically address sustainability issues. IANUS is one of these new approaches. It highlights the importance of the development of explicit indicators for sustainability and the need for the participation of a full range of actors concerned with the building or infrastructure; this is not always easy to achieve. Evaluations of individual buildings, as well as infrastructures, can be useful snapshots but become more powerful as part of benchmarking studies with other facilities (e.g. via the IANUS database) or longitudinal studies of the same facility over time. Such comparisons enable progress towards greater sustainability to be measured.

About IANUS

The IANUS research programme was funded by the European Union under the Fifth Framework Programme 1998–2002, Thematic Programme: Environment and Sustainable Development, contract no. EVK4-CT-1999-00010.

Contributors were:

Diputació de Barcelona (DIBA)
Institut de Programmation en Architecture et Aménagement (IPAA)
Deutsches Institut für Urbanistik (DIFU)
Ambiente Italia Instituto di Ricerche (Ambiente Italia)
Institut Ildefons Cerdà (Institut Cerdà)
Poliprogram (PL)
University of West England, Bristol (UWE)
Provincia Regionale di Caltanissetta (PROV.CL)
Università degli Studi di Firenze (DPMPE)
The IANUS Handbook was edited by: Caroline Brown and Martin Symes, University of the West of England, Bristol
Further information about IANUS is available from the project website: www.project-IANUS.org

NOTES

1   'Evaluation project representatives' is used here to mean the person or group of people who have commissioned the evaluation. This may be the property owner, manager, responsible department of a local authority, a management or steering committee, etc.

2   For that reason benchmarking analysis is strongly dependent on the number of applications present in the database and therefore it is seen as one of the future characteristics of the IANUS modular approach.

170 | Mark Deakin, John Hudson and Martin Symes

REFERENCES

Action Energy (2004) www.actionenergy.org.uk (21 July 2004).

Association of British Insurers (2001) *Investing in Social Responsibility*, London: Association of British Insurers.

Atkin, B. and Brooks, A. (2000) *Total Facilities Management*, Oxford: Blackwell.

Barrett, P. and Baldry, D. (2003) *Facilities Management*, 2nd edn, Oxford: Blackwell Science.

Beggs, C. and Moodley, K. (1997) Facilities management of passively controlled buildings, *Facilities* 15(9/10): 233–240.

Bentivegna, V., Curwell, S., Deakin, M., Lombardi, P., Mitchell, G. and Nijkamp, P. (2002) A vision and methodology for integrated sustainable urban development: BEQUEST, *Building Research and Information* 30(2).

BEQUEST (2004) http://research.salford.uk/bqtookit (July 2004).

BIFM (2004) http://www.bifm.org.uk/?pd/competence.html (21 July 2004).

Bordass, B., Leaman, A. and Cohen, R. (2002) Walking the tightrope: the Probe team's response to BRI commentaries, *Building Research and Information* 30(1): 62–72.

BREEAM (2004) www.breeam.org (2 July 2004).

Brundrett, G. (2003) Preventing Legionellosis: is your action plan complete? *Facilities* 21(11/12): 275–279.

Campbell, L. and Finch, E. (2004) Customer satisfaction and organisational justice, *Facilities* 22(7/8): 178–189.

Chanter, B. and Swallow, P. (1996) *Building Maintenance Management*, Oxford: Blackwell Science.

Cohen, R., Standeven, M., Bordass, B. and Leaman, A. (2001) Assessing building performance in use 1: the Probe process, *Building Research and Information* 29(2): 85–102.

Cooper, I. (2001) Post-occupancy evaluation – where are you? *Building Research and Information* 29(2): 158–163.

Cowles, D. (2001) Legionnaires disease, and the Legionella risk assessment process explained, *Facilities* 19(1).

Dabson, A. (2000) Managing the journey to work in Nutt, B. and McLennan, P. (eds) *Facility Management: Risks and Opportunities*, Oxford: Blackwell Science, pp. 117–125.

Deakin, M. (1999a) Valuation, appraisal, discounting, obsolescence and depreciation: towards a life cycle analysis and impact assessment of their effects on the environment of cities, *International Journal of Life Cycle Assessment* 4(2):

Deakin, M. (ed.) (1999b) *Local Authority Property Management: Initiatives, Strategies, Reorganisation and Reform*, Aldershot: Ashgate.

Deakin, M. (2002) *The Transition to Property Management*, Estates Gazette, London.

Deakin, M. (2004) *Property Management: Corporate Strategies, Financial Instruments and the Urban Environment*, Aldershot: Ashgate Press.

Deakin, M. and Curwell, C. (2004) Sustainable urban development: the framework and directory of assessment methods. In Deakin *et al.* (2004) *Models and Instruments for Rural and Urban Development*, Aldershot: Ashgate Press.

Deakin, M., Curwell, S. and Lombardi, P. (2001) BEQUEST: The framework and directory of assessment methods, *International Journal of Life Cycle Assessment* 6(6):

Deakin, M., Huovila, P., Rao, S., Sunikka, M. and Vreeker, R. (2002) The assessment of sustainable urban development, *Building Research and Information* 30(2): 95–108.

Department of Work and Pensions (2004) http://www.disability.gov.uk/ (22 July 2004).

Donaldson, T. (2002) The stakeholder revolution and the Clarkson principles, *Business Ethics Quarterly* 12(2): 107–111.

Dow Jones (2004) http://www.sustainability-indexes.com/ (29 June 2004).

Edwards, S. (2004) Opportunities to address sustainability, *Essential FM Report 35*, Croydon: LexisNexis Butterworth, pp. 8–9.

Elkington, J. (1999) *Cannibals with Forks*, Oxford: Capstone.

Fisk, D. (2001) Sustainable development and post-occupancy evaluation, *Building Research and Information* 29(6): 466–468.

Fitzsimmons, J., Noh, J. and Thies, E. (1998) Purchasing business services, *Journal of Business and Industrial Marketing* 13(4/5): 370–380.

FTSE4Good (2004) http://www.ftse.com/ftse4good/index.jsp (29 June 2004).

Hood, C. (1991) A public management for all seasons? *Public Administration* 69: 3–19.

Hood, C. (1995) The 'new public management' in the 1980s: variations on a theme, *Accounting, Organizations and Society* 20(2/3): 93–109.

Hudson, J. and Curwell, S. (2004) Sustainable facilities management, *Essential FM Report 35*, Croydon: LexisNexis Butterworth, pp. 2–3.

Hui, E. and Tsang, A. (2004) Sourcing strategies of facilities management, *Journal of Quality in Maintenance Engineering* 10(2): 85–92.

Keeping, M. and Shiers, D. (1996) The 'green' refurbishment of commercial property, *Facilities* 14(3/4): 15–19.

Langston, C. and Lauge-Kristensen, R. (2002) *Strategic Management of Built Facilities*, Oxford: Butterworth-Heinemann.

Managing Buildings Sustainably (2003) www.ecde.co.uk/projects/mbs/index.html

McGregor, W. and Then, D. (1999) *Facilities Management and the Business of Space*, London: Arnold.

Preiser, W., Rabinowitz, H. and White, E. (1988) *Post-Occupancy Evaluation*, New York: Van Nostrand Reinhold.

Sustainable Development in Government (2004) *Framework for Sustainable Development on the Government Estate*, http://www.sustainable-development.gov.uk/sdig/improving/index.htm (22 July 2004).

Then, D. (1999) An integrated resource management view of facilities management, *Facilities* 17(12/13): 462–469.

Turner, N., Bennett, L., Prescott, G. and Gronow, S. (1994) Assessing and managing the environmental risks of property ownership, *Property Management* 12(2): 4–15.

Wastebusters (2000) *The Green Office Manual: A Guide to Responsible Practice*, 2nd edn, London: Earthscan.

Wordsworth, P. (2001) *Lee's Building Maintenance Management*, 4th edn, Oxford: Blackwell Science.

Part III

The Environmental Assessment Methods

8

The Directory of Environmental Assessment Methods
Mark Deakin and Patrizia Lombardi

In drawing attention to Mitchell *et al.*'s (1995) and May *et al.*'s (1997) environmental assessment, Cooper (1997) proposes that if we are to bridge the gap between buildings and cities and evaluate the sustainability of urban development, it will be necessary to compile an extensive list of environmental assessment methods: a list of methods able to operate at various levels of assessment – from building to city scale – and not just with the environmental, but also the economic and social issues underlying the evaluation process (see also Cooper and Curwell 1998; Curwell *et al.* 1998; Nijkamp and Pepping 1998). In the interests of compiling such a list of assessment methods, Cooper (1997) and Cooper and Curwell (1998) propose that the evaluations in question should be able to engage the 'pole of actors' in the built environment and meet the demands which exist for cities to be sustainable in terms of:

• the ecological integrity of the built environment;
• the equity of the economic and social structures underlying the city;
• the ability the public in turn have to participate in decisions taken about the future of the urban development process.

This chapter sets out how BEQUEST has sought to meet these demands and the particular challenges they pose for environmental assessment. It begins by setting out how the network has gone about compiling such an extensive list of environmental assessment methods. Having done this, the chapter then goes on to outline the post-Brundtland directory of environmental assessment methods assembled to evaluate the sustainability of urban development.

ASSESSING THE SUSTAINABILITY OF URBAN DEVELOPMENT

It is the question of how to compile such an extensive list of environmental assessment methods that Deakin *et al.* (2001, 2002a, 2002b) have sought to tackle head on. This has been done by:

- referring to the framework accompanying the integrated methodology and vision of SUD;
- scoping SUD in terms of both the protocols and environmental assessment methods needed to evaluate the sustainability of urban development;
- undertaking a survey of the environmental assessment methods that can be made use of to carry out such an evaluation;
- compiling a master list of the said assessments, their scope, methodology and vision;
- classifying the methods in terms of their type of evaluation and what they contribute to the sustainability of urban development: for example whether the value of the assessment method lies with its ecological integrity, or equitable or participative qualities and whether the evaluation in question is environmental, economic or social in nature.

THE FRAMEWORK AND PROTOCOL(S)

The framework underlying BEQUEST's vision and methodology of an integrated SUD has been set out by Bentivegna *et al.* (2002) and Deakin *et al.* (2002a, 2002b). The protocol(s) to follow in extending this vision and methodology of an integrated SUD into a process of environmental assessment have also been discussed by Deakin *et al.* (2002b). They are developed in this volume by the authors of Chapters 2 and 3 to 7 respectively. This chapter and the following will focus on the directory of assessment methods for evaluating the sustainability of urban development.

TOWARDS A DIRECTORY OF ENVIRONMENTAL ASSESSMENT METHODS

While Chapters 2 to 7 provide a framework and protocol, they do not address the key question of how decision makers can reverse the current trend of resource depletion, conserve resources and protect the environment. That is to say, build the environmental capacity which is needed to ensure the *ecological integrity, equity, participation and futurity* of urban development and in turn the sustainability of cities. To achieve this it is necessary to: (a) qualify the environmental capacity of the urban development process and (b) evaluate the actions taken to build the environmental capacity needed for the urban development process to sustain the city.

Qualifying environmental capacity and evaluating the actions taken

Here 'environmental capacity' is taken to mean the ability the environment has to carry urban development and the pressure which the weight of resource consumption loads on to the eco-system as part of the relentless pursuit of economic growth, competitiveness and social cohesion that cities amass as forms of human settlement. In line with current knowledge on climate change, the ability of cities to bear such pressure and carry the sheer weight of such a loading is understood to be threatened by the environmental degradation and ecological damage this in turn produces. If this trend of depletion is to be reversed by resource conservation and environmental protection measures, then it is evident that cities need to take actions which are best termed 'capacity building', if they are to be able to absorb such pressure and carry the said weight. This in a nutshell is what environmental assessment methods set out to do. That is to say, *qualify* the environmental capacity in question – whether it can carry the pressure and the said weight – and go on to *evaluate* if the actions which are taken by cities to build environmental capacity – by reversing the current trend of resource depletion and conserving resources – allow this loading to be absorbed into the urban development process. Absorbed, it should also be noted, into an urban development process whose 'environmentally friendly' approach towards economic growth, competitiveness and social cohesion in turn offers up the possibility of balancing such forces, allowing cities to become sustainable.

The survey

In responding to this, the partners of BEQUEST have surveyed the environmental assessment methods currently available to carry out such qualifications and undertake the related evaluations. So far, the survey has identified sixty such methods which are available to assess the sustainability of urban development. It has also shown that the said methods have been applied to the planning, property development, construction and operational activities of the urban development process and used to analyse the sustainability issues these raise within cities at the various scales of assessment. The survey can be accessed via the website address for the BEQUEST project: http://www.surveying.salford.ac.uk/bq/extra. The website provides a list of the methods surveyed and in a number of cases offers hypertext links to the case studies they have been drawn from. This provides the opportunity for the readers to explore the implications of applying the method in further detail and satisfy themselves as to whether the technique is appropriate for the assessment under consideration.

The master list

The list of methods is drawn from a survey of the scientific literature and unpublished technical reports, written by professional members of the community. The methods have been drawn from textbooks, scientific journals and professional reports on the methodology of environmental assessment. The master list provides a survey of the methods that it is possible to select and deploy in Europe and North America and case-study reviews of how the assessment methods have been applied to evaluate the sustainability of urban development. In certain cases they represent assessment methods the partners and extranet members of BEQUEST have been engaged in developing, or have a detailed knowledge of (Deakin *et al.* 2001, 2002a provide further details of the survey). The complete list of the assessment methods can be found in Box 9.1 (see pages 204–5).

Review of the assessments

The case-study reviews contained in the master list show how the assessment methods have been applied to qualify whether the city has the capacity to reverse the current trend of resource depletion, and evaluate whether resource conservation builds the environmental capacity needed for the city to sustain the urban develop-ment. The case-study reviews indicate that a large number of assessment methods have been used to:

*   underpin the growing commitment to sustainable development and qualify how planning policies form part of the regulative framework to conserve resources (Bentivegna 1997, Davoudi 1997, Therivel 1998);
*   evaluate the property development programmes designed to construct the infrastructures (energy, water and drainage, transport, telecommunication tech-nologies) needed to build environmental capacity (Banister and Button 1993, Nijkamp and Pepping 1998, Graham and Marvin 1996, William *et al.* 1996, Fusco and Nijkamp 1997, Marvin and Guy 1997, Jones *et al.* 1997);
*   assess what the said design and construction projects do to build the environ-mental capacity of the urban development process and make cities sustainable (Prior 1993, Vale and Vale 1993, Cole 1997, Curwell *et al.* 1999, Deakin 1999).

The review also revealed that scientific opinion about the potential of environmental assessment is currently divided. First, there are those who are of the opinion that environmental assessment methods can be used to promote sustainable development (Brandon *et al.* 1997a, b, Bergh 1997, Nijkamp and Pepping 1998). Second, there are others who are of the opinion that the all-pervasive marketisation and privatisation of the environment, and resultant risk and uncertainty surrounding the nature of public goods, mean the methods currently available are no longer appropriate (Guy and Marvin 1997). This division of opinion is important for two reasons. First, because it illustrates that the scientific community is divided about the value of assessment methods. Second, it tends to undermine the certainty the professional community needs in order to be confident about the worth of such assessments (Cooper 1997).

The position the network has taken on the matter tends to align with the first opinion. This is because the network is of the view that the environmental assessment methods can be used to promote sustainable urban development and that the uncertainty and risk which surround the process of privatisation represent a particular, but not insurmountable, challenge for the scientific community. The BEQUEST network is of the opinion that the source of such division lies in the absence of appropriate frameworks and the less than systematic approach which has previously been taken towards SUD and its associated sustainable development issues, spatial levels and time scales (Curwell *et al*. 1998, Cooper and Curwell 1998).

The assessment methodology adopted

The assessment methodology BEQUEST adopts is based upon an understanding that the growing international and increasingly global nature of the relationship between the environment and economy is uncertain, resulting in as yet incalculable degrees of risk associated with environmental policy and any actions which member states take on resource conservation. This in turn means that standard methods of assessment – for example cost-benefit analysis – are of limited help in building the environmental capacity needed for the urban development process to sustain the economic and social structures of cities. This is because such assessments increasingly require the use of non-standard valuation (multi-criteria, contingency and hedonic type) methods.

More importantly, the network is of the opinion that methods of this kind are of limited use in assessing sustainable development and it is necessary to transcend such valuations as part of a co-evolutionary approach to environmental assessment – an approach to sustainable development that represents the environmental, economic and social as complementary, in the sense that resource conservation reduces depletion rates, protects the environment and builds the capacity of the urban development process to carry the economic and social structures of cities (Faucheux *et al*. 1997, O'Conner 1998, Faucheux and O'Conner 1998). This is the environmental capacity – it should be added – which the urban development process needs to carry economic and social structures in cities that are sustainable in terms of the quality of life which such values in turn institute. It should perhaps also be noted that this concern with the quality of life is significant because this moves both the academic and scientific communities beyond the issues which are of current concern to environmental valuation (property rights, landscape, recreation and leisure), and shifts attention to valuing the environment in terms of ecological integrity (resource consumption, pollution, land use and bio-diversity) and the scientific basis of such assessments.

What such assessments do is turn attention towards the ecology of resource consumption. The advantage of this lies in the opportunity that assessments of this kind provide to develop methods which apply the so-called 'hard' certainties of bio-physical science to the more uncertain, risky social relations – relations that are 'softer' and which are by nature more difficult to predict (Faucheux and O'Conner 1998). This is done by emphasising the co-evolutionary nature of the bio-physical and social in a framework for analysis that integrates the environmental, economic and social and which in turn provides the methodology for assessing the sustainability of development. What this does is focus attention on the hard and soft issues of sustainable development (Fusco and Nijkamp 1997, Capello *et al.* 1999). These are the issues which in this instance are integrated in the form of the environmental appraisals and impact analyses which provide statements about the sustainability of development. Environmental appraisals and impact analyses that transcend – overcome the limitations of – existing valuation techniques and which in turn develop as forms of sustainability assessment.

What is significant about such methods is the tendency they illustrate not only to transcend the limitations of existing valuation techniques, but to transform environmental assessment per se. This is because, as forms of sustainability assessment, such methods not only transcend existing valuation techniques, but go a long way to transform environmental assessment methodology. These methods form a post-Brundtland directory of environmental assessment methods, to evaluate the sustainability of urban development and build the environmental capacity needed to ensure the *ecological integrity, equity, participation and futurity* of the urban development process and sustainability of cities.

TOWARDS A POST-BRUNDTLAND DIRECTORY OF ASSESSMENT METHODS

In the interests of capturing these methodological developments and reflecting the direction they are pushing environmental assessment, the network has produced a post-Brundtland directory of environmental assessment methods. The objective of the said directory is fourfold. First, to direct decision makers towards the master list of assessment methods currently in existence and its possible use in evaluating the sustainability of urban development. Second, to provide a standard description of each assessment method for consideration. Third, to illustrate the classes of assessment the methods represent. Fourth, to classify the assessment methods based on the complexity of the evaluations they advance.

Directing the decision makers

The framework for analysis shows that the pole of actors associated with the urban development process is diverse. They are represented as planners, property developers, designers (architects and engineers), building contractors and operators, either as the users or managers of the installations. Representing a range of stakeholders in the community, each group is seen as responsible for taking specific actions and evaluating what this contributes towards SUD. As each group offers expertise at various stages of the urban development process, it is recognised that each decision maker requires to be directed towards a method of assessment which provides a detailed description of what each evaluation contributes to the sustainability of cities. This is what the standard description of the assessment methods proposes to do. In providing a standard description of the assessment methods, it allows stakeholders to source the information of interest to them and to direct decision makers towards the nature of the evaluation the techniques of analysis offer.

Given the number of stakeholders in the urban development process and interests they represent, it is felt important to provide such a description because it is not always clear which sector of the community the assessment method is directed towards and what stage of the urban development process it addresses. The standard description aims to clarify these matters and avoid any such confusion over the use of the assessment methods. Ultimately, of course, the effects of the decisions taken on SUD are assumed to be fed back to the community so they can inform further research into the sustainability of cities.

The reason for this stakeholder approach is fourfold. First, it focuses attention on the agents of change (planners, architects, engineers, surveyors, building contractors, etc.). Second, the attention paid to the agents of change, and activities they undertake, means the analysis is not limited to the statutory planning instrument. Third, in taking this approach, it becomes possible to also take the property development, design, construction and operational interests into account. Fourth, it allows the analysis to concentrate on the built environment and the relationship this has to the economic and social structures of the city – the environmental, economic and social structures in turn make up the urban development process and sustainability of cities that it is the object of the analysis to evaluate. In taking on this form, the stakeholder analysis might be seen as a 'grass roots' approach by activists responsible for making urban development sustainable and supported by a growing body of professional knowledge and deepening academic understanding of the process. The benefits of this approach are seen to lie in the capacity the analysis has to unify, rather than further fragment, our knowledge and understanding of the urban development process. For rather than dividing the subject into sectional interests, professional fields and academic disciplines, the analysis makes it possible to circumvent such divisions, something which it achieves by recognising the cross-sectional and inter-professional nature of what are trans-disciplinary issues.

The standard description

Given the diverse range and spread of methods currently in existence, the survey has sought to provide a standard description of the assessments in terms of the following characteristics:

- name of method
- description
- data required
- status (well-established, or experimental)
- activity (planning, design, construction and operation)
- environmental and societal (economic, social and institutional) issues
- scale of assessment (spatial level and time frame)
- references.

Box 8.1 provides an example of how the standard description has been used to characterise the assessment methods in question. The description is of the SPARTACUS assessment method and its particular characteristics as a tool for evaluating the sustainability of urban development.

This description of the assessments method's characteristics can be found in the decision support system developed by the BEQUEST network as an electronic toolkit, linking the framework and protocols to the assessment methods. This in turn connects the framework, protocols and assessment methods to the actions taken in evaluating the sustainability of urban development (see Curwell *et al.* 1998, Hamilton *et al.* 2002). These matters, however, do not concern this volume. The assessment methods form the focus of Volume 2 of this series, and the development and use of the toolkit is examined in Volume 3. The following discussion will instead examine the classes and classification of the assessment methods drawn from the network's review of how they have been used to evaluate the sustainability of urban development.

The classes

The classification BEQUEST has undertaken reveals that the methods can be divided into two: those used for the purposes of carrying out 'environmental valuations'

BOX 8.1

Standard description of the SPARTACUS assessment method

ASSESSMENT METHODS: SPARTACUS (**System for Planning and Research in Towns and Cities for Urban Sustainability**)

Explanation of the BEQUEST classification. **Please read before using this document**. Each link will bring its relevant heading to the top left of your screen.

Summary

Activity: Strategic Planning

Environmental & Societal Issues: Natural resources, environmental pollution, land use, bio-diversity, production, buildings, transport & utility infrastructure, finance, access/accessibility, safety and security, health & well-being, community and human capacity, governance, justice.

Spatial Level: Global: National: Urban Region: City

Time Scale: Medium: 5–20 years: Long: 20 years plus

----

1.   **Name – SPARTACUS** – System for Planning and Research in Towns and Cities for Urban Sustainability

2.   **Description**:

a.   General

SPARTACUS is a method for assessing sustainability implications of urban land use and transport policies. The core of the system is a computerised land use transport interaction model, MEPLAN.

This model can be used for analysing the impacts of e.g. transport investment, regulatory, pricing or planning policies on e.g. overall mobility, modal split, journey times, movements of households and jobs and production costs of firms.

The SPARTACUS method builds on the results of the model to calculate values for sustainability indicators. Sustainability is understood as consisting of environmental and social sustainability and economic efficiency. The environmental and social indicators are aggregated into indices using user-given indicator-specific weights and value functions. The social indicators include a set of justice indicators which assess the justice of the distributions of certain impacts among socio-economic groups. The methodology is being further developed in the PROPOLIS project.

b.   Data requirements

Setting up the MEPLAN model requires a great deal of data on land use and transport: floor spaces, jobs, households (all by category and area), transport networks, traffic volumes, modal split, speeds etc. etc. Building the indicator system requires further information on e.g. the emission and noise characteristics of the vehicle fleet and meteorological conditions. The coarse zonal system of the model is refined into a raster system, and this requires detailed information about the location of land uses and population.

c.   Status

The MEPLAN model is well established, but the SPARTACUS system as a whole is experimental and under further development in the PROPOLIS project where two other transport land use models, TRANUS and DORTMUND, are involved in addition to MEPLAN.

3.   **Activity** – Strategic planning.

4.   **Environmental & social issues** – Natural resources, environmental pollution, land use, bio-diversity, production, buildings, transport & utility infrastructure, finance, access/accessibility, safety and security, health & well-being, community and human capacity, governance, justice.

5.   **Scale of assessment**:

a.   Space: Global, national, urban region, city.

b.   Time: Medium and long term, 5–20 years plus.

6.   **References** – Presentations and publications:

Lautso, K. and Toivanen, S. (1999) 'SPARTACUS System for Analysing Urban Sustainability'. Transportation Research Record No. 1670, pp. 35–46.

Lautso, K. and Toivanen, S. (1998) 'System for planning and research in towns and cities for urban sustainability – SPARTACUS'. Presentation at the 8th World Conference on Transport Research, Antwerp, July 1998.

Toivanen, S. (1997) 'System for planning and research in towns and cities for urban sustainability' in Elohimji, F. Parra-Luna and E.A. Stuhler (eds) Pre-Conference Publication of the 14th International Conference of the World Association for Case Method Research and Case Method Applications (WACRA-Europe) on Sustainable Development: Towards Measuring the Performances of Integrated Socio-economic and Environmental Systems, Madrid, September 1997.

Web resources:
SPARTACUS:http://www.ltcon.fi/spartacus/
MEPLAN.:http://www.meap.co.uk/meap/ME&P.htm
PROPOLIS:http://www.ltcon.fi/propolis/

Provided by: Sami Yli-Karjanmaa
Date: 25 July 2000

and those which are augmented to become particular forms of 'sustainability assess-ment'. The classification shows that the *environmental valuations* provide assessments which focus on ecological integrity. It also shows that those methods which move into particular forms of *sustainability assessment* tend to focus on building the envi-ronmental capacity needed not only to qualify the ecological integrity of the urban development process, but to evaluate the equity, participation and futurity of the economic and social structures underlying the sustainability of cities.

Examples of the 'environmental valuation' class include: contingent valuation, cost-benefit analysis, hedonic analysis and multi-criteria analysis. The forms of sustainability assessment have been sub-classified as simple baseline qualifications, complex and advanced and very advanced evaluations. The simple baseline qualifications include: the AHP (analytical hierarchy process), compatibility matrix and eco-profiling measures carried out to support ecological footprinting exercises. They

Table 8.1 Assessment methods

Environmental valuations	Environmental, economic and social evaluations	
	Simple	Complex, advanced and very advanced
Contingent valuation	AHP	(Complex)
Cost-benefit analysis	Compatibility matrix	Regime analysis
Hedonic analysis	Ecological footprinting	(Advanced)
Multi-criteria analysis	Eco-profiling	BEES
Travel cost theory	Environmental auditing	BREEAM
	Flag method	Eco-points
	Spider analysis	Eco-prop
		Green Building Code
		LCA
		Meta-analysis (Pentagon Method)
		Multi-model analysis
		NAR model
		(Very Advanced)
		ASSIPAC
		AQM
		MASTER Framework
		Neighbourhood model
		Quantifiable City model
		SPARTACUS
		Sustainable city
		Sustainable communities
		Transit-orientated settlement
		W&D model

also include environmental auditing techniques required for such purposes. These exercises are also supported by the AHP method (analytical hierarchy process), flag method and spider analysis. The complex, advanced and very advanced methods include: BEES, BREEAM, Eco-points and the Green Building Code (complex). They also include: AQM, the MASTER Framework, the Pentagon model, the Quantifiable City model, regime analysis, SPARTACUS, the sustainable city model, sustainable communities, transit-orientated settlement and W&D models. Examples of these two classes and their evaluations are set out in Table 8.1.

The classification

The wide range of methods that exist for the assessment of SUD can be divided into five main classes in terms of the complexity and completeness of the overall evaluation they provide:

1   Environmental valuations, in the form of contingent valuation, cost-benefit analysis, travel cost, hedonic and multi-criteria analysis, to assess the environmental sustainability (in this instance, ecological integrity) of urban development.

2   Simple base-line or benchmarking methods to assess the environmental, economic and social issues underlying the policy commitment to SUD. Examples of such methods include the use of compatibility, eco-profiling and ecological footprinting exercises. They also include the use of environmental auditing techniques such as the flag method, or spider analysis.

3   More complex methods to assess whether the planning, property development, design and construction of infrastructure projects (servicing, energy, water and drainage, and transport) provide the environmental capacity (in this instance ecological integrity and equity) that is needed for the urban development process to carry the economic and social structures of cities.

4   Advanced methods that assess the contribution of construction to SUD, that is, how particular construction projects and installations – for example, energy systems, waste management provisions, repair and maintenance technologies – operate and what effect they have upon the environmental sustainability of cities. This includes an assessment of whether they have levels of energy consumption and emissions that have an adverse effect, or an impact which is more environmentally friendly – more environmentally friendly in the sense that the construction and operation of such installations augments, rather than diminishes, the environmental capacity (ecological integrity and equity) the urban development process has to carry the economic and social structures of cities. These evaluations include BREEAM (Building Research Establishment Environmental Assessment Method), Eco-points, the Green Building Code, the NAR (net annual return) model, Pentagon model and multi-model form of analysis.

5   Very advanced models that assess the ecological integrity and equity of the alternative developments which it is possible for the public to participate in and select as those designs, constructions and operations which augment, rather than diminish, the environmental capacity – in this instance, ecological integrity, equity, participation and futurity – of the urban development process and the ability it has to carry the economic and social structures of cities. These methods include ASSIPAC, AQM, the MASTER Framework, the Quantifiable City model, SPARTACUS, the sustainable city, sustainable communities, transit-orientated settlement and W&D models. They evaluate the environmental, economic and social sustainability of cities.

Irrespective of whether the environmental valuations are applied to policy planning, property development programmes, infrastructure designs, construction projects, or the installation of operations, the object of the 'environmental valuations' is to assess the ecological integrity of the sustainable development issues (natural resources, land use, pollution and bio-diversity) under consideration. With this class of assessment, it is also noticeable that any economic analysis is confined to the planning, property development and design stage of the policy, programme and infrastructure provision and does not extend into the construction of projects, or installation of operations. This is also the case for any social issues that surface from the application of such assessment methods. With the 'environmental, economic and social assessments' the situation is different. This is because these methods address development activities that run from planning through to operation and which evaluate the ecological integrity, equity, participation and futurity of the sustainability issues (including those surrounding the construction and installation of operations) in both economic and social terms. These assessments take SUD to include environmental sustainability, in terms of ecological integrity and the equity, participation and futurity of the building stock, transport, safety, security, health and well-being of the economic and social structures of cities. This is a key point because it is here that the assessment of SUD begins to become integrated, in the sense that environmental sustainability is evaluated in terms of the economic and social structures that underlie the city. These methods assess the environmental capacity – *ecological integrity, equity, participation and futurity* – of the urban development process in terms of the ability to build the stock, transport, safety, security, health and well-being (economic and social structures) that are needed for cities to institute a quality of life which is sustainable – in terms of the districts, neighbourhoods and estates which this process of urban development produces as forms of sustainable community.

However, it is also evident that most of the methods still fail to address the institutional issues which underlie the assessment of SUD. It is clear that in their current form the methods find it difficult to address issues relating to the governance, morality and ethics of the urban development process. The reasons for this are not currently known and require further investigation. It may be because most attention has been focused on environmental, economic and social issues and this has resulted in relative under-development of the institutional considerations. So it appears that if the assessment methods are to provide an appropriate basis for such evaluations, the governance, morality and ethics of the urban development also need to be integrated into assessments concerning the sustainability of cities. This is important because without an evaluation of the institutional structures it will not be possible to throw light on the consensus building, commitment and leadership issues surrounding the measures and actions taken to augment environmental capacity, and support the ecological integrity, equity, participation and futurity of the urban development process, with all this in turn means for the economic and social sustainability of cities.

CONCLUSIONS

All this suggests a great deal of headway has been made in progressing the theory, science and practice of assessment. This is because the survey and classification of the post-Bruntdland directory provides the evidence that is needed to counter the recent criticisms which have surfaced about environmental assessment methods. Being inter-disciplinary in nature and providing evidence of environmental, economic and social evaluations, the directory also goes some way to setting out the classes, type, range and spread of methods currently available to undertake an integrated assessment of SUD – and in turn throw light on what might best be referred to as the 'trans-disciplinary' issues underlying the sustainability of cities.

In addressing this particular matter, the chapter has found such trans-disciplinary issues lying in three of the advanced assessment methods: the quantifiable city, sustainable communities and transit-orientated settlement models. The trans-disciplinary issues are those of urban metabolism (quantifiable city model), urban sprawl, economic growth, competitiveness and the social cohesion of settlements. In addition to this, there are also issues raised about the transport and mobility of the urban development proposed in the sustainable communities and transit-orientated settlement models of SUD.

REFERENCES

Banister, D. and Button, K. (eds) (1993) *Transport, the Environment and Sustainable Development*, E & FN Spon, London; Island Press, Washington, DC.

Bentivegna, V., Curwell, S., Deakin, M., Lombardi, P., Mitchell, G. and Nijkamp, P. (2002) A vision and methodology for integrated sustainable urban development: BEQUEST, *Building Research and Information* 30(2).

Bentivegna, V. (1997) Limitations in environmental evaluations. In: Brandon, P., Lombardi, P., Bentivegna, V. (eds) *Evaluation of the Built Environment for Sustainability*, E&FN Spon, London.

Bergh, van den (ed.) (1997) *Meta Analysis in Environmental Economics*, Kluwer, Dordrecht.

Brandon, P., Lombardi, P. and Bentivegna, V. (1997a) *Evaluation of the Built Environment for Sustainability*, E&FN Spon, London.

Brandon, P., Lombardi, P., Bentivenga, V. (1997b) Introduction. In: Brandon, P., Lombardi, P. and Bentivegna, V. (eds) *Evaluation of the Built Environment for Sustainability*, E&FN Spon, London.

Capello, R., Nijkamp, P., Pepping, G. (1999) *Sustainable Cities and Energy Policies*, Springer-Verlag, Berlin.

Cole, R. (1997) Prioritising environmental criteria in building design. In: Brandon, P., Lombardi, P. and Bentivegna, V. (eds) *Evaluation of the Built Environment for Sustainability*, E&FN Spon, London.

Cooper, I. (1997) Environmental assessment methods for use at the building and city scale: constructing bridges or identifying common ground. In: Brandon, P., Lombardi, P. and Bentivenga, V. (eds) *Evaluation of the Built Environment for Sustainability*, E&FN Spon, London.

Cooper, I. (1999) Which focus for building assessment methods? *Building Research and Information* 27(4).

Cooper, I. (2000) Inadequate grounds for a 'design-led' approach to urban design, *Building Research and Information* 28(3).

Cooper, I. and Curwell, S. (1998) The implications of urban sustainability, *Building Research and Information* 26(1).

Curwell, S. and Deakin, M. (2002) Sustainable urban development and BEQUEST, *Building Research and Information* 30(2).

Curwell, S., Hamilton, A. and Cooper, I. (1998) The BEQUEST Network: towards sustainable urban development, *Building Research and Information* 26(1).

Curwell, S., Yates, A., Howard, N., Bordass., B. and Doggart, J. (1999) The green building challenge in the UK, *Building Research and Information* 27(4/5).

Davoudi, S. (1997) Economic development and environmental gloss: a new structure plan for Lancashire. In: Brandon, P., Lombardi, P., Bentivegna, V. (eds) *Evaluation of the Built Environment for Sustainability*, E&FN Spon, London.

Deakin, M. (1999) Valuation, appraisal, discounting, obsolescence and depreciation: towards a life cycle analysis and impact assessment of their effects on the environment of cities, *International Journal of Life Cycle Assessment* 4(2).

Deakin, M. (2000) Developing sustainable communities in Edinburgh's South East Wedge, *Journal of Property Management* 4(4).

Deakin, M. (2002) Modelling the development of sustainable communities in Edinburgh's South East Wedge, *Planning Practice and Research* 17(3).

Deakin, M., Curwell, S. and Lombardi, P. (2001) BEQUEST: the framework and directory of methods, *International Journal of Life Cycle Assessment* 6 (6).

Deakin, M., Curwell, S. and Lombardi, P. (2002a) Sustainable urban development: the framework and directory of assessment methods, *Journal of Environmental Assessment Policy and Management* 4(2).

Deakin, M., Huovila, P., Rao, S., Sunikka, M. and Vrekeer, R. (2002b) The assessment of sustainable urban development, *Building Research and Information* 30(2).

European Commission (EC) (2000) Common position of the Council on an amended proposal for a directive on the assessment of the effects of certain plans and programmes on the environment, *Official Journal of the European Communities*, No. C137, 16.5.00.

Faucheux, S. and O'Conner, M. (1998) Introduction. In: Faucheaux, S. and O'Conner, M. (eds) *Valuation for Sustainable Development*, Edward Elgar, Cheltenham.

Faucheux, S., Pearce, D. and Proops, J. (1997) Introduction. In: Faucheaux, S., Pearce, D. and Proops, J. (eds) *Models of Sustainable Development*, Edward Elgar, Cheltenham.

Fusco, L. and Nijkamp, P. (1997) *Le Valutazioni per lo Sviluppo Sostenibile della Città e del Territorio*, Angeli, Milan.

Graham, S. and Marvin, S. (1996) *Telecommunications and the City*, Routledge, London.

Guy, S. and Marvin, S. (1997) Splintering networks: cities and technical networks in 1990s Britain, *Urban Studies* 34(2).

Hamilton, A., Nitcell, G. and Yil-Karjanmaa, S. (2002) The BEQUEST Toolkit: a decision support system for urban sustainability, *Building Research and Information* 30(2): 109–115.

Jones, P., Vaughan, N., Cooke, P. and Sutcliffe, A. (1997) An energy and environmental prediction model for cities. In: Brandon, P., Lombardi, P. and Bentivegna, V. (eds) *Evaluation of the Built Environment for Sustainability*, E&FN Spon, London.

Marvin, S. and Guy, S. (1997) Infrastructure provision, development process and the co-production of environmental value, *Urban Studies* 34(12).

May, A., Mitchell, G. and Kupiszewska, D. (1997) The development of the Leeds quantifiable city model. In: Brandon, P., Lombardi, P. and Bentivenga, V. (eds) *Evaluation of the Built Environment for Sustainability*, E&FN Spon, London.

Mitchell, G., May, A. and McDonald, A. (1995) PICABUE: a methodological framework for the development of indicators of sustainable development, *International Journal of Sustainable Development World Ecology* 2.

Nijkamp, P. and Pepping, G. (1998) A meta-analytic evaluation of sustainable city initiatives, *Urban Studies* 35(9).

Nijkamp, P. and Perrels, A. (1994) *Sustainable Cities in Europe: A Comparative Analysis of Urban Energy and Environmental Policies*, Earthscan, London

O'Conner, M. (1998) Ecological-economic sustainability. In: Faucheaux, S. and O'Conner, M. (eds) *Valuation for Sustainable Development*, Edward Elgar, Cheltenham.

Palmer, J., Cooper, I. and van der Vost, R. (1997) Mapping out fuzzy buzzwords – who sits where on sustainability and sustainable development, *Sustainable Development* 5(2).

Prior, J. (1993) *Building Research Establishment Environment Assessment Method, BREEAM, Version 1/93, New Offices*, Building Research Establishment Report, Watford.

Therivel, R. (1998) Strategic environmental assessment of development plans in Great Britain, *Environmental Impact Assessment Review* 18(1).

UNCED – United Nations Conference on Environment and Development (1992) *Earth Summit 92 (Agenda 21)*, Regency Press, London.

Vale, B. and Vale, R. (1993) Building the sustainable environment. In: Blowers, A. (ed.) *Planning for a Sustainable Environment*, Earthscan, London.

WCED (Brundtland Commission) (1987) *Our Common Future*, United Nations, New York.

William, P., Anderson, P. and Kanaroglou, E. (1996) Urban form, energy and the environment: a review of issues, evidence and policy, *Urban Studies* 33,(1).

9

Assessing the Sustainability of Urban Development
Mark Deakin and Patrizia Lombardi

The post-Brundtland directory of environmental assessment outlined in the previous chapter provides the evidence that is needed to counter much of the recent criticism which has recently surfaced about evaluating the sustainability of urban development. Being inter-disciplinary in nature, the directory of environmental assessment also goes some way to setting out the classes, type and range of methods currently available to carry out such evaluations. The object of this chapter is to examine how the environmental assessment methods in question have been applied in evaluating the sustainability of urban development. This will be done by:

- studying the results of an exercise that has been undertaken by BEQUEST to map out the extent to which the assessment methods making up the post-Brundtland directory evaluate the sustainability of urban development;
- providing an example of how the assessment methods have been applied to evaluate one of the sustainable urban development issues;
- examining the findings of the said exercises and the degree to which it is possible to suggest that the evaluations in question offer the opportunity to carry out an integrated assessment of SUD;
- reflecting on whether this transformation of environmental assessment builds the environmental capacity needed to sustain cities.

THE MAPPING EXERCISE

Figure 9.1 maps how the methods have been applied to assess the sustainability of all the urban development issues. The exercise maps the applications by interrelated activities (planning, property development, design, construction and operation) of the urban development process, sustainability (environmental, economic, social and institutional) issues, spatial level and time frames. These are the issues, spatial level and time frames that form the subject of the assessment and which are carried out with the object of evaluating the sustainability of urban development.

The exercise illustrates how the said classes and types of assessments are represented across the range of activities making up the sustainability of the urban development process. The purpose of mapping the assessment methods by such

		Planning	Property development	Design	Construction	Operation
Sustainable development issues	Environmental					
	Economic					
	Social					
	Institutional					
Spatial level	City					
	District					
	Neighbourhood					
	Estate					
	Building					
	Component					
Time frames	Long					
	Medium					
	Short					

Policies
Programmes
Infrastructures
Projects
Installations

Note: This shows the results of the mapping exercise carried out on twenty of the assessment methods. The shading shown is indicative of the 'intensity scores', or 'frequency' with which each method addresses the sustainable urban development issues, spatial level and time frames of assessment. The shadings score the frequency with which the assessment methods address the issues in terms of high, medium, low and no representation. The five degrees of shading roughly approximate to 75–100%, 50–75%, 25–50% and 0% representation of the issues at the specified spatial level and time frames.

9.1 Mapping of the assessment methods

co-ordinates is fourfold. First, it illustrates the range and spread of methods currently available. Second, it provides the means to identify how the assessment methods are being used. Third, it identifies the strength of representation by sustainable development issue, spatial level and time frame. Fourth, it draws attention to the gaps that exist in the range and spread of methods which are needed to provide an integrated (environmental, economic and social) assessment of SUD. The exercise also provides the opportunity to direct further research aimed at developing the methodology of such assessments.

What the mapping exercise suggests is that the scientific and professional communities are using the assessment methods needed to evaluate the sustainability of urban development. It provides evidence to suggest that a range of assessment methods is being used to evaluate whether the urban development process has the capacity – i.e. urban planning policies, property development programmes, infrastructure designs, construction projects and operational installations – needed for the built environment to carry the economic and social structures underlying the city. The exercise also illustrates that it is the sustainable development issues, spatial levels and time frames of the urban planning policies, property development programmes and infrastructure design activities, which are the most strongly represented forms of assessment. This is because the other forms of assessment (construction and operation) are not as well covered in terms of sustainable development issues, spatial level, or time frame (see Figure 9.1). This suggests that the gaps which exist in the range and spread of methods needed to provide an integrated assessment of SUD are located here in the construction of projects and operation of installations.

It should be noted that Figure 9.1 does not map how the assessment methods evaluate the ecological integrity, equity, participation and futurity issues underlying the sustainability of the urban development process. To be explicit about this further analysis will need to be carried out. This will need to extend the analysis beyond the matrix-based mapping set out in Figure 9.1 and introduce a more comprehensive grid-referencing system. One that can map the sustainability issues, spatial levels and time frames as shown, but also go on to cross-reference these evaluations with the ecological integrity, equity, participation and futurity components of the assessment methods. While this would be one line of enquiry for the mapping exercise to adopt in furthering our knowledge of the environmental assessment methods, it is not one the following discussion chooses to take. Instead the rest of this chapter chooses to revisit the mapping exercise and look again at the underlying issues. This is done for the following reasons:

- It provides the opportunity to take a further look at the issues underlying SUD and how the environmental assessment methods have sought to evaluate them.
- It allows for a more in-depth study of how a particular underlying issue has been tackled by the environmental assessment methods and what has been subject to an evaluation.
- It evaluates whether the urban development process has the capacity (urban planning policies, property development programmes, infrastructure designs, construction projects and operational installations) needed for the built environment to carry the city's underlying economic and social structures.
- It evaluates if the built environment is able to carry the city's underlying economic and social structures and do so in sustainable forms of settlement.

This will be tackled by providing an example of how the assessment methods have been used to evaluate the sustainability of a particular urban development issue. The example in question concerns the evaluation of the transportation and utilities issues surrounding the sustainability of urban development.

Table 9.1 draws attention to the evaluation of the transport and utility issues surrounding the sustainability of urban development. As can be seen, the left-hand column uses the post-Brundtland directory of environmental assessment to classify the methods. The right-hand column goes on to highlight the transport and mobility-related issues the assessment methods address in evaluating – in this instance – the

Table 9.1 Assessment methods for evaluating the transport-related issues

Assessment methods	Evaluation of the transport-related issues
Environmental valuations	
Contingent valuation	Value of 'clean air', pollutant-free emissions, amenity and bio-diversity
Cost-benefit analysis	Value of transport-related planning and development
Hedonic analysis	Effect of noise and emissions on land and property values, health and well-being
Multi-criteria analysis	(as cost benefit analysis and contingent value)
Travel cost theory	(ditto)
Environmental, economic and social assessments:	
Simple	
Compatibility matrix	Compatibility of land-use development plans with transport investment programmes
Eco-profiling	–
Ecological footprint	Effect of growth on energy consumption, air quality and emissions
Environmental auditing	(as ecological footprint)
Flag method	Benchmarking of the effects noise and emissions have on the environment
Spider analysis	Measuring the 'interconnections' between transport and other land-use development plans
Complex and advanced	
Strategic:	
• environmental	Impact of transport investment programmes on the environment
• economic	Impact of traffic management schemes on land and property values
• social	Value of car-free environments on health and well-being
Community evaluation	Adverse impact of transport investment programmes on traffic flow, safety and economic security and social cohesion
BEES	–
BREEAM	Impact of building and infrastructure design on transport demand, energy efficiency and environmental emissions

Eco-points	–
Green Building Code	–
ASSIPAC	Impact of transportation networks on the environment
MASTER Framework	Appraisal of transport-related planning polices
Meta-analysis (Pentagon method)	–
NAR model	Effect of (re)development programmes on transport demand
Regime analysis	Impact of transport investment on economic competitiveness and social cohesion
Very advanced	
Quantifiable City model	Impact of emissions on eco-system, health and well-being
SPARTACUS	Effect of alternative transport policies
Sustainable city model	Environmental benefits (cleaner air, reduced emissions) of reductions in 'car dependency', increased public transport provision and road pricing
Sustainable communities	Effects of high-level public transport provision on the environment and benefits of energy-efficient forms of mobility
Sustainable regions	Impact of major transportation investment programmes on economic growth, employment and output
Transit-orientated settlement	Economic and social impact of 'reduced trip', energy-efficient and 'environmentally friendly' settlement patterns

Source: Deakin (2003)

sustainability of transport and utilities-related urban development. It serves to highlight the classes, range and extent of assessment methods made use of to evaluate the sustainability of transport and utility-related urban development. For, as can be seen, the evaluations carried out use both classes of assessment method and cut across a whole range of issues. What is noticeable is that the assessment methods are not limited to environmental valuations (ecological integrity) but include those which extend to environmental, economic and social assessments (covering ecological integrity, equity, participation and futurity) – the assessment methods whose respective interests rest with air quality pollution issues etc. (ecological integrity), growth, efficiency, employment, health and well-being (economic and social). As such it demonstrates the respective capabilities of the assessment methods in terms of what they can evaluate.

Under the BEQUEST framework, transport and utility-related issues are classified as primarily economic. However, if we compare this with the classification of the environmental assessment methods, it is evident that the secondary impacts are much wider than this and require evaluations which are environmental, economic and social (see Table 9.1). While at first this may appear alarming – the fact that transport and utility-related matters tend to ignore the environment, and focus on the economic at the expense of the social – it ought not to be seen as a matter of particular concern. This is because while the issues surrounding transport and utility provision may be seen as primarily economic, the framework links them to the secondary impacts, first on the environment and then on both the economy and society. As such it provides a framework of analysis that allows us to get around seeing such matters too narrowly and view them as environmental, economic and social issues. This wider vision is further reinforced by the protocols that allow us to scope the issues in such terms and screen their impacts as part of a methodology for an integrated assessment – an assessment that connects the environmental, economic and social in the evaluations which are carried out to tackle such issues.

It should perhaps also be pointed out that this is not unique to transport and utility-related issues, but indicative of all the issues which underlie the sustainability of urban development. This is because, irrespective of what issues are under consideration, it is this line of reasoning that underlies the framework's vision and methodology of an integrated SUD and protocols supporting the environmental assessments which are undertaken to evaluate the sustainability of urban development not only in environmental, but also economic and social terms.

Turning our attention back to the matter of transport and utility-related issues, perhaps the first thing to note from Table 9.1 is the range of assessment methods that are available to evaluate the transport and utility-related issues, along with the spread of evaluations carried out and the extent to which they are tackled – first of all as environmental valuations, as with the use of cost-benefit analysis to evaluate transport-related planning and development. Then, secondly, as environmental, economic and social evaluations: for example, as seen with the use of assessment methods by the sustainable communities model of SUD and with the evaluation of the effects public transport provision has not only on the environment, but also in terms of the economic and social benefits it brings in the form of more energy-efficient mobility.

THE FINDINGS

From the mapping exercise and case study example, it is evident that a number of assessment methods exist to evaluate the sustainability of urban development and these include:

- Environmental valuations in the form of cost-benefit analysis, contingent valuation, travel cost, hedonic and multi-criteria analysis, to assess the environmental sustainability (in this instance, ecological integrity) of urban development.

- Simple baseline methods to assess the environmental, economic and social issues underlying the policy commitment to SUD. Examples of such methods appear under the title of simple base-line evaluations and include: the use of compatibility, eco-profiling and ecological footprinting exercises. They also include the use of environmental auditing techniques, the flag method and a spider analysis exercise.
- The use of more complex methods to assess whether the planning, property development, design and construction of infrastructure projects (servicing energy, water and drainage, transport, telecommunication technologies, leisure and tourism) provide the city of tomorrow with the capacity (in this instance, ecological integrity and equity) that is needed to carry its cultural heritage. Examples of such methods include project, strategic, economic, social and community evaluations.
- The development of advanced methods that assess what the construction and installation of particular operations contribute to SUD. How, that is, particular construction projects and installations – for example, energy systems, waste management provisions, repair and maintenance technologies – operate and what effect they have upon the environmental sustainability of urban development. Whether they have levels of energy consumption and emissions that have an adverse effect, or an impact which is more environmentally friendly – in the sense that the construction and operation of such installations augments, rather than diminishes, the capacity (ecological integrity, and equity) which the built environment has to sustain the city's economic and social structures.

  These evaluations include BREEAM, Eco-points, the Green Building Code and the NAR (net annual return) model.
- The emergence of very advanced methods that assess (at the level of policy planning) the ecological integrity and equity of the alternative developments which it is possible for the public to participate in and select those designs, constructions and operations that augment, rather than diminish, the capacity (in this instance, ecological integrity, equity, participation and futurity) which the environment has to sustain the city's building stock, transport, safety, security, health and well-being (economic and social structures). Furthermore, to do so in forms of settlement (districts, neighbourhoods and estates) that institute a quality of life which is in turn sustainable.

  These methods include ASSIPAC, the MASTER Framework, the Pentagon model, the Quantitative City model, SPARTACUS, the sustainable city, sustainable region, sustainable communities and transit-orientated settlement models.

Environmental valuations

Irrespective of whether the methods in question are applied to policy planning, property development programmes, infrastructure design, construction projects, or the installation of operations, the object of the 'environmental valuations' is to assess the ecological integrity of the sustainable development issues (natural resources, land use, pollution and bio-diversity) under consideration. With this class of assessment, it is also noticeable that any economic analysis is confined to the planning, property development and design stage of the policy, programme and infrastructure provision and does not extend into the construction of projects, or installation of operations. This is also the case for any social issues that surface from the application of such assessment methods.

Environmental, economic and social assessments

With the 'environmental, economic and social assessments' the situation is different. This is because with these assessments there is evidence to suggest that the assessment methods cover the planning, property development, design, construction and operational stages and go on to evaluate the ecological integrity, equity, participation and futurity of the sustainability issues (including those surrounding the construction and installation of operations) in economic and social terms. This in turn suggests such evaluations take SUD to include environmental sustainability in terms of eco-system integrity *and* the equity, participation and futurity of the building stock, transport, safety, security, health and well-being (economic and social structures) underlying the city.

The findings of the mapping exercise and case study provide evidence to suggest that it is here – with the methods which are adopted to evaluate the environmental sustainability of the economic and social structures underlying the city – that the assessment of SUD becomes integrated – integrated in the sense that the assessment methods evaluate environmental sustainability *in terms of* the economic and social structures which underlie the city.

Institutional issues

From the mapping exercise it is evident that most of the applications fail to address the institutional issues underlying the assessment of SUD. It is clear that, in their current form, the methods find it difficult to address issues relating to the governance, morality and ethics of the urban development process. The reasons for this are not currently known and will require further investigation. It may be because most attention has focused on environmental, economic and social issues and this has resulted in a relative under-development of the institutional considerations. However, it would appear that if the environmental, economic and social issues of SUD are to provide an appropriate basis for such assessments, the governance, morality and ethics of the urban process also need to be integrated into the exercise.

Spatial configurations and time horizons

The mapping exercise also shows that both classes of assessment relate to particular spatial configurations and time horizons. With the environmental valuations there is evidence to suggest that the spatial configuration rests with the city and its districts. With the environmental, economic and social assessments, it is evident that the simple baseline and complex evaluations tend to be more explicit about the spatial configuration of SUD and extend to the city, district, neighbourhood, estate, building and component levels of analysis. It is also noticeable that it is the advanced methods which assess the regional, cumulative national, growing international and global sustainability of urban development over the long, medium and short term. This suggests that the advanced assessment methods appreciate the need for a pan-European understanding of the urban development process. This in turn recognises the need to develop methods that are urban in the sense that they transcend the city and assess the regional, cumulative national, growing international and global issues that SUD faces.

THE POST-BRUNDTLAND TRANSFORMATION OF ENVIRONMENTAL ASSESSMENT

It is also common to see the methods of environmental valuation embedded in and providing the foundation for the type and range of evaluations undertaken in the other (in this instance, environmental, economic and social) class of assessments. This is common irrespective of whether the assessment is of the simple, complex, or advanced type. Examples of this occur with the use of cost-benefit analysis in simple and advanced forms of evaluation (Glasson *et al.* 1994, Lichfield 1996, Therivel 1998, Deakin 1997, 1999). It is also evident in the use of the multiple-regression component of the hedonic technique – the technique forming the meta-analysis of policy planning, property development and infrastructure design (Bergh *et al.* 1997, Nijkamp and Pepping 1998). Another example of this can also be found in the transformation of multi-criteria assessments into regime analysis and the use of this technique to support actions taken over the development of property and the design of infrastructures (Bizarro and Nijkamp 1997).

There is also evidence to suggest that this 'post-Brundtland' transformation of environmental valuation is mediated through other assessment methods – methods that take on the function of mechanisms which support the transformation as part of the search for an integrated assessment of SUD. This is evident in the use of the analytical hierarchy process to transform CBA both in environmental appraisal (the flag method) and in the impact assessments undertaken as part of regime analysis. It is also seen in the use of life-cycle analysis to transform CBA into the NAR model – the model also adopted for the assessment of sustainable communities. Another observation that can be drawn from this transformation relates to the way in which the 'hard' and 'soft' issues of sustainable development form part of the assessment methodology. With methods of sustainability assessment – for example, BEES and the quantifiable city model – the bio-physical aspects of the eco-system are the main issues. Here the sustainable development issues under assessment are those of energy consumption, material flows, waste and pollution. This is also the case for the quantifiable city model. While useful in focusing attention on eco-system integrity, it should perhaps also be noted that such methods do not integrate either the economic or the social to the same degree that other assessments have managed to do. Methods that manage to integrate the bio-physical aspects of the eco-system within an economic and social assessment include: BREEAM, the MASTER Framework, SPARTACUS, sustainable communities, city, region and transit-orientated settlement models.

PROGRESS MADE

It should be recognised that the mapping exercise suggests a great deal of headway has been made in progressing the theory, science and practice of assessment. This is because the survey of methods, classification of assessment and mapping exercise provide the evidence that is needed to counter the recent criticism which has surfaced about environmental assessment. Being inter-disciplinary in nature and providing evidence of environmental, economic and social evaluations, the mapping exercise also goes some way to set out the classes, type, range and spread of methods currently available to undertake an integrated assessment of SUD and which in turn throw light on what might best be referred to as the trans-disciplinary issues currently underlying the sustainability of urban development.

In addressing this particular matter, the mapping exercise has found such trans-disciplinary issues lying in three of the advanced assessment methods: the quantifiable city, sustainable communities and transit-orientated settlement models. The trans-disciplinary issues are those of urban metabolism (quantifiable city model), urban sprawl, economic growth, competitiveness and social cohesion (sustainable communities model), and mobility questions the aforesaid issues in turn raise about urban development (transit-orientated settlement model). However, by way of a qualification to this finding, it ought perhaps to be also recognised that the following tend to restrict the degree of progress which has been made in advancing the theory, method and practice of assessment. These factors are:

- The need to extend the analysis beyond the matrix-based mapping set out in this chapter and to introduce a more comprehensive grid-referencing system – one that can not only map the urban development process in terms of the sustainability issues, spatial levels and temporal scale, but cross-reference them with the ecological integrity, equity, participation and futurity components of the assessment.
- The tendency for the policy planning, programmes of property development and infrastructure design considerations to overshadow the assessment needs of the construction and installation stages (Cooper 1997, 1999, 2000, Deakin 2000, 2002).
- The relative absence of any institutional assessment.
- The paucity of environmental, economic and social (sustainable urban development) indicators it is possible to draw upon as a means of benchmarking the effect planning policies, property development programmes, infrastructure designs, construction projects and installations have upon the sustainability of urban development (Mitchell *et al.* 1995, Mitchell 2000).
- The fact that this in turn makes it difficult – in methodological terms – to assess the aggregate effect policy planning, property development programmes, infrastructure designs, construction projects and the installation of operations have upon attempts to sustain cities and carry their economic and social structures in forms of settlement which are sustainable in terms of the quality of life which they institute (Cooper 2000).

These are seen as being restrictive because they tend to highlight the rather limited nature of the data-sets currently available to provide an integrated assessment of SUD.

CONCLUSIONS

This chapter has examined the questions that have surfaced over the use of assessment methods to evaluate the sustainability of urban development. It has suggested that the assessment methods in question fall into two classes: 'environmental valuations' and 'environmental, economic and social assessments' of SUD. It has proposed that the valuations which have been carried out tend to focus on assessing environmental sustainability in terms of eco-system integrity. The chapter has also proposed that the 'environmental, economic and social assessments' are different. It has suggested that this is because there is evidence to suggest these methods provide a more integrated assessment of SUD – more integrated in the sense that they take SUD to include environmental sustainability in terms of eco-system integrity

BOX 9.1

List of assessment methods (19 September 2000)

Analysis of Interconnected Decision Areas (AIDA)
Analytic Hierarchy Process (AHP)
ASSIPAC (Assessing the Sustainability of Societal Initiatives and Proposed
    Agendas for Change)
ATHENA
BEPAC
BRE Environmental Assessment Method (BREEAM)
BRE Environmental Management Toolkits
Building Energy Environment (BEE 1.0)
Building Environmental Assessment and Rating System (BEARS)
Building for Economic and Environmental Sustainability (BEES 2:0)
Cluster Evaluation
Community Impact Evaluation
Concordance Analysis
Contingent Valuation Method
Cost-Benefit Analysis
Eco-Effect
Eco-Indicator '95
Eco-Instal
Economic Impact Assessment
Ecological Footprint
Eco-points
Ecopro
Eco-Profile
EcoProP
Eco-Quantum
ENVEST
Environmental Impact Analysis
Environmental Impact Assessment
Environmental Profiles (The BRE Methodology for Environmental Profiles of
    Construction Materials, Components and Building Materials)
EQUER
ESCALE

Financial Evaluation of Sustainable Communities
Flag Model
Green Building Code
Hedonic analysis
Green Guide to Specification (An Environmental Profiling System for Building
 Materials and Components)
Hochbaukonstruktionen nach ökologischen Gesichtspunkten (SIA D0123)
INSURED
Leadership in Energy and Environmental Design Green Building Rating System
 (LEEDTM)
Life Cycle Analysis (LCA)
Mass Intensity Per Service Unit (MIPS)
MASTER Framework
Meta Regression Analysis
Multi-criteria Analysis
Net Annual Return (NAR) Model
Optimierung der Gesamtanforderungen (Kosten/Energie/Umwelt) ein Instrument
 für die Integrale Planung (OGIP)
PAPOOSE
PIMWAQ
Project Impact Assessment
Regime Analysis
Quantitative City Model
Planning Balance Sheet Analysis
Risk Assessment Method(s)
SANDAT
Semantic Differential
Social Impact Assessment
SPARTACUS
Sustainable Cities
Sustainable Regions
Transit-oriented Settlement
Travel Cost Theory

and the equity, public participation and futurity of the economic and social structures that underlie the city. The chapter went on to suggest that it is here that the environmental, economic and social assessments which are carried out become integrated – in the sense that the assessment methods which are made use of evaluate environmental sustainability in terms of the economic and social structures underlying the city.

While the chapter has gone some way to counter the recent criticism of environmental assessment by showing how existing methods provide the opportunity to evaluate the sustainability of urban development plans, programmes and projects, by outlining the trans-disciplinary issues underlying such matters it has also sought to highlight some of the problems associated with the use of the assessment methods. In this respect, it has been recognised that methods able to overcome such difficulties and build the environmental capacity needed to sustain the city are currently in the research phase, and the tools which are needed for a fully integrated assessment of SUD are still some years away. In the meantime, the toolkit being developed by BEQUEST (see Hamilton *et al.* 2002) provides a decision support system able to assist with such actions. It enables the appropriate assessment methods to be selected and used for the purposes of evaluating the sustainability of urban development.

REFERENCES

Bergh, J., Button, K., Nijkamp, P. and Pepping, G. (1997) *Meta-Analysis of Environmental Policies*, Kleuwer, Dordrecht.

Rizarro, F. and Nijkamp, P. (1997) Integrated conservation of cultural built heritage. In: Brandon, P., Lombardi, P. and Bentivegna V. (eds) *Evaluation of the Built Environment for Sustainability*, E&FN Spon, London.

Cooper, I. (1997) Environmental assessment methods for use at the building and city scale: constructing bridges or identifying common ground. In: Brandon, P., Lombardi, P. and Bentivegna, V. (eds) *Evaluation of the Built Environment for Sustainability*, E&FN Spon, London.

Cooper, I. (1999) Which focus for building assessment methods? *Building Research and Information* 27(4).

Cooper, I. (2000) Inadequate grounds for a 'design-led' approach to urban design, *Building Research and Information* 28(3).

Deakin, M. (1997) An economic evaluation and appraisal of the effects land use, building obsolescence and depreciation have on the environment of cities. In: Brandon, P., Lombardi, P., Bentivenga, V. (eds) *Evaluation of the Built Environment for Sustainability*, E&FN Spon, London.

Deakin, M. (1999) Valuation, appraisal, discounting, obsolescence and depreciation: towards a life cycle analysis and impact assessment of their effects on the environment of cities, *International Journal of Life Cycle Assessment*, 4(2).

Deakin, M. (2000) Developing sustainable communities in Edinburgh's South East Wedge, *Journal of Property Management*, 4(4).

Deakin, M. (2002) Modelling the development of sustainable communities in Edinburgh's South East Wedge, *Planning Practice and Research* 17(3).

Deakin, M. (2003) The new deal for transport: the BEQUEST protocol for assessing the sustainability of urban development, in Hine, J. and Preston, J. (eds) *Integrated Futures and Transport Choices*, Ashgate, Aldershot .

Glasson, J., Therival, R. and Chadwick, A. (1994) *Environmental Impact Assessment*, University College London, London.

Hamilton, A., Mitchell, G. and Yil-Karjanmaa, S. (2002) The BEQUEST Toolkit: a decision support system for urban sustainability 20(2).

Lichfield, N. (1996) *Community Impact Evaluation*, University College London, London.

Mitchell, G. (2000) Indicators as tools to guide progress on the sustainable development pathway. In: Lawrence, R. (ed.) *Sustaining Human Settlements: Economy, Environment, Equity and Health*, Urban International Press, London.

Mitchell, G., May, A. and Mcdonald, A. (1995) PICABUE: a methodological framework for the development of indicators of sustainable development, *International Journal of Sustainable Development World Ecology* 2.

Nijkamp, P. and Pepping, G. (1998) A meta-analytic evaluation of sustainable city initiatives, *Urban Studies* 35 (9).

Therivel, R. (1998) Strategic environmental assessment of development plans in Great Britain, *Environmental Impact Assessment Review* 18(1).

Part IV

The Assessment Community

10

Networked Communities, Virtual Organisations and the Production of Knowledge
Ian Cooper, Andy Hamilton and Vincenzo Bentivegna

This chapter examines the scientific and professional community undertaking evaluations of the sustainability of urban development. It illustrates that this is becoming a 'networked' community, displaying the characteristics of an interdisciplinary 'virtual organisation', using decision support systems that, in turn, require underpinning by modern communications and information technology. Using BEQUEST as an example, the chapter focuses attention on the interdisciplinary nature of this networked community, operating as a virtual organisation in order to develop the decision support system for integrated sustainable urban development described in this book. It argues that the development of the 'post-Brundtland' approaches to integrated environmental assessment set out in the previous chapters of this volume depends on the emergence – and successful operation of – such communities. The communication systems underpinning these developments have been, and will continue to be, supported by web-based information technology. The decisions that need to be taken cannot be made without it and the involvement of all appropriate sectors of society in the making of these decisions cannot be sustained without it.

The chapter also places BEQUEST within the context of a discussion that has arisen, within the last decade, about the so-called 'new production of knowledge'. Where such production occurs, short-life interdisciplinary teams collaborate by engaging in a dynamic form of research characterised by practical problem-solving through negotiated and consensually produced knowledge. In BEQUEST, such knowledge production was electronically mediated – collaboration and dissemination occurred predominantly over the internet. Attention is drawn to BEQUEST's modus operandi for dealing with contentious issues – sustainable development, interdisciplinary working, and the design and management of virtual organisations. The chapter closes by commenting on the implications of crossing discipline boundaries and electronically mediated working for the organisation and conduct of research and practice in the production and management of the built environment.

COMMUNICATIONS TECHNOLOGIES AND SUSTAINABLE URBAN DEVELOPMENT

Information communication technologies (ICTs) loom large in the European Union's policies for sustainable development. Much hangs on their assumed capacity to generate and maintain more sustainable patterns of living and working. Their capacity for transformation has been evoked to tackle three EU policy imperatives:

* economic competitiveness
* social inclusion
* environmental sustainability

And ICTs are expect to deliver this transformation on at least four spatial scales:

* the EU as a whole
* its regions
* cities
* individual workplaces.

At the highest of these spatial scales, for example, the EU is committed to creating a European Research Area (ERA) through networking existing centres of excellence in Europe to act as 'virtual centres through the use of new interactive communications' (EC Research Directorate 2002). This is necessary (Lawton 2002) to redress 'the fragmentation of the European research community' as well as to capture 'the richness and synergies that working internationally can bring'. The current Framework Six Programme has been identified as an important instrument for implementing the ERA – as the primary mechanism for 'integrating research efforts and activities on a European scale' (EC Research Directorate 2002). The aim here is:

> to create rapid growth based on world-class research and innovation [by agreeing] to focus the bulk of Community money on supporting research in a small number of crucial areas key to the EU's ability to compete on the world stage in the coming years . . . [by creating] a critical mass across the EU in key frontier technologies such as . . . information technology.
>
> (Sainsbury 2002)

In this formulation, ICTs are both means and end. They are not only the means of achieving the desired integration of the ERA, they will also be one of its principal areas of activity. However, as the Director of the European Research Area has acknowledged (Escritt 2002), if an integrated ERA is to be achieved, Framework Six will need to deliver a 'structuring effect' by promoting capacity building in 'human resources, mobility, and infrastructures'.

ICTs are seen as crucial at the regional scale too. For instance, they are cast in the role of making not just cities, but whole regions, more economically and socially sustainable. According to Dabinett, the EU sought to mainstream ICTs into regional development policy during the 1990s because:

> The key issue is the pace and scale of these developments within the EU, as the use of ICTs will continue to play a global role in creating new markets, opportunities and wealth over the next decade.
>
> (2001: 168)

However, the impact of ICTs on regional development remains contested. For example, Christie and Hepworth have argued:

> In many visions of the new economy, geography is seen as something to be transcended by technology. The electronic revolution brings about the 'death of distance' and ICTs free us to work anywhere, tele-commuting and connecting effortlessly with people and websites around the planet. Perhaps it will turn out this way; but for the moment, this vision of the irrelevance of geography is quite wrong. Place matters, and it has a significant bearing on the social and environmental sustainability of the emerging information economy.
>
> (2001: 140–1)

As they pointed out, 'e-commerce' could be a powerful vehicle for sustainable development but:

> it has no intrinsic dynamic that makes it socially equitable or environmentally friendly in terms of its impact on living patterns. The e-economy maps on to the existing geography of car-intensive commuting. If it is to become more socially inclusive, and if its potential for contributing to more environmentally sustainable lifestyles is to be harnessed, policy will need to be devised to shape its evolution in a more positive direction.

ICTs are also central to EU policy on bringing about social inclusion in cities because, as Van Winden observed:

> Currently, a new optimism can be observed about the possibilities of fighting social exclusion, mainly based on the seemingly endless opportunities of information and communications technology. . . . [But] The degree to which the new opportunities of ICT can be capitalized on depends to a large extent on the capacity of urban management to influence the population's uptake and application of ICT.
>
> (2001: 861)

This too is unlikely to be simple to achieve. As Norton has commented:

> The challenge of digital inclusion is like a Russian doll. Each time you try to solve an issue, and thus open up the doll, there is another issue inside. Once physical access to the internet is resolved, the next challenge is access to payment systems for those who, through personal choice or exclusion, exist outside conventional banking and hold no debt or credit cards. Once this is resolved, there is the question of functional illiteracy, building voice and picture-based systems to support the surprisingly large minority in the UK who cannot easily use existing systems.
>
> (2001: 163–4)

ICTs are also seen as a major driving force for economic and social change in the workplace by the EU's Advisory Group on the Information Society:

> Many tasks that were once exclusive to particular locations can now be performed anywhere in the world. ICT have overcome the barriers of distance and time and economic activity is becoming characterised by a close and complex cross-border networking of commercial transactions. . . . As we move further into a service and information-based economy, the challenge is to ensure that it is an information society that is economically, socially and environmentally sustainable. ICT can provide an essential contribution to an increase in resource productivity and dematerialization.
>
> (IST 1999: 4)

There is, the Advisory Group argued:

> a widespread belief that ICT necessarily leads to sustainability [but] this is not an automatic result. ICT can as well harm the social quality of organisations (e.g. by increasing stress, centralising control mechanisms, etc), can increase energy consumption (e.g. by stimulating travelling, changing settlement patterns, etc), and can harm the environment (cf. the explosive increase in the use of computers, of electrical energy and paper, and the by-products resulting from the increased travelling).
>
> (ibid.: 6)

These unwanted increases, it argued, will have to be countered through the introduction of more sustainable workplaces. However, at present, the Advisory Group acknowledged: 'the dynamic effects of ICT-supported sustainable development are not yet well understood' (ibid.: 5).

Given the breadth and depth of the EU ambitions listed above, it is difficult to exaggerate the importance of successful exploitation of ICTs to the delivery of sustainable urban development in Europe.

But ICTs have become important to the delivery of sustainable development in another crucial sense too. When they reviewed for the Planning Directorate of the Department of the Environment, Transport and the Regions the policy relevance of the research undertaken for the UK's Sustainable Cities programme, Cooper and Palmer concluded that:

> the impact of variables under consideration in sustainable urban development is highly interactive and inter-dependent. Decision-making mechanisms and support systems, used to formulate, implement, and monitor sustainable development policies and practices need to be able to encompass this inter-dependency.

> (1999: 113)

To achieve the required levels of integration, they argued, such decision support systems need to be computer-based and capable of drawing on output from complex 'what if' scenarios.

Subsequent EU-funded research has pursued this line of development. The INTELCITY roadmap (Curwell *et al.* 2003) has explored new opportunities for sustainable development of cities through the intelligent use of information and communication technologies (ICTs). The INTELCITY network integrated the knowledge of experts in sustainable urban development (SUD) and ICTs to deliver a roadmap that related the range of potential ICT development options to planning and urban re/development processes. This roadmap culminated in the vision of an e-gora – a communally shared place in virtual space where professionals, citizens, and their elected representatives can engage in more inclusive dialogue about how best to develop cities more sustainably. Implementation of this vision is currently being pursued with major European cities through the INTELCITIES project, funded by the EU under its Framework Six Programme (INTELCITIES 2004).

Yet experience in BEQUEST suggested that successful dialogue and decision making through the use of ICTs cannot be taken for granted. The exploitation of ICTs will have to be explicitly and carefully managed. The remainder of this chapter offers one particular instance of the specific and critical attention that needs to be given to developing and disseminating 'good practice' advice on how to exploit ICTs for virtual teamworking in a manner that does not impact adversely on sustainability.

BEQUEST AS AN EXAMPLE OF INTERDISCIPLINARY WORKING

An embryonic BEQUEST network existed before the partnership described in this book. As noted earlier, it arose out of a conference on evaluating the sustainability of the built environment held in Florence in 1995 (Brandon *et al.* 1997). This conference identified discipline-based factors that both unite and divide those involved in assessing urban sustainability. For instance, specific differences were suggested (Cooper 1997: 4) in the predominant focus of attention of those operating at the building scale (architects and engineers) and at the city scale (planners). The BEQUEST network was intended not just to bridge such differences, but to build a shared platform across these disciplines for assessing sustainable urban development (SUD). This underlying motivation explains the network's emphasis on creating consensus – on developing a common language and on constructing a shared analytical framework for SUD (see Chapter 2).

According to Thompson Klein (1996: 1), who conducted a detailed review of the extent and occurrence of 'interdisciplinarity', two claims about knowledge are widely made today:

- Knowledge is increasingly interdisciplinary.
- The crossing of discipline boundaries has now become a defining characteristic of production of knowledge.

As a result, she contended (ibid.: 2), the interactions and re-organisations that boundary crossing creates are now as central to the production and organisation of knowledge as boundary formation and maintenance had been previously. Yet mapping interdisciplinary activity remains difficult because interdisciplinary activities 'compose a complex and contradictory set of practices' that are located along 'shifting co-ordinates'. As a consequence, she argued (ibid.: 52–3), the implications of boundary permeations are significant but are not immediately apparent because 'the boundaries of fields are not always easy to discriminate'. In other words, how, when and how discipline boundaries are crossed, in the production of knowledge, is now highly important but remains difficult to discern. As BEQUEST illustrates (Cooper 2002a), this is particularly evident in decision making about sustainable urban development.

Because so little agreement exists about what the words 'multidisciplinary' and 'interdisciplinary' mean, there is a need to explain how these terms are used in this chapter. 'Multidisciplinary' is used when work is undertaken by two or more disciplines – working either in series or in parallel – without any of the disciplines involved having to step outside their own traditional discipline boundaries (see Figure 10.1).

Multidisciplinary research
(disciplines operating in parallel)

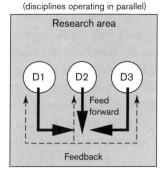

(disciplines operating in series)

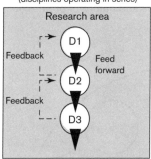

Discipline boundaries remain unpermeated

Interdisciplinary research
(disciplines operating jointly)

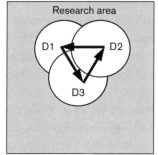

Discipline boundaries inter-penetrated
with some requirement for shared perspective

10.1 Comparison of multidisciplinary and interdisciplinary research

Source: Eclipse Research Consultants 1997

'Interdisciplinary' is used when two or more disciplines work together through the development of some form of shared perspective. Through constructing and then sharing a common theoretical position, conceptual framework, or methodological approach, discipline boundaries become permeable and are transcended. Of course, this short description simply raises other, more detailed questions about its implementation.

* How permeable are the discipline boundaries involved?
* What level of permeability/penetration is required for effective interdisciplinary working?
* How is this to be achieved?
* What level of shared perspective is required?
* And who is responsible for negotiating/achieving this?

Just the first of these questions is considered here. It can be addressed diagrammatically by using the 'wheel of cognate disciplines' involved in research on sustainable cities (Eclipse Research Consultants 1997: 13), shown in Figure 10.2. It is suggested that the closer disciplines are located, the more likely they are to share a common parentage and so the more open their boundaries are likely to be to each other. The further apart disciplines are, the less cognate their origins and the less compatible their modes of practice, and so the more impermeable their boundaries are likely to be to each other. In BEQUEST, the three disciplines most represented amongst the project partners fell within an arc formed by engineering, architecture and planning. Given their relatively cognate origins, collaboration across these discipline boundaries could be thought relatively straightforward. However, experience in BEQUEST suggests otherwise. Even with cognate disciplines, interdisciplinary working is difficult to achieve. In part, this can be explained by the situated nature of professional learning and expertise:

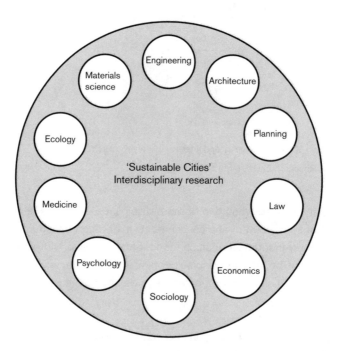

10.2 The wheel of cognate disciplines involved in research on sustainable cities

Source: Eclipse Research Consultants 1997

> Learning can be viewed as situated activity . . . [in which] learners inevitably participate in communities of practitioners . . . [where] mastery of knowledge and skill requires newcomers to move towards full participation in the socio-cultural practices of the community [which is being joined]. 'Legitimate peripheral participation' provides a way to speak about the relations between newcomers and old-timers and concerns the process by which newcomers become part of a community of practice. This social process includes, indeed subsumes, the learning of knowledgeable skills.
>
> (Lave and Wenger 1991: 29)

In BEQUEST, this problem of newcomers and old-timers was compounded since there was no dominant discipline or domain. In this sense, all the participants were newcomers, having to construct not just a shared conceptual space, but the social processes employed to achieve and maintain this position. This problem was made more difficult by the tacit nature of much of the knowledge and expertise that members of the network sought to share. And, through its consideration of issues such as costs and benefits and 'quality of life', BEQUEST also involved – and sought to draw into its deliberations – many other disciplines, including economics, psychology, sociology, health studies and ecology. As Rock observed:

> Disciplined knowledge is a collective pursuit, and its manufacture does not rest on explicable or explicit procedures alone. Even when coherent intellectual worlds collide, there may be insufficient common territory for them to resolve all issues that are in dispute.
>
> (1979: 13)

In the absence of such common territory, BEQUEST's members had to carve out a shared space that they could then jointly agree to occupy.

BEQUEST AS AN EXAMPLE OF A NETWORKED COMMUNITY

Developing a toolkit for assessing urban sustainability required consultation and negotiation with a wide range of stakeholders from both the demand and supply sides of the property and infrastructure industrial sectors across Europe (see Chapter 4). To achieve this, BEQUEST held specially convened international workshops every quarter. Between these workshops, BEQUEST had to exploit electronic communications in order to operate as a networked community to allow widely geographically dispersed stakeholders to play an active part in the project (Hamilton *et al.* 2002). The internet was used to host activities at three levels:

- an intranet set up to facilitate collaborative working between members of the research team;
- an extranet whose purpose was to provide workspaces in which wider representatives of stakeholder communities could play an active role in the project;
- the internet − a website open to the public on the internet designed to act as a major vehicle for raising interest in and disseminating outputs from the project.

While the intranet provided a discussion forum for project partners and held documents in the process of production, the extranet contained details of workshops, electronic reports, prototypes of the toolkit, and questionnaires to capture comment and feedback from extranet members. The public website was used as a continuously updated source of information on urban sustainability during the life of the project and held completed documents, periodic newsletters, and links to other appropriate organisations and related work.

Through these three web-based mechanisms, BEQUEST sought to do more than just build consensus amongst its immediate project partners. It also attempted to reach out to form a wider supportive community, particularly through its extranet. Indeed one of the deliverables specified by EU funding was 'an effective, multi-professional, international, interactive networked community', electronically mediated over the internet (BEQUEST 2001: 5). As a networked community, BEQUEST set itself two extremely high ambitions:

1 To deliver a multi-professional consensus around the assessment of urban sustainability.
2 To achieve this consensus predominantly through electronically mediated interactions.

In practice, this meant that, to be successful, BEQUEST had to operate effectively as a 'virtual organisation'.

BEQUEST AS AN EXAMPLE OF A VIRTUAL ORGANISATION

According to Harris (1998: 75), there have been many attempts to establish a comprehensive definition of the 'virtual organisation': 'But the concept, like the more popular notion of cyberspace, is characterized by semantic instability which may render it ultimately resistant to empirical investigation.'

'Virtual' is usually taken to mean something that does not exist in reality. However, when applied to organisations, a not untypical definition is:

> A temporary network of independent companies linked by IT to share skills, costs and access to one another's markets – or – an organization distributed geographically and whose work is co-ordinated through electronic communications.
>
> (Virtual Organization Net 2001)

Bradt (1998) has suggested a simple taxonomy for virtual organisations:

- *The alliance* built around horizontal networks between multiple business partners, rather than vertical integration within a single organisation.
- *The displaced* where members are geographically apart, usually working by computer e-mail and groupware, while appearing to be a single, unified organisation with a real physical location.
- *The invisible* where the organisation is characterised not so much by scattered locations but by the absence of any physical structure at all.

BEQUEST did not fit neatly into any one of Bradt's categories but they can usefully be plundered to shed light on how it operated. Throughout the 'concerted action', it acted as a temporary alliance of geographically displaced academic institutions and private companies, presenting itself not through the bricks and mortar of any of its partner organisations but primarily via the presence of its website on the internet. Part of BEQUEST's remit was to agree a framework for assessing sustainable urban development. Its modus operandi for achieving this was predominantly over the internet. Three monthly face-to-face meetings between partners were initially held to weld them into a team and to develop consensus about what needed to be done and how to move forward. Later such meetings were held to monitor progress and resolve conflicts. Face-to-face workshops were also held with members of the extranet to collect evidence from them and disseminate findings. However, outside these intermittent meetings, BEQUEST operated as a virtual organisation conducting its business over the internet.

Most international virtual teams are reported to fail (Lipnack and Stamps 2000, GlobalWorkshop.com 2002). And, according to Haywood (1998: 11) who surveyed 514 managers' experience of being responsible for the performance of geographically distributed teams, even when they do not fail, such teams take longer to complete tasks and have serious communications problems. In short, as Lipnack and Stamps concluded (2000: xxvii), 'Everything that goes wrong with in-the-same-place teams also plagues virtual teams – only worse.'

A composite list of reasons for the failure of virtual teams, compiled from just these three sources alone, includes:

- insufficient experience of, or preparation for, operating virtually;
- inadequate access to shared best practice about 'working together apart';
- a dearth of critical analyses allowing learning from successes or failures;
- difficulties building trust and generating motivation amongst dispersed team members;
- members' feelings of isolation and lack of inclusion;
- conflicting loyalties caused by allegiance to a team and to a parent organisation;
- in-house management resistance to staff's membership of virtual teams;
- difficulties communicating across organisational boundaries and in-house reporting lines, using only tenuous electronic links;
- problems crossing geographical boundaries, time zones, language and cultural differences;
- management skills and methods developed to correct problems in face-to-face teams that do not translate well to virtual teams.

E-mail and other forms of electronic communication – often cited as bridging such boundaries – were, in practice, found to be 'actually fraught with complications' (GlobalWorkshop.com 2002).

The problems listed above map well on to the difficulties experienced in working virtually reported by the BEQUEST partners, whose competence in using internet-based communication techniques varied widely from anxious first-time users to the highly skilled and motivated (Cooper 2002b). Their reported problems fall into three broad categories (see Table 10.1).

If such problems are to be tackled effectively, Lipnack and Stamps (2000: 6) advised that the skills required to lead virtual teams should not be treated as a given but addressed as a new set of requirements. Even when appropriate technology and connections are in place, they argued, the really difficult part of the 'virtual equation' still has to be faced – 'the people element'. Haywood agreed (1998:18). She proposed four key principles to support communicating effectively at a distance:

1   Agreement between team members about when and how they will be available for collaboration.
2   Actions by team members to replace lost context in their communications, with special attention to both the sender's and receiver's frames of reference.
3   Regular use of one-on-one phone conversation to clarify local priorities and concerns.
4   Senders taking responsibility for prioritising electronic communications to avoid information overload and communications fatigue.

Table 10.1 Problems encountered in the use of ICTs by BEQUEST partners

Problems encountered	Solutions proposed
Technologies	
Lack of common platform	Resolvable in-house but not cross-organisationally
System incompatibilities for data handling and transfer, especially attachments	Limit size of attachments transmitted to ensure information received Resort to snail mail or fax Need standard agreed format for all team members
Loss of richness of dialogue: lack of spontaneity and visual clues in electronic communication: dehumanised nature of electronic communication	Organise workshops to bring people together Use phone calls Invest inordinate amounts of time in clarifying
Problems with ISDN	With ISDN, disconnection between users has to be accepted as norm
Working practices	
Dynamic communications of (often abstract) ideas	Organise workshops to bring people together
Meeting deadlines/time pressures/disruptions	Organise face-to-face meetings or phone calls/avoid sending unexpected e-mails containing unexpectedly short deadlines
Agreeing responsibilities	Organise face-to-face meetings of phone calls
Reaching consensus on work to be done	Referring to contract specifications
Over-use of new media, especially in terms of over-long circulation lists	Talking to experienced users can be successful but inexperienced ones need access to in-house advisers
Lack of response from recipients to electronic communications	Use notation to signal the urgency of communication/reply
Cultural/social/psychological issues	
Motivation	Organise workshops to bring people together
Trust	Organise workshops to bring people together
Communications overload	Delete e-mails after reading subject line Avoid making internet connection to get work done 'Work longer hours or not respond at all.'
Unwillingness to try new technologies, e.g. chat room	Retreat to established technologies such as e-mail
Lack of capability of users	Resolvable in-house but not cross-organisationally
Language problems create confusion for non-native speakers	Use simple everyday as well as technical language

Klein and Pena-Mora's work (2001) on virtual teams suggests two more principles:

5   Invest the time team members would have spent travelling to identify and manage cultural differences and geographical disparities at the outset of the project.
6   Develop meeting norms and protocols that preserve and integrate cultural differences, e.g. expectations about punctuality, frequency of e-mail checking, etc.

As this brief set of principles illustrates, there is an emerging body of work offering advice on how to manage virtual teams. The focus and source of this advice is typically commercially based virtual teams, not international, interdisciplinary research teams seeking to operate across the academic/industry or private/public sector divides. Yet much of the advice generated does appear to read directly on to managing such virtual research teams as well.

However, there remains a highly significant area not covered by such guidance on how to run virtual teams or e-businesses effectively. As Wilsdon observed:

> One aspect of business remains strangely untouched by the revolutionary hand of the internet. Hardly anything has been said about the relationship between e-commerce and corporate sustainability . . . [but] alongside the economic opportunities created by e-commerce, there are a host of social and environmental opportunities that must be seized if the new economy is to be more sustainable than the old. . . . Now, in the early stages of this revolution, is the right time to pose some IAQs (infrequently asked questions) about the potential of e-commerce to bring wider benefits to society.
>
> (2001: 72–3)

The size of the potential environmental problems posed by rebound effects arising from using ICTs should not be under-estimated. Those who work geographically dispersed over the internet do need to meet, even if only occasionally. For instance, the final meeting of BEQUEST was held in Venice and brought together face-to-face thirty-five members of the networked community. The energy consumed in assembling these participants in one place was calculated as the equivalent of the global per capita annual allowance for 5.5 people as established in Kyoto (Cooper 2002b).

BEQUEST AND THE NEW PRODUCTION OF KNOWLEDGE

In the mid-1990s, Gibbons *et al.* (1994) suggested that the way in which knowledge was being produced in advanced capitalist societies was changing. For instance, they pointed to an increase in the number of sites where knowledge could be produced (ibid.: 4). This now occurs not just in universities, or non-university research institutes and centres, government agencies, industrial laboratories, think tanks, or private consultancies but, more importantly, they argued, in the interactions between these 'through functioning networks of communications'. BEQUEST can be seen as one example of what Gibbons *et al.* meant by 'a functioning network of communications' since it displays many of the characteristics which they said typified the 'new production of knowledge'. These characteristics are summarised in Table 10.2.

Table 10.2 'Old' v. 'new' production of knowledge

Old knowledge production	New knowledge production
Single discipline-based	Interdisciplinary – involving diverse range of specialists
Problem formulation governed by interests of specific community	Problem formulation governed by interests of actors involved in application
Problems set and solved in (largely) academic context	Problems set and solved in application-based context
Newtonian model of science specific to field of enquiry	Emergent theoretical/conceptual framework not reducible to single discipline
Research practice conforms to norms of discipline's definition of 'scientific'	Research practice reflexive and socially accountable
Quasi-permanent, institutionally based teams	Short-lived, problem-defined, non-institutional teams
Hierarchical and conservative team organisation	(Non) hierarchical and transient team organisation
Normative, rule-based, 'scientific' knowledge produced	Consensual, continuously negotiated, knowledge produced
'Innovation' seen as production of 'new' knowledge	'Innovation' also seen as reconfiguration of existing knowledge for new contexts
Separate knowledge production and application	Integrated knowledge production and application
Dissemination discipline-based through institutional channels	Dissemination through collaborating partners and social networks
Static research practice defined by 'good science'	Dynamic research practice characterised by on the move problem-solving
Static research practitioners operating within discipline/institution	Mobile research practitioners operating through networks
Mediated through face-to-face or paper-based communications	Electronically mediated over the internet

Source: Constructed from Gibbons *et al.* (1994: 3–16)

It is not possible here to discuss BEQUEST and how it operated against each of the characteristics listed in Table 10.1. Just a few illustrative examples are offered. For instance, under Gibbon *et al.*'s discussion of the 'new' knowledge production, research teams, as they work together, evolve an emergent conceptual framework that transcends those owned by any single discipline. As a consequence of this, acceptance of any knowledge produced has to be continuously negotiated between the parties involved until a consensus is reached. This is a description of how BEQUEST operated throughout the concerted action. Task groups, with members deliberately selected from several disciplines, would draw on their members' experience and expertise to propose how a specific portion of BEQUEST's remit should be tackled. Initially, such negotiations would take place within the task group. Once consensus had been reached between the disciplines represented within the task group (if this was achievable – see below), then their proposals were brought to all the partners for plenary discussion. At this point, the task group's recommendations were accepted, directly modified, or returned for further negotiation within the task group. This cycle was reiterated until a consensus position was reached.

According to Gibbons *et al.*'s description of the 'new' production of knowledge, innovation occurs, not just through producing new knowledge, but through taking existing knowledge and reconfiguring it so that it can be used in new contexts or by new sets of users. This reconfigured knowledge is then both disseminated and applied through the networks to which the research team members belong and out into their practitioner communities. Again, this is how BEQUEST sought to operate. Two related examples of the first tendency can be offered. The first concerns the construction of the BEQUEST framework (see Chapter 2). This was built from a combination of pre-existing and newly developed elements. The second concerns the use of this framework as a means of locating and classifying existing assessment methods – developed for a variety of purposes, many of which predate interest in sustainability – in order to identify which aspects of urban sustainability they can be used to address. The second tendency is illustrated by the dissemination pathways employed by BEQUEST – most immediately via its own extranet but beyond this through the wider networks to which its partners themselves belong.

When Gibbons and his colleagues wrote in the mid-1990s, they recognised (e.g. 1994: 101–2) the increasingly important role that information technologies were playing in both the generation and dissemination of knowledge. Subsequently this role was further stressed by Mansell and Wehn (1998) in their work for the UN on 'knowledge societies'. They signalled (ibid.: 100–18) the significance of information technology for the achievement of sustainable development – especially for the sharing of information between most and least developed countries. Their work allows a further characteristic to be added to Gibbon *et al.*'s set that draws attention to the importance of the internet to the new production of knowledge – see added bottom row of Table 10.2. For such production is now quite clearly mediated, not just by working face to face, but electronically over the internet. Drawing on this extended list, it is possible to summarise what seem the most significant of the ways in which BEQUEST operated as an example of the new production of knowledge throughout the concerted action:

- interdisciplinary working
- interaction electronically mediated over the internet
- application-based problem-solving
- emergent conceptual framework
- transient, problem-defined team
- consensual, negotiated knowledge production
- innovation predominantly through reconfiguring existing knowledge
- dissemination through partners and networks.

Applied research on urban sustainability will increasingly need to display such characteristics since the topic respects no spatial, temporal or discipline-based boundaries. BEQUEST is, in this sense, a clear example of the type of boundary crossing required to tackle sustainable urban development as an area of practical activity.

CONCLUSION

It is difficult to exaggerate the importance to EU policy imperatives of successfully exploiting ICTs to deliver sustainable urban development in Europe. The widespread application of ICTs is seen as an extremely positive engine for change, enabling radically new ways of working and e-business patterns to energise and revitalise a wide range of human activities in all communities, creating new forms of growth and prosperity, loosely described as the knowledge economy. EU policy has also explicitly cast cities in the role of motors for change in regional, national and European economic progress. Hence, from an EU policy perspective, the interaction between cities and ICTs is expected to act both as the key driver and as the primary location for the delivery of the knowledge economy and society. From the macro-scale of regional economic competitiveness and social inclusion in cities, through to the micro-scale of the role of innovative workplaces in the information society, ICTs have been invested with high significance as major levers for change.

The 'post-Brundtland' approaches to integrated environmental assessment set out in the previous chapters of this volume are already highly computer-dependent. They require the emergence – and successful operation of – integrated decision making across a wide range of currently functionally separate disciplines. The decision-support systems needed to underpin such integration are becoming increasingly computer-based. Likewise the communication systems underpinning the dialogue between the professionals required to use such decision-support systems will increasingly be supported by web-based information technology. But this dependence on computers goes further. For, if robust and acceptable decisions about urban development and regeneration are indeed going to require active involvement from citizens as well as professionals, then their engagement is also likely to be mediated by ICTs, eventually perhaps in the form of some kind of e-agora. It is these kinds of developments, identified in BEQUEST, that are currently being pursued through further EU-funded projects such as the INTELCITY roadmap and its immediate successor, INTELCITIES.

However, experience in BEQUEST suggested that successful dialogue and decision making through the use of ICTs cannot be taken for granted. The exploitation of ICTs will have to be explicitly and carefully managed. Specific and critical attention needs to be given to developing and disseminating 'good practice' advice on how to exploit ICTs for virtual team working in a manner that does not impact adversely on sustainability.

There are discipline-based factors that both unite and divide those who need to collaborate in assessing urban sustainability. The members of BEQUEST tackled the absence of common territory by carving out a shared space that they could jointly agree to occupy. They constructed not just this shared conceptual space, but also the social processes they employed to achieve and maintain this position. BEQUEST exploited electronic communications in order to operate as a network community in order to engage widely geographically dispersed stakeholders. Through use of ICTs, BEQUEST sought to do more than just build consensus amongst its project partners. It also attempted to reach out, through its extranet, to form a wider supportive community amongst practictioners. BEQUEST acted as a temporary alliance of geographically displaced academic institutions and private companies, presenting itself primarily via the presence of its website on the internet. In operating in this way throughout the concerted action, BEQUEST displayed many of the characteristics of what Gibbons has called the 'new production of knowledge'.

The experience of the partners (Deakin 2004) indicates that ICTs were indispensable in the knowledge production processes used in BEQUEST. The network employed the internet as its main form of communication (for exchanging information, developing arguments, structuring complex issues) because, without this technology, it would not have been possible – indeed highly improbable – for the partners to have delivered the concerted action's objectives. Progressing from a model (with the required vision and scope) to a methodology (a framework, set of protocols and assessment methods) with the integrity required to evaluate SUD could not have been achieved without this technology. ICTs were used (to form the virtual organisation and networked communities operating through the internet and extranet) because they are able to:

- cast the vision of SUD agreed by the network into the community – as part of the scoping exercise;
- use the methodology of this exercise to build capacity and carry the sheer weight of material needed to frame the issues in question;
- work these issues through the protocols also agreed by the various stakeholders to represent the pathways to SUD;
- support stakeholders in selecting the assessment methods needed to evaluate – provide the evidence to prove, demonstrate and so forth – the sustainability of urban development;
- offer the technology (websites, e-consultations) to effectively inform stake-holders about ongoing research on SUD and place findings on relevant action in the public domain.

Hence, without ICTs, it would simply not have been possible to link the vision and scoping exercises with the framework, protocols and assessment methods and then to connect them to one another in the form of a toolkit. BEQUEST experience suggests that, without the internet, the tasks involved would have been too complex. As a result, the partners would have sunk under the sheer weight of material needed to manage the required data streams and information flows. Beyond such technical issues, employing ICTs had a strong social benefit as well. As Deakin (2004) observed, the shared construction of the virtual organisation also allowed participants to 'drop all the vested interests of their own institutional settings – this in itself was liberating – "freeing" them to consider new ways of tackling issues and working up solutions to problems'.

Using electronic communications to bridge organisational, professional and discipline boundaries encountered was found to be fraught with complications. BEQUEST drew on the emerging body of work offering advice on how to manage virtual teams, to deal with these. However, one highly significant area remains uncovered by such guidance – how to seize the social, economic and environmental opportunities offered by ICTs without incurring unwanted and unsustainable rebound effects.

REFERENCES

BEQUEST (2001) *Final Report 2000–1*, Contract No. ENV 4 CT/97–607, EC Environment and Climate Programme, Research Theme 4: Human Dimension of Environmental Change, University of Salford, UK.

Bradt, R. (1998) *Virtual Organisations: A Simple Taxonomy*, available online at www.infothink.com

Brandon, P., Lombardi, P. and Bentivegna, V. (eds) (1997) *Evaluation of the Built Environment for Sustainability*, E&FN Spon, London.

Christie, I. and Hepworth, M. (2001) Towards the e-region. In Wilsdon, J. (ed.) *Digital Futures: Living in a Dot-com World*, Earthscan, London, pp. 140–162.

Cooper, I. (1997) Environmental assessment methods for use at the building and city scales: constructing bridges or identifying common ground. In Brandon, P., Lombardi, P. and Bentivegna, V. (eds) *Evaluation of the Built Environment for Sustainability*, E&FN Spon, London, pp. 1–5.

Cooper, I. (2002a) Transgressing discipline boundaries: is BEQUEST an example of 'the new production of knowledge'? *Building Research and Information* 30(2): 116–129.

Cooper, I. (2002b) *Delivering Sustainability Through ICTs: How Robust are Virtual Research Teams?* Building Sustainable Cities Conference, Venice, 18–20 April.

Cooper, I. and Palmer, J. (1999) The Sustainable Cities programme in the United Kingdom, *Urbanistica* 112: 83–87 (English summary, pp. 112–113).

Curwell, S. *et al.* (eds) (2003) *INTELCITY Final Report*, Project Number IST-2001-37373, EU Information Society Technologies 2002 Work Programme, University of Salford, www.scri.salford.ac.uk/intelcity

Dabinett, G. (2001) EU mainstreaming of the information society in regional policy development, *Regional Studies*, 35(2): 168–173.

Deakin, M. (2004) private communication, School of the Built Environment, Napier University, Edinburgh (8/1/2004).

Eclipse Research Consultants (1997) *Support for Inter-disciplinary Research*, a workshop prepared for the Research and Graduate College, University of Salford, and for the Committee for Inter-disciplinary Environmental Studies, University of Cambridge, ERC, Cambridge.

Escritt, R. (2002) *Framework Programme 2002–2006: An Overview*, OST Framework 6 Conference, Office of Science and Technology, Department of Trade and Industry, London, January, www.dti.gov.uk/ostinternational

EC (European Commission), Research Directorate General (2002) *Research and Technology Development Beyond 2002: The European Research Area*, www.cordis.lu/rtd2002/era-debate

Gibbons, M., Limoges, C., Nowotny, H., Schwartzman, S., Scott, P. and Trow, M. (1994) *The New Production of Knowledge: The Dynamics of Science and Research in Contemporary Societies*, Sage Publications, London.

GlobalWorkshop.com (2002) *Global Team Training*, Chicago, www.globalworkshop.com/globalteams.html

Hamilton, A., Cooper, I. and Bentivegna, V. (2002) An assessment of collaboration, supported by electronic communications, in the BEQUEST project, *Urbanistica* 117.

Harris, M. (1998) Rethinking the virtual organisation, in Jackson, P. and van der Wielen, J. (eds) *Teleworking: International Perspectives – From Telecommuting to the Virtual Organisation*, John Wiley & Sons, London, pp. 74–92.

Haywood, M. (1998) *Managing Virtual Teams: Practical Techniques for High-technology Project Managers*, Artech House, Boston.

INTELCITIES (2004) www.INTELCITIESproject.com

IST (1999) *Sustainable Workplaces in a Global Information Society: New Methods of Working*, Report of a Thematic Programme Consultation Meeting, User-friendly Information Society, EU Framework 5, Brussels.

Klein, J. and Pena-Mora, F. (2001) *MIT Team Reports Tips for Successful Virtual Collaborations*, Sloan School of Management, MIT, Cambridge, Mass., http/web.mit.edu/newsofficer/nr/2001/vcollaboration.html

Lave, J. and Wenger, E. (1991) *Situated Learning: Legitimate Peripheral Learning*, Cambridge University Press, Cambridge.

Lawton, J. (2002) *Opportunities for the UK – a View from the Research Councils*, OST Framework 6 Conference, Office of Science and Technology, Department of Trade and Industry, London, January, www.dti.gov.uk/ostinternational

Lipnack, J. and Stamps, J. (2000) *Virtual Teams: People Working across Boundaries with Technology*, John Wiley & Sons, New York.

Mansell, R. and Wehn, U. (1998) *Knowledge Societies: Information Technology for Sustainable Development*, Oxford University Press on behalf of the United Nations, Oxford.

Norton, J. (2001) Response, in Wilsdon, J. (ed.) *Digital Futures: Living in a Dot-com World*, Earthscan, London, pp. 163–164.

Rock, P. (1979) *The Making of Symbolic Interactionism*, MacMillan Press, London.

Sainsbury, Lord (2002) Opening address, OST Framework 6 Conference, Office of Science and Technology, Department of Trade and Industry, London, January, www.dti.gov.uk/ostinternational/

Thompson Klein, J. (1996) *Crossing Boundaries: Knowledge, Disciplinarities and Interdisciplinarities*, University Press of Virginia, Charlottesville.

Van Winden, W. (2001) The end of social exclusion? On information technology as a key to social inclusion in large Eurpoean cities, *Regional Studies* 35(9): 861–877.

Virtual Organization Net (2001) Virtual organizations, *Journal of Virtual Organizations*, available online at www.virtual-organization.net/cgi/main.asp

Wilsdon, J. (2001) Dot-com ethics: e-business and sustainability. In Wilsdon, J. (ed.) *Digital Futures: Living in a Dot-com World*, Earthscan, London, pp. 72–93.

11

Conclusions

Mark Deakin, Martin Symes and Steven Curwell

This volume on *Sustainable Urban Development* (SUD) has sought to outline the underlying concepts, models, vision and methodology of an integrated SUD and to support the BEQUEST framework of analysis. In addition, particular attention has been drawn to the protocols BEQUEST members argue should be followed in carrying out an environmental assessment and evaluating the sustainability of urban development. The book is based on, and extends, proposals made by the BEQUEST network of academics and practitioners. It argues:

- SUD's goal is to improve the quality of life in an increasingly urban population;
- actions aiming to improve the quality of life need a simple, clear framework for analysing the sustainability of urban development;
- this framework for analysis needs to provide a vision and methodology which brings such concerns into the scope of actions targeting improvements in the quality of life;
- within this vision and methodology, protocols provide a middle ground between our general understanding of sustainability issues surrounding the quality of life and the particular evaluations that can help in selecting the urban development proposals which best address them;
- in carrying out such actions, these evaluations must transcend purely environmental factors and embed themselves securely in more comprehensive and integrated environmental, social and economic assessments of SUD;
- a community of academic and professional advisers is emerging, willing and able to use new information technology as a means of undertaking these evaluations and making the knowledge of SUD they produce, available to local, regional, national and international agencies.

In this concluding chapter, the editors start by reviewing the chapters in the volume and then go on to reflect on the contribution the BEQUEST network has made to our knowledge and understanding of SUD.

THE UNDERLYING CONCEPTS AND MODELS

The introduction to this volume provided a wide-ranging discussion of the underlying concepts and models applicable to SUD. This examination showed that, while it is frequently held that sustainable development is a concept which can be articulated in many different ways, the literature reviewed suggests that there is an emerging consensus on what the concept refers to and on the means by which it can be put it into effect.

Initial concern over the impact of modern technology on the environment has led directly to consideration of the economic, social and institutional changes which have accompanied such developments. World summits, commissions, international conferences and their related programmes have focused research and technical development on the global trend towards urbanisation and the growth of cities. In the EU this trend is particularly strong: it is leading to a notable increase in the quality of life. However, the resulting increase in resource consumption has been seen to produce a situation whereby the capacity of the environment to carry such a level of economic growth and social change has been brought into question. This in turn has resulted in questions being asked about the sustainability of urban development.

The work reviewed in the introduction argues that there is a strong convergence in the definitions offered for conditions under which sustainability can be achieved. Most widely accepted is the goal of a developmental process which 'meets the needs of the present without compromising the ability of future generations to meet their needs and aspirations as regards quality of life'. Using this representation as a reference point, the BEQUEST network has sought to build on earlier publications by some of its members and create a fourfold definition of sustainable development – ecological integrity, equity, participation and futurity – and draw on this vision to propose a methodology of concerted action and consensus building – to integrate the underlying issues, activities, spatial levels and time frames of SUD. This in turn provides the network with the common language and terms of reference forming the glossary of terminologies – syntax, semantics, ontological structure and taxonomies – needed to model the stages of sustainable development. This in turn makes it possible to model the planning, property development, design, construction and operational interests of key stakeholders in the built environment and engage with the economic and social issues underlying the sustainability of urban development.

In Chapter 2 the four dimensions of sustainable development were described as follows. The *ecological integrity principle* recognises the undeniable fact that people are entirely dependent upon the natural world, and without the resources and eco-system services it provides, life and development are impossible. Therefore, in order to maintain the viability of ecological systems in perpetuity, development must not degrade or deplete them to such an extent that they are unable to function effectively. The *equity principle* (also known as social or intra-generational equity) is concerned with fairness for all. This principle requires us to recognise that the most vulnerable people in society need to have a satisfactory quality of life, particularly with respect to access to resources and development opportunities and freedom from threat. The *participation principle* argues that sustainable development is not about achieving a desired balance between competing needs at any one time, but about achieving this balance continuously over a long time frame and in a world where natural and human systems are both dynamic and uncertain. Fourthly, there is the *futurity principle*, which recognises that the development aspirations of future generations must not be impaired by actions that we take today, and for this reason futurity is also known as inter-generational equity, or simply ensuring 'fair shares' for us and our descendants. Futurity demands that the value of all assets which are passed on to future generations, including natural resources, cultural heritage and human knowledge, should not decline, and is supported by the following guidelines:

- renewable resources must not be consumed faster than the rate at which they are renewed;
- non-renewable resources must not be consumed at a rate faster than that at which they can be substituted by a renewable resource;
- waste substances must not be discharged to the environment faster than they can be assimilated without impairment of eco-system functions.

Taken together, the environment, equity, participation and futurity principles are central to ensuring the bio-physical conditions for sustainable development and the socially inclusive decision making required to ensure fairness for all.

The BEQUEST network has primarily been concerned with the built environment. Hence the BEQUEST framework for analysis classifies development processes in four particular ways. First, it classifies them as functions of the main actors in the development process (planners, property developers, designers, the construction sector and those responsible for the operation and use of facilities). Second, it classifies them as environmental, economic and social representations of such actions. Third, it classifies them as expressions of such development activity at different spatial levels (from global through national, regional, and urban, down to cities, districts, neighbourhoods and estates, then finally on to buildings and their materials and components). Finally, it classifies them as development activities having effects over long, medium and short time scales. Conceived in this manner, the development activity is represented as creating, or responding to, a number of environmental, economic and social pressures: for example, the depletion of natural resources, the distribution of income, access to services and various means of influencing govern- mental decision making.

The discussions which have taken place on the BEQUEST framework argue that it represents a structuring device, allowing academics and practitioners alike to locate and specify their own position in the development process, to benchmark the current situation, and to identify the sustainability issues of particular significance – be they environmental, economic, or social. Clearly this is an important development because in framing the sustainability issues and qualifying them as environmental, economic or social, it does not lose sight of the fact there are also institutional issues at stake. These institutional issues – it should be noted – also need to be addressed if the moral and ethical shifts required for bringing about cultural change in the governance of urban development are to be identified. It is clear that if such a cultural change is to take place, institutions must address the ecological integrity, equity, participation and futurity of SUD and make every effort to ensure the outcomes of such action produce a balanced environmental, economic and social structure.

THE PROTOCOLS

A major section of this first volume has been concerned with explaining the structure, form and content of SUD. Consideration of this process was one of the major objec- tives of the BEQUEST network. The structure of the process is termed a protocol and has been subdivided into five sections (the BEQUEST protocols). This subdivision derives from the five main development activities of the BEQUEST framework. The form and content of these five 'second level' protocols were discussed in the five chapters making up the second part of this book.

The BEQUEST protocol relates to the selection and application of assessment methods available to evaluate the sustainability of urban development. It states that there are eight aspects of this process:

- Preparation
- Planning an assessment
- The content of an assessment
- The assessment process
- Consultation
- Reporting
- Providing information
- Monitoring.

Most often, these considerations are addressed in sequence, so the eight aspects of the assessment process become eight steps towards the procurement of a sound evaluation. The BEQUEST framework divides development into five activities, and each of these can be evaluated with assessment methods procured in broadly the same sequence of steps. However, the activities do not necessarily always occur as a linear sequence of events and it is possible that they are undertaken in parallel, rather than sequentially. So this description of the process allows for the possibility that a number of assessment methods, each selected for their suitability in evaluating the effects of any one of the development activities, may be in use simultaneously. It is, therefore, possible to talk of an assessment process composed of several methods and of evaluating a set of sustainable development issues over a variety of spatial configurations and time frames. Preparing for one assessment could occur while consultation is taking place on the findings of another evaluation, and while a report is being received from a third, and so forth. Thus, while the five chapters on protocols each address a distinct need – planning, property development, design, construction and operation – they overlap in content and suggest there is a diversity of gateways to pass through en route to SUD.

The protocol on planning showed that sustainability assessments could be mounted for plans concerned with a whole range of geographical scales, from the pan-European to the local. It also highlighted that the major issues which need to be resolved and the legal context within which the planning process occurs are liable to be different at these different scales. A common difficulty is that of understanding the assessment methods by which plans are put into practice: are they advisory, or statutory, and if statutory, are they implemented in advance of development (constraining action) or after the fact (acting as a form of control)? In some instances, planners will provide only guidance, in others clear regulation. Sustainability of the development proposed may be a specific objective of the planning system, or it may be a consequence of the approach taken. Chapter 3 used the British planning system as an example. In it, the view has been taken that planning provides a forum in which development is contested, conflicts emerge and sustainability issues must be negotiated. The procurement of assessment methods can be tailored to this condition.

The chapter on property development first gave the reader a traditional representation of how this activity is carried out and followed with a description of some alternative visions. The clear implication of this examination is that the property market is changing and the package of measures needed to meet the challenge which sustainable development poses is now starting to be delivered. As the examination established, in the traditional representation, property development is a kind of pipeline, taking raw materials (land, labour and capital) and combining them in such a way that the use of land is changed and the productivity of the sites concerned is improved. Here a number of assessment methods can be found already in use: property market analysis, valuation, investment appraisal and so on. However, in these the evaluation of the environmental, economic and social aspects of sustainable development tend to be under-represented and are poorly integrated with each other. When the chapter discusses recent changes in property development, as in the example of the development of new settlements (sustainable communities), new representations arise. One of the most significant is that known as the 'institutional approach'. From this perspective, a change in the market – for example, an interest in 'environmentally friendly, green settlements' (urban villages and eco-neighbourhoods) – emerges and is transmitted to producer institutions, which then undergo economic and social reorganisation and cultivate new practices. This demonstrates that if such an interest in sustainable communities is going to produce environmentally friendly, green settlements, a different set of values must be developed, those which perhaps most significantly of all begin to challenge the predominantly commercial culture of property development.

The third chapter in this sequence was concerned with urban design. It argued that two quite separate meanings of the word design must be separated from each other before a clear idea of the possibilities for evaluation can be gained. The first is that of design as a process: a variety of actors are involved, a series of sub-processes take place, a large number of criteria are brought into the decision-making process, and this in itself is sometimes more tacit than overt, so potentially opaque to the assessment community. The second meaning of design is that of three-dimensional descriptions of the physical object, and in this case, evaluation of its consequences for human behaviour, or environmental quality, is more straightforward. The chapter included a case study of design objectives developed for the sustainability of urban neighbourhoods in another EU project. This showed a great variety of criteria which appeared relevant (they are organised as twenty-one objectives in five target areas: the heritage, the local environment, diversity, integration and social capacity). The conclusion was drawn that evaluation methods should be selected which dealt in a holistic way with a complex group of factors: examples include 'impact matrix analysis' and 'social cost-benefit analysis'. The selection of appropriate indicators for inclusion in such sophisticated methods is another area of difficulty which has implications for evaluating the sustainability of urban development.

The following chapter dealt with construction. This examination explored how construction can and should be made more sustainable and addressed two main areas of good practice. First, the design of more sustainable buildings and urban landscapes (sustainable architecture). Second, the procurement of materials and components, and the process of assembly and/or refurbishment of a building, or element of the infrastructure and/or landscape, in a more sustainable manner (sustainable construction). Embracing them both under the heading of sustainable construction, the chapter sought to explore the environmental, economic, social and institutional issues arising from the construction of a sustainable built product, in terms of individual buildings, civil structures and urban landscape.

Arguing that the neo-liberal, free-market model fails to represent the complexity of the interactions necessary for the creation of a high-quality 'sustainable' built environment, the chapter sought to address the wider socio-economic dimensions of the principles outlined in the four-dimensional model of sustainable development, particularly those of ecological integrity, equity and participation in decision making. The examination also drew attention to the inability of the construction sector to address the futurity principle of sustainable development. As the examination pointed out, buildings and associated infrastructure are very long-lived artefacts that contain community activities and which over time, individually and/or collectively, become part of the cultural heritage – which in turn requires preservation and whose conservation has become an additional sustainability issue which needs to be addressed.

The chapter identified the main sustainability issues and factors that could and should be borne in mind in each of the main steps in producing the built product, from inception through to occupation. Arguing that construction needs to reduce environmental impacts and become more sustainable, the examination set out a protocol for sustainable construction, setting out the objectives, briefings, and management actions needed to operationalise the protocol. With this aim, the examination went on to draw attention to the matrix of nine activity zones and ten distinct steps (grouped into four main process phases) that are needed for the protocol in question to break with tradition and successfully procure the construction services that are required for built products to become sustainable.

Finally in this set of detailed discussions of the procurement protocol for sustainable urban development, a chapter has been included on the operation and use of buildings. This chapter took us full circle, from the 'upstream' concerns of planning, property development, design and construction and towards more 'downstream' activities concerning the operation and use of buildings as products. The chapter established that, as a distinct stage of the urban development process, the sustainability issues underlying the operation and use of buildings are complex. It argued that while understanding them is in itself challenging, any proposal to turn this into a set of guidelines for property and construction managers to follow in making the operation and use of buildings sustainable, is particularly so. This chapter aimed to meet this challenge by outlining a protocol to follow in making developments surrounding the operation and use of buildings sustainable. With this aim, the chapter began by setting out the organisational context of the study and in that sense the legacy of how the operation and use of buildings has previously been dealt with by property and construction managers. Critical of the limited developments that have previously taken place in this field, this section of the chapter took the opportunity to set out recent changes which point to the sustainable development agenda and how to address it.

From here the chapter developed a framework for understanding the sustainable operation and use of buildings. Six criteria were set out for property and construction managers to take account of in ensuring the sustainable operation and use of buildings. Examining these criteria, the chapter drew attention to the procurement and evaluation of building products and their infrastructure services. It then went on to set out how post-occupancy methods of assessment can be made use of to evaluate the sustainability of such products and their services.

THE ASSESSMENT METHODS

The third part of the book introduced the BEQUEST Directory of Environmental Assessment Methods, and the experience gained in relation to the use of these methods in evaluating the sustainability of urban development.

The first chapter in this part of the book, Chapter 8, was about the Directory. It reported the findings of the BEQUEST network's survey of the methods currently available for evaluating the sustainability of urban development and described the master list of published and unpublished assessment methods suitable for use in Europe and North America. The authors of this chapter argued that scientific opinion concerning the value of available methods is currently divided. One opinion is that the use of these methods can promote sustainable development, another that there is so much uncertainty surrounding the nature of public goods, that the methods available for assessing their value are inappropriate. The issue is whether the degrees of risk which are associated with any particular environmental actions are so great that it causes conventional methodologies, such as cost-benefit analysis, to be of little real value. If the answer is negative, then only a new generation of methods, termed 'co-evolutionary methods' by the authors, will suffice. These show how closely the factors involved in a traditional environmental evaluation (property rights, landscape, recreation, leisure) are linked with those of concern to the assessment of ecological integrity (resource consumption, pollution, land use and bio-diversity). The authors suggest, however, and ask the reader to note, that even with the most sophisticated co-evolutionary – environmental, economic and social – assessments, there is currently a gap in the ability of such methods to address the institutional questions surrounding such evaluations of SUD. This chapter included a classification of methods uncovered in the survey. This places them in three categories: environmental evaluations; simple environmental, economic and social evaluations; and complex environmental, economic and social evaluations. The chapter is illustrated by a typical description of one of the complex assessment methods, SPARTACUS. Importantly, this description includes information on the developmental status of the method and its data requirements.

The second chapter in this part of the book, Chapter 9, 'Assessing the Sustainability of Urban Development', takes the reader into a more detailed 'mapping' of the range of methods available. The 'map' shows the comparative frequencies of assessment methods which cover the aspects of the development process identified by the BEQUEST framework and dealt with by the protocols outlined in the previous section. It showed, *inter alia*, that a majority of methods deal with the planning activity, at the city level and over a long time scale. It also established that a number of them deal with environmental, economic and social issues which underlie the search for sustainable communities – whether surfacing in the form of city, district, or neighbourhood-wide developments.

NEW WAYS OF WORKING

The final part of this volume included a chapter on the scientific and professional community which is emerging to carry out the evaluations which have been described.

Of course, the BEQUEST network was interdisciplinary and it was an international community. But more than this, it made intensive use of new information technology, some of the difficulties of which are described in this chapter, and formed a virtual organisation, with its intranet and extranet of, respectively, core and associated partners. It was in this respect that the BEQUEST team worked in a new way.

This chapter refers to the ideas of Michael Gibbons, who has proposed that we talk about the 'new production of knowledge'. This is knowledge production in which innovation is generated by taking existing knowledge and reconfiguring it so that it can be used in new contexts or by new sets of users. Other writers quoted by the authors of this chapter argue that it is important to ensure that an information society is created which is economically and environmentally sustainable, seeks to fight economic inequality and social exclusion and is based on increasing the capacity of urban management to govern in a more positive direction.

Arguably, the BEQUEST framework, protocols and careful selection of assessment methods described in earlier chapters will support these aims. It should perhaps also be noted that the use of new technology which is set out in this chapter does not necessarily result in improvements to the urban development process, or make it sustainable. But the community of academics and practitioners which was formed in the BEQUEST project appears to have shown that a real opportunity for doing so can be created by adopting these new ways of working.

Before going on to set out the specific contribution made by the BEQUEST network, we feel it is worthwhile to illustrate how our understanding and knowledge of SUD set out in the Introduction to this volume has developed from the aforementioned examination of the BEQUEST framework, protocols and assessment methods. Figure 11.1 attempts to capture these developments. As can be seen, the simplicity of the linear logic set out in the introduction is relaxed in this illustration, with the framework running in parallel to the protocols and assessment methods – the framework relating to the 'top level' issues, the protocols taking the 'middle ground' and providing the content required to 'fill out' the assessment methods in their evaluation of SUD. This process of moving between the 'top' and 'middle' levels of analysis itself requires a considerable degree of reflection when linking the framework to the protocols and to the assessment methods available for evaluating the sustainability of urban development. It should perhaps also be noted that the connection which the protocols in turn have to the assessment methods is also subjected to critical evaluation. The sum of the said reflections and critical evaluations on the links and connections between the protocols and assessment methods are then brought together synthetically as a set of protocols and assessment methods for evaluating the sustainability of urban development (see Figure 11.1).

CONTRIBUTIONS MADE BY THE BEQUEST NETWORK

If we look at the representation of BEQUEST first set out in Brandon et al.'s (1997) *Evaluation of the Built Environment for Sustainability*, it is possible to see what the network has added to our knowledge and understanding of SUD. In the introduction to the said book, Brandon et al. state:

> This volume includes several studies on the evaluation of the built environment for sustainability, considering the built environment as a dynamic scenario that changes over time. As already said, it represents the 'product' of urban planning, [property development] and architectural design processes and of various construction activities that take place in defined spatial organisation . . . Unfortunately, at present there does not exist a transdisciplinary language across the built environment that can bring together the diversity of interests necessary to assess the built and natural environmental impacts. In evaluating the built environment for sustainability, the disciplines involved bring their own classification system and techniques to the problem and they are unwilling (or unable) to consider the views represented by others, because there is not a common vocabulary or a systematic methodology which will allow a fruitful dialogue to take place. Therefore, the task is to find an integrating mechanism, or tool for helping decision making processes in planning [property development] design and construction.
>
> (1997: xiv–xv)

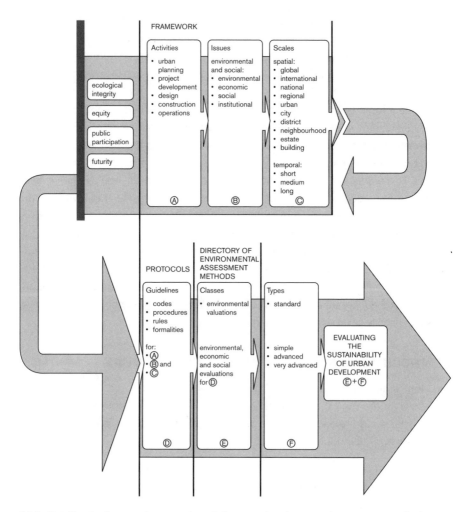

11.1 Detailing the framework, protocols and directory of environmental assessment methods

The integrating mechanism, or tool, in question is, it is suggested, the BEQUEST framework, vision and methodology of an integrated SUD. This provides the 'trans-disciplinary language' of the consensus-building methodology adopted by BEQUEST to 'bring together the diversity of interests' – planners, property developers, designers, constructors and operators – who act as stakeholders in the environmental, economic and social structure of the urban development process. Also noticeable is that in this framework, the common vocabulary and systematic methodology it offers have provided a fruitful dialogue between representatives of the stakeholder groups, until now missing, and has enabled them to devise, agree and adopt a trans-disciplinary language previously absent from the debate on sustainability. For not only has the BEQUEST network undertaken an extensive review of existing literature, but its academic partners have also sought to frame the debate as a set of 'gateways' for practitioners to pass through as part of the search for SUD. Further to this, it has sought to formalise these gateways as 'hard and soft' junctions – crossing points – in the stakeholders' journey towards SUD. At these junctions, members of the network argue, stakeholders cross over their own boundaries of knowledge and embark on a journey that takes them into other domains en route to SUD. The process by which the stakeholders 'beat a path' to SUD and proceed to 'stay on track' is by means of the BEQUEST protocols. These should represent an accepted or established code, procedure, set of rules and formalities, which set out a pathway to follow 'en-route' to SUD.

While the BEQUEST framework itself represents a significant step forward in our knowledge and understanding of SUD, the contribution made by the protocols should not go unrecognised. This is because they provide a formal link which both casts back to the issues, spatial levels and time frames of the framework and forward to their connection with the assessment methods. As such they provide a 'roadmap' which not only links the 'top level' issues, spatial levels and time frames to the middle-ground of 'first and second level' protocol(s), but also connects them together as a set of co-ordinates to follow in 'getting to the bottom of the matter' and adopting the assessment methods capable of evaluating the sustainability of urban development. Taking this form, it is possible to say that the BEQUEST framework, protocols and assessment methods set out 'grid references' which allow the network – along with its representative community of stakeholders – to take the matter of evaluation full circle. That is to say, take it from a framework for analysis, to a protocol to follow and procedure to adopt in selecting the assessment methods which are best able to evaluate the sustainability of urban development.

It is perhaps these qualities which have led Kohler (2002), who wrote a full review of work previously published by the BEQUEST network, to propose:

> BEQUEST is without doubt one of the really interesting network research programmes with an excellent input/output relation and a high multiplication effect. . . . [It] provides an excellent state of the art report and a point of departure for projects on 'the City of Tomorrow', helping them to define their own approach and focus.

Under the heading of 'Principal achievements' and referring to the four-sided definition of SUD – ecological integrity, equality, participation and futurity – Kohler's review goes on to say that the principal achievements of the BEQUEST network relate to the following.

The definition of SUD

Here he draws attention to the achievement of the vision and methodology of an integrated SUD, in particular the manner in which it 'scopes' SUD and 'enlarges' what is normally considered to represent the environment. In including the economic and social dimensions he suggest one of the principal achievements is that in this form SUD:

> increasingly becomes a complete alternative to the actual development model of late modernisation (globalisation and its widening of social inequalities etc.). By enlarging the scope, the difficulties of finding aggregate models for the different components of SUD have led to an abandonment of classical optimisation models.

Clearly, Kohler is in favour of this approach and draws attention to the manner in which this has developed into the BEQUEST framework.

The BEQUEST framework

On this matter, Kohler (2002) says: 'The principal advantage of the framework is its simplicity which makes it [SUD] understandable to lay people and therefore usable in the public sphere.'

The protocol

Kohler sees this instrument as a guideline helping key stakeholders take decisions about how to proceed in procuring sustainable planning, property development, design, etc. of the built environment (defined as inclusive of its economic and social qualities).

The directory of assessment methods

It is noticeable here that Kohler is more guarded in his comments. He sees the linking of the framework and protocols to assessment methods as a challenging exercise because many of the assessments have not been originally developed with such connections in mind. However, he is complimentary about the standard reporting system devised for this purpose and the classification of assessment methods drawn from the analysis of case study applications. This he suggests shows great promise and provides an ideal opportunity to spread best practice across stakeholders, at various spatial levels and over a number of time frames.

Summing up these principal achievements, Kohler (2002) writes:

> The BEQUEST project is exemplary in several ways: 1. By advancing the basic definitions of SUD and establishing common agreements. 2. By producing material which has been brought to a wide audience in a short time. 3. By the very dynamic information exchanges

and international discussions made possible through the workshops and above all, the extranet.

Stanghellini (2002) also provides a positive review of the BEQUEST network's concerted action on SUD and echoes the sentiments of Kohler in his reference to the exemplary nature of the project.

These reviews by Kohler (2002) and Stanghellini (2002) are taken from 'Special Issues' of *Building Research and Information* (Curwell and Deakin 2002) and *Urbanistica* (Lombardi 2002) on BEQUEST and SUD respectively. What also comes through from these reviews is the extent of the challenge the BEQUEST network has taken on in searching to first of all define, and second, find the instruments to operationalise its concepts, and third, going on to gain a deeper knowledge and understanding of SUD. Whether this challenge has been met is, of course, for others to judge. However, the editors are of the opinion that much of what the BEQUEST network adds lies in its vision and methodology of an integrated SUD and the way the framework, protocols and directory of assessment methods allow stakeholders to evaluate the sustainability of urban development.

The relationship between the principles, the framework, protocols and assessment methods, drawn from the examinations presented in this volume, is set out in Figure 11.1 (see page 242). It provides a useful reference point from which to compare the form that it takes in the introduction and which is now presented here in the conclusions. Here the additional degree of detail represented in this illustration is noticeable, with the activities, issues, types of protocol and assessment methods becoming clear and more definite in terms of both form and content.

THE CRITICAL CONTRIBUTION BEQUEST MAKES

If asked to summarise what can be drawn from Figure 11.1 in terms of the critical contribution BEQUEST makes to our knowledge and understanding of SUD, the response would be as follows:

- The BEQUEST framework has the advantage of being based on concerted action and consensus building within the network and wider community of stakeholders.
- The vision and methodology of an integrated SUD, emerging out of the concerted action and consensus building, has moved from the PICABUE indicator model to the four principles of ecological integrity, equity, participation and futurity. These are clearly set out and represent the key reference points for the BEQUEST network, and the values it stands for and represents.

- This provides the common language, syntax and terms of reference – semantics, ontological structure and taxonomies – adopted for a glossary of terminology – modelling the stages and issues of sustainable development.

- While the above point has been agreed, the network recognises that SUD is not a linguistic exercise based only on semantics, but grounded in the activities and actions of key stakeholders in the built environment. In that sense SUD is not about the formulation of theoretical constructs, but concerted action. This is because a level of consensus requires to emerge between stakeholders before it is possible to build a vision and methodology with the scope and foresight needed for the planning, property development, design, construction and operational stages to be integrated with the environmental, economic and social dimensions of SUD. To do this there is also a requirement for the stakeholders – in their capacity as agents of change – to address the institutional structures – moral and ethical codes of governance – because they need to be tackled 'head-on' if SUD is to surface.

- The instruments the BEQUEST network has assembled to meet this challenge and bring about such a transformation are triangulated, taking the form of a framework, protocols and directory of assessment methods.

- The framework sets out the activities, actors – planners, property developers, designers, contractors and operators – stages and environmental, economic and social issues underlying SUD.

- The five protocols cover all the activities and stages of SUD and direct decision makers towards the assessment methods for evaluating the sustainability of urban development. It is noticeable that some of the protocols are sufficiently developed to get beyond environmental, economic and social issues and tackle many of the underlying institutional issues, drawing particular attention to the cultural dimension of SUD. They propose tackling the moral and ethical position of the market and replacing this form of governance with a culture better able to balance the environmental, economic and social issues and in so doing make urban development sustainable. Examples of this ability to tackle the moral and ethical position of the market were found in the chapter on property development and suggest transformative capacities for institutional change currently exist at the cultural level of SUD.

- BEQUEST has compiled a directory of assessment methods to consider in undertaking such evaluations and, while it is recognised that scientific opinion concerning the strength of certain available techniques is sometimes divided, the network has identified a new generation of assessments, termed 'co-evolutionary methods'. These show how closely the factors involved in a traditional environmental evaluation (property rights, landscape, recreation, leisure) can be linked with those of concern to the contemporary assessment of ecological integrity (resource consumption, pollution, land use and bio-diversity). The network partners suggest, however, and ask readers to note, that even with the most sophisticated co-evolutionary environmental, economic and social assessments there is currently a gap in the ability of such methods to address the institutional questions which surround the evaluations of SUD.

• The interdisciplinary nature of the concerted action, with consensus building, and sharing of a vision and methodology for an integrated SUD, means that BEQUEST has emphasised the environmental, economic and social issues as much more than institutional. Having said this, the network has gone to some length to highlight the critical nature of the institutional issues because it is with them that the cultural change which is needed to transform the urban development process and make it sustainable will be won or lost. What the BEQUEST network suggests is that the change needed to bring about such a transformation is locked away in the organisations responsible for the plan-ning, property development, design, construction and operation of the urban development process – and in the relations they have with the wider community of stakeholders. The network members also argue that in order to unlock this potential it is first necessary to operate as a virtual organisation, using semantically rich text to link stakeholders – be they professional bodies, or members of the public – who were previously disconnected from one another as a community. What is more, it is felt that this cannot be done just through electronic exchanges about ecological integrity, or the equity of environmental, economic and social issues, but needs to involve discussion of institutional issues. This is because, in the absence of compulsory measures, it will be the underlying concerns about morality, ethics and issues of governance which shall provide the pretext for cultural change and a substantive reorganisation of the urban development process. The type of cultural change required is, it can be argued, in line with the values of BEQUEST's PICABUE origins – in this instance its concern with public participation and futurity.

FURTHER DEVELOPMENTS

From the reviews of BEQUEST, there is evidence to suggest that the network and its research have been well received by both the academic and professional com-munities. An important question for the BEQUEST network to now address is how to take this forward and build upon the achievements made. The first step was for the network's partners to invite the editors of this volume to publish material on the framework, protocols and assessment methods. The second step taken to advance our knowledge and understanding even further relates to the proposal for further volumes on BEQUEST and SUD. In this respect it is proposed that Volume 2 of this series should examine the environmental assessment methods for evaluating SUD. It is further proposed that Volume 3 should progress this examination by elaborating the toolkit which the network has assembled for assessing the sustainability of urban development.

Volume 2, *Sustainable Urban Development: The Environmental Assessment Methods*, will bring together a number of contributions from recognised experts on sustainable urban development and leading authorities in environmental assessment. Many of the contributions are drawn from the BEQUEST project's study of SUD in terms of protocols and a directory of environmental assessment methods. Others have been commissioned especially for this volume. Together the contributions provide a unique insight into a matter of critical importance to SUD and provide the opportunity to focus attention on the environmental assessment methods currently available to evaluate the sustainability of urban development.

Organised around the themes of environmental assessment, methods and the evaluation of SUD, the volume also offers case studies on the application of specific environmental assessment methods and serves to provide examples of best practice in evaluating the sustainability of urban development. Adopting the BEQUEST classification of environmental assessment methods, there are case studies on the statutory instruments of environmental assessment and of environmental, economic and social evaluations undertaken to qualify the sustainability of urban development. Best practice examples in environmental valuations are also provided. Examples of such valuations include multi-critieria analysis, contingent valuation and cost-benefit analysis. Particular attention is given to what are referred to as environmental, economic and social evaluations.

Volume 3, *Sustainable Urban Development: A Toolkit for Assessment*, examines the toolkit needed to link the protocols with the assessment methods and form an integrated methodology and vision for sustainable urban development. It studies the BEQUEST toolkit and investigates the information system and decision-support system needed for the assessment of SUD. The toolkit in question links the framework, protocols and assessment methods as an information system and, as such, provides the technology of the integrated methodology and vision of SUD. Taking this form, it links the tools – the framework, protocols and assessment methods – together and connects them with the kit – information system, and protocols and assessments technology of the framework's vision and methodology, available for evaluating the sustainability of urban development. The examination of the toolkit thus brings the subject full circle. Having begun with a discussion of the framework, protocols and assessment methods, and the second volume having then gone on to examine the vision and methodology of the assessments underlying the evaluation of SUD, the third volume on the toolkit will turn attention to the links and connections between them and their ability to deliver SUD.

REFERENCES

Brandon, P., Lombardi, P. and Bentivegna, V. (1997) Introduction. In Brandon, P. *et al.* (eds) *Evaluation of the Built Environment for Sustainability*, Spon, London.

Curwell, S. and Deakin, M. (2002) (eds) Sustainable urban development: BEQUEST, *Building Research and Information* 30(2): 79–138.

Kohler, N. (2002) The relevance of BEQUEST: an observer's perspective, *Building Research and Information* 30(2): 130–138.

Lombardi, P. (2002) (ed.) The BEQUEST Project for sustainable urban development, *Urbanistica* 118: 20–93.

Stanghellini, S. (2002) Evaluation in planning: the BEQUEST network and tool-kit contribution, *Urbanistica* 118: 62–63.

Index